Aimée & Jaguar

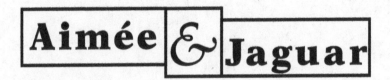

Aimée & Jaguar

A Love Story, Berlin 1943

Erica Fischer

TRANSLATED FROM THE GERMAN BY EDNA McCOWN
WITH ALLISON BROWN

HARPER ⬤ PERENNIAL

NEW YORK • LONDON • TORONTO • SYDNEY • NEW DELHI • AUCKLAND

HARPER ● PERENNIAL

AIMÉE & JAGUAR. Copyright © 1994 by Kiepenheuer & Witsch. English language translation © 1995, 2015 by HarperCollins Publishers. All rights reserved. Printed in the United States of America. No part of this book may be used or reproduced in any manner whatsoever without written permission except in the case of brief quotations embodied in critical articles and reviews. For information, address HarperCollins Publishers, 195 Broadway, New York, NY 10007.

HarperCollins books may be purchased for educational, business, or sales promotional use. For information, please e-mail the Special Markets Department at SPsales@harpercollins.com.

Originally published as *Aimée & Jaguar* in hardcover in Germany in 1994 by Kiepenheuer & Witsch.

FIRST U.S. EDITION PUBLISHED BY HARPERCOLLINS PUBLISHERS IN 1995.

FIRST HARPER PERENNIAL EDITION PUBLISHED 2015.

Library of Congress Cataloging-in-Publication Data has been applied for.

ISBN 978-0-06-239037-0 (pbk.)

HB 03.06.2024

For Felice

ACKNOWLEDGMENTS

My thanks to:
        Ingrid Lottenburger, Margot Scherl, Sonja Wohlatz and Inge Keller, for letting me stay at their apartment in Berlin;

Gerd W. Ehrlich, who entrusted me with his unpublished manuscript;

Annette Leo, for providing me with material on Gross-Rosen;

Susanne Pollak, who offered encouragement on this project from the very beginning;

Christel Becker-Rau, who took the wonderful photographs of Lilly;

Robert S. Mackay, Lilly's agent and friend, for establishing contact with Kiepenheuer & Witsch;

the Omina Freundeshilfe Foundation for their financial support;

the Ministry of Culture of North Rhine-Westphalia for providing a work grant;

Mieczysław Mołdawa, who sent me his book on Gross-Rosen and provided me with valuable suggestions;

Stella Leibler, for her report on Peterswaldau;

Friederike Cohensius, for her memories of the Peterswaldau camp;

Andrea Rudorff, for the information she gave me on the Kurzbach women's subcamp;

my mother, Irena Fischer, who translated Stella Leibler's letters and excerpts from Mieczysław Mołdawa's book for me from Polish;

the women of Vienna, whose appreciation and warmth during the first reading I gave from the unfinished manuscript encouraged me to go on;

Erwin Buchwieser, Gerd W. Ehrlich, Siegfrid Gehrke, Elenai Pollak, Olga Selbach, Lola Sturmova, Inge Wolf and Dörthe Zivier, as well as Lilly's sons, Albrecht, Bernd, and Eberhard Wust, for opening themselves to my questions;

Beate Mohr of San Francisco, for a conversation;

Christa-Maria Friedrich, a former classmate of Felice, who offered important details about Felice and her family;

my editor, Erika Stegmann, who always believed in the book and as in other projects saw me through its development with affectionate severity;

and finally to the central character, Lilly Wust, who, in countless and at times distressing conversations with me, allowed her memories to be uprooted from the past, and whose trust in me never faltered, even when I was impatient and intemperate.

LIST OF CHARACTERS

The Major Characters:

Elisabeth Wust, also called Lilly and Aimée

Felice Schragenheim, also called 'Lice, Fice, Putz, and Jaguar

Albrecht, Bernd, Eberhard, and Reinhard Wust, Lilly's sons

Inge Wolf, bookseller and Lilly's domestic aide for one year

Günther Wust, Lilly's husband

Günther and Margarethe Kappler, Lilly's parents

Erwin Buchwieser, Albrecht's father

Käthe Herrmann, Lilly's best friend

Dr. Albert and Erna Schragenheim, Felice's parents

Irene Schragenheim, Felice's sister

Käte Schragenheim, née Hammerschlag, also called "Mulle," Felice's stepmother

Hulda Karewski, Felice's grandmother

Dr. Walter Karewski (Karsten), Felice's uncle in the United States

Felice's friends: Elenai Pollak, Nora, Ilse Ploog, Christine Friedrichs, Luise Selbach, also called "Mutti," and Olga Selbach, Mutti's daughter and Felice's classmate

Hilli Frenkel, Felice's best friend from school

Georg Zivier, called Gregor, a writer and a friend of Felice

Dörthe Zivier, Gregor Zivier's wife

Gerd W. Ehrlich, an acquaintance of Felice and member of a Jewish underground group

Fritz Sternberg, a friend of Felice

Lola Sturmova, Lilly's subtenant who had been bombed out of her home

Lucie Friedlaender, Dr. Rose Ollendorf, called Petel, Katja Laserstein—Lilly's "three witches"

Willi Beimling, Lilly's second husband

Liesl Reichler, Günther Wust's fiancée

Senator of the Interior Lummer yesterday presented the Federal Service Cross, awarded by the Federal President, to Elisabeth Wust (68), of Lichterfelde. In the years from 1942 to 1945 Elisabeth Wust hid and cared for four Jewish women in her apartment in Schmargendorf. One of the women was hunted down by the Gestapo and died at the Auschwitz concentration camp. Three of the women survived the Nazi regime. This is the twenty-first Federal Service Cross awarded in Berlin to "unsung heroes," those persons who offered aid to victims of Nazi persecution.

DER TAGESSPIEGEL, SEPTEMBER 22, 1981

Aimée & Jaguar

ONE

The broad wooden stairs under the rust-red runner creaked as Inge Wolf took them two at a time to the fifth floor of Friedrichshaller Strasse 23. The bright and colorful lead-glazed windows of the landings looked out onto a leafy back courtyard and the modest lower wing where the lower-income families lived. With each floor she climbed, Inge gained a better view of the roofs of the Schmargendorf district of Berlin and the linden trees tinged with the colors of fall.

It was the first of October, and Inge Wolf was in a hurry to find a suitable position for herself. If she did not begin her compulsory year of domestic service soon, she would be called up by the National Labor Service. The Friedrichshaller Strasse address was her second attempt at finding work on this Thursday morning.

A slender redhead in rimless glasses opened the door marked "Wust."

"Good day."

Inge breathed a sigh of relief. She already had been received by four different housewives, all in apron dresses, with a "Heil Hitler," and "Oh, how nice that you've come!" and she had given up hope of a simple "Good day." The overabundance of Nazi women she was encountering was probably due to the fact that Inge, at twenty-one, was required to fulfill her obligatory service in a family with at least four children. Were she only sixteen, a family with one child would have been acceptable. It was bad enough that someone like herself, who had more on her mind than cooking and cleaning, had to work for others, but this pack of Nazis was really too much. If a woman invoked the Führer in her own home it was not hard to imagine what all would follow.

"You know, I have so many choices, I think I'll look around a bit more," she would hasten to say each time, and make her getaway.

Was it Inge's scrawny figure, her big ears, tousled short hair and intense dark eyes that caused Elisabeth Wust to greet her with "Good day," or was this the first unmistakable sign of Elisabeth's doubt in her husband's convictions? She had been dissatisfied for some time now, without knowing exactly why. She had no apparent reason to complain: her sons were doing splendidly and would some day attend the *Napola*, the elite Nazi school. On August 12 Elisabeth had received the Maternal Cross in bronze, on her fourth son's first birthday. Günther Wust was serving as a soldier in Bernau, near Berlin, far from the front, thank God. In civilian life he was a clerk at the Deutsche Bank, soon to become an authorized signatory, a dashing fellow, tall, slim, with dark hair and good manners, the type of man every girl dreamed of. After meeting Günther at a club run by the bank, Elisabeth—engaged to be married to someone else—sent her fiancé packing.

With another sigh of relief Inge Wolf stuck into her jacket pocket the stack of white index cards with addresses from the Labor Service and decided her search was ended. The two women sat down at the freshly scrubbed kitchen table to take care of formalities. It was agreed that Inge would work each day from eight to five.

"I'll show you around."

The spacious four-room apartment with its decorative plaster ceilings had a large balcony that overlooked shady Frie-drichshaller Strasse and a smaller one off the kitchen, with a view of the roof of the rear wing. Scarcely had Inge entered the living room through the wide double doors before she realized she had made a fatal mistake. A highly polished relief of the Führer, and in bronze! What could she do? The time had come for her to utter her usual excuse and quickly disappear. But her papers lay filled out on the kitchen table and a retreat could arouse suspicion. All she needed was for someone to denounce her. Inge felt sad and weary at this latest disappointment. How long would she have to wander through Berlin before she found a family that had resisted the brownshirts? Did such a family even exist after what soon would be a decade of Hitler's dictatorship?

She decided to swallow the bitter pill. "There's something I must say right off," she remarked, searching for one last way to back out of her decision. "I'm an absolute washout when it comes to housework." After all, the compulsory year of domes-tic and agricultural service introduced in 1938 for all single women under twenty-five was supposed to "arouse joy at one's domestic and social vocation," as had appeared in the paper recently. Inge most certainly would not be able to demonstrate this commitment to the *Reichsfrauenführerin*, leader of the women of the Third Reich.

But in the face of ever scarcer domestic help Elisabeth Wust was not about to be scared off. "Oh, child, you have no idea what a washout I myself am. Together we'll manage." She gave Inge a deep-throated laugh and showed her to the door.

"Until tomorrow, then."

Lilly:

I'm sorry, but we never had a picture of Hitler. Inge most certainly imagined that. She simply assumed I was a Nazi, that's all. We were a loyal German family, of course, that's true. I admit that. My home was furnished like millions of other German households, I admit that too. I never voted for Hitler, but I was married to a Nazi. My husband was a Nazi, not a party member, but a good German and Nazi he was. And that's when Inge got to know me. He was a real Prussian, though actually he was a Sorb. We had a copy of *Mein Kampf*, I think. Yes, we did. And we had the *Völkischer Beobachter*, the Nazi newspaper, lying around. I don't like to talk about it. I don't like to admit that my husband was a Nazi and a bit of an anti-Semite, it ran in his family, the usual anti-Semitism without much reflection on it. My parents were always needling me, my father objected to my having married a Nazi. And my brother didn't approve of it at all, for as long as he remained in Germany. And then he forgot about me entirely. But I

wouldn't have listened to them even without their objections.
I did what I pleased at the time, and I definitely wanted to go
through with it. I was silly and foolish, but above all I wanted
to get away from home. I didn't give a thought to the rest
of it. He was good-looking, everyone liked him, he wanted
to be somebody. It was Günther I married, after all, not the
Nazi! And I married without my parents' blessing. Even my
parents-in-law didn't attend the wedding; in their eyes I was
too young and spirited. They disapproved of my entire way of
life. My father was in the mountains, in the Altvater (Jeseník)
range, when I got married. We had to talk him into giving us
his written permission, as I was not yet twenty-one. My father
was so terribly dogmatic. I didn't see him again until Bernd
was born. Our animosity ended once his grandchild arrived.
And then I turned into a good little housewife and had children. Basically, I was brought up to have a family and run a
household, and that's what I did. That's how I spent those first
years—with children and diapers, running the house, taking
care of my husband. I was always cross with him, even more
so as time went by. The least he could have done was give me
a rest on Sundays, but no, the food always had to be on the
table at a certain time. Or he could have taken the children for
a walk once in a while. He had no idea what to do with small
children. He was incredibly proud of his sons, but taking care
of them once in a while, there was never any question of that.
There were thousands of households like ours, households that
had no interest in anything but their offspring. We women
swapped recipes, that was more important to us than anything
else. *Napola*? Don't make me laugh. My husband would have

had to be in the party for that, right? Only the children of bona fide party members could enroll at the *Napola*. Never, he truly was not that kind of Nazi. There were many like him, thousands. Germany was going to make something of itself again, that's the way it was. A lot of people went along, even became party members, because they believed Hitler could get something done. What it later turned into. . . . But people didn't really envision any of that at first. *Napola*—it's the first time in how many years that I've heard that word. My goodness, it must be over fifty years now! No, for God's sake, he was a good bank clerk, that's the path he would have followed. The children perhaps would have joined the Deutsche Bank as well, or gone to university. The path was foreordained, so to speak. He was a good German, that's all.

On October 5, 1942, *Reichsmarschall* Hermann Göring, in a speech celebrating the harvest festival, said of the "great race war": "Whether it is the German or the Aryan who endures, whether the Jew will rule the world, that is what it is about in the end, and that is what we are fighting for in the battlefield." The newspapers printed his speech in its entirety, and that same day *Reichsführer-SS* Heinrich Himmler issued the order that all Jews held in concentration camps within the German Reich be deported to Auschwitz.

Meanwhile, Inge Wolf had begun to adjust to life in the Wust household. Reluctantly, she learned how to arrange the growing pile of *Völkischer Beobachter* newspapers in the study so that the center fold lined up exactly with the edge of the small glass cabinet. But in only a few days she had taken the adorable Wust children to heart. Elisabeth Wust, at twenty-nine, had borne a child with remarkable regularity, every two years: Bernd was seven, Eberhard five, Reinhard three, and Albrecht was one year old.

Inge's first task of the day was to relieve Albrecht—two of his brothers would deliver him from the children's bunker with his diapers close to overflowing—of his burden. Otherwise, she was primarily busy taking care of the two middle brothers. Each day Eberhard ran to greet "Aunt" Inge, his gingerbread grin sweetly revealing a charming row of rotten teeth. Reinhard, whose alert and serious eyes took in everything, was always begging her to take him to the movies, where he would sit on her lap contented and still as a mouse. Bernd, tall and the eldest, paid little attention to Inge, preferring to spend his afternoons on the street playing war.

Elisabeth Wust had her children so well trained that she could indulge in a bit of leisure activity odd for a Nazi woman. With disarming trust she included Inge in her preparations for visits from her gentlemen friends, so that the two women became something like accomplices, though Inge Wolf neither understood nor wished to understand her employer's political or sexual preferences. Her afternoon visitors were colleagues of Günther Wust, men with good manners who were well dressed and of stately bearing. "She's the major sweetheart of minor officials," Inge scoffed at home, in revenge for the insult of having to polish Hitler's bronze nose. When a gentleman caller was scheduled, Elisabeth arranged her pale green nightgown to reveal her cleavage, and Inge put fresh sheets on the bed.

Then she took the children to the zoo. Lilly was particularly flushed with excitement when expecting a certain Herr Patenheimer, a bank official and "old warrior"—that's what they called someone who joined the Nazi party before Hitler came to power in 1933—with a shadow on his lung, who for this reason had been excused from duty in the Wehrmacht. When he was scheduled to visit, Lilly ran around the apartment like a teenager, putting up her hair and continuously searching for something, rearranging everything. She could do it best with "old warriors," she said.

Lilly:

They were men from our circle of friends, the same age as my husband. They were on leave or had some position or other in Berlin. There had to be some men to keep things running, after all. I've never suffered from a lack of men. But most of them, well, they couldn't perform, more or less, it was a sad fact. When I think about it, Günther was the best of them all. I can only explain it by saying that I took very little part in any of it. An orgasm, as they say today, was totally strange to me. But they wanted me, and I didn't say no. It's flattering to a young woman, of course, if men are always after her. Morals always loosen up a bit when men are conscripted. No one knew what would happen tomorrow, so we enjoyed life as best we could. The men as well. After all, my husband had Liesl.

I liked him, Günther, I wouldn't have married him otherwise, that wouldn't have made sense. But I was much too young and foolish at the time. I didn't wake up until I was twenty-six, and by then I had three children. Suddenly I no

longer wanted to be the little wife and mother, didn't want
only to be obedient and maternal. That's when my husband
and I had our first disagreements. I began to grow up and
defend myself. He liked to go out and have a beer by himself.
I never wanted to go to the pub with him, it's true, but neither
did I want merely to take care of the children, good God
in heaven. I wanted to go to the theater, do something nice
together with him. And suddenly it occurred to me: What
are you going to do now? It was then that I began to detach
myself from my husband. It began with the war, actually.
One day we decided to spend a few days with our friends the
Herrmanns. Ewald worked at the bank with Günther, our
oldest children were the same age, and so we had got to know
each other. And Käthe was my best friend. Then I noticed
that something was going on. When my husband was called
up in 1940 he complained to me in a letter that he hadn't
heard from Käthe. I went to see her, furious. "When Günther
sends letters they at least should be written to me," I hissed at
her. Then Käthe began to cry. "Do you love each other that
much?" I asked. "Yes," she sobbed. So I put my arms around
her and comforted her. "Love each other then, but leave me in
peace."

Actually, I didn't hold it against him. My motto was: Just
don't desert the family, otherwise do what you want. I just
didn't want to know about it. Once I suggested to him that we
live apart for five years, in the same apartment. I'll take care
of the household, I said, I'll do that, but nothing else, please.
And my husband just tapped his forehead. I needed an escape.
I jumped the fence. Before, I could never have imagined

cheating on my husband, but he went a bit too far. And later I threw it in his face. We were having some fight or other—Albrecht, my fourth, was barely nine months old—and all of a sudden I got furious and said to him: He's not your child, by the way. That really got him, mostly because he knew Erwin, you see. But then I told him it was his own fault. Why was he always running around with other women? I felt like I was alone, damn it all, so I gave in, you see. I didn't have a long relationship with Erwin, it must have happened the third time we saw each other. That was a wild year as it was, he wasn't the only one. My husband knew that Erwin was chasing me. Right up to the altar Erwin begged me to marry him and not my husband. We always stayed in contact. We moved all over Berlin and he was always right behind us. When he became a clerk at the city hall at Wilmersdorf it was he who got us the apartment in Schmargendorf.

No, I didn't want that many children. I wanted Bernd and Eberhard; I wanted Bernd to have a little brother. But Reinhard was an accident, I didn't speak to my husband for three days after I found out. I had just gotten over the last birth. When Eberhard was three weeks old he got a cramp in the lower part of his stomach, and almost died. For more than six months I had to feed him every other hour. He was thin as a stick. And then another child—it was too much for me. But then my nature prevailed. I never would have considered an abortion, not even with Albrecht. I accepted it as my fate, and I enjoyed having my children. But the way they were made, *that's* another story.

Erwin Buchwieser, Albrecht's biological father:

> I met Lilly at the beginning of 1933. We were both in a steno
> and typing course that the Deutsche Bank organized to get
> the unemployed off the streets. My father was at a local branch
> of the bank and Lilly's father was in the foreign section,
> but they didn't know each other. I was twenty-one and had
> trained to be an auto mechanic, but was out of work. I would
> like to have been an engineer, but I couldn't manage it finan-
> cially. The course was a gesture with which the bank hoped to
> get in good with the new regime, a kind of "emergency relief."
> And it didn't cost them much, after all.
>
> Lilly was simply what I had always wanted. Red hair—
> that was the first impression—something that for me has
> always remained a largely unrealized dream. Her spirit, her
> self-assurance and her good manners impressed me greatly.
> I lacked all of these. I was awkward. I was shy and retiring,
> but somehow we connected right off, without a lot being said.
> But she was already taken. I never tried to change her mind.
> That would have been futile, it had all been arranged. Both
> Lilly's and Günther Wust's parents were a bit above my social
> position. I was only a proletarian, really. My father was an em-
> ployee of the bank, that's true, but we lived in quite reduced
> circumstances socially. I was nothing and had nothing. And
> then I got to know Günther Wust as well, when he came to
> pick up Lilly after the class. He made a very good impression
> on me. A bit affected, but he already had a higher post at the
> bank and had to display a certain attitude toward his clientele.
> He was very correct, polite, refined. Lilly was refined too, of

course. She had her secondary school diploma; I didn't. And Wust almost surely did not take me seriously. My father was an insignificant clerk who had come to Berlin from a small town and had never really coped well there. So Lilly was some-one to strive for in every sense, but marriage was something that was always out of the question. I was unemployed and Günther Wust had a solid position. The Deutsche Bank didn't let anyone go, not even in times of crisis, it was always reliable.

I married someone else in August of 1938, but I contin-ued to be taken with Lilly. She was something precious to me, a kind of jewel, something fragile perhaps as well, not to mention her erotic allure. She was everything I wanted—red-haired, more intelligent than I, more educated. She was short-sighted and wore glasses. I was always telling her to take them off, so it would be harder for her to see my weaknesses. When finally we went to bed together, I didn't feel I had done anything wrong. In January 1941, after the French campaign, we were camped south of Berlin in a village called Schöne-weide, for a little respite, so to speak, before being sent on to Russia. I had a great deal of freedom to move around in. It must have happened then.

I don't remember a picture of Hitler in her living room. But that was the rule then, so I probably wouldn't even have noticed it. Or would I have? Perhaps I would have said some-thing like, "Good old Adolf, already here too," or something like that. But an image of Hitler was also used as a cover then. When the block warden came by to collect for the NSV, the Nazi public welfare organization, or for Winter Relief, one had to reckon with the fact that he would look around to see

if you at least had a picture of Hitler on the wall, or a Nazi
banner hanging outside the window. Half the population
were spies and informers, after all. But is that so important?
I never noticed Lilly exhibiting any sort of enthusiasm for
Hitler. I myself was a National Socialist out of conviction.
I joined the party in 1931 because I liked its platform. And
there was nothing in the platform about those things. I'm still
glad today that I was a soldier and didn't have to participate in
the things that party members did here. That Jews were taken
to concentration camps and killed there. . . . Nowhere was it
written that they wanted to destroy them. And if there was,
then I thought: economically. It all boiled down to the Jews
apparently having influence everywhere, due to their wealth.
Yes, I believed that, that they played a dominant role in economic life. We were told, for instance, that most bankers were
Jewish, and that Hollywood was run by Jews. They're just
harder-working, for God's sake, but we didn't see it that way
at the time. I never did any Jew harm, not even verbally, but
everyone says that. Today I sometimes ask myself: Why did we
take so little notice? But do you think any of us little people
took it seriously when they sang their vicious songs against the
Jews? And then they had to assume a middle name, one that
sounded Jewish. God, what all went on. . . . What I felt about
it at the time, I can't tell you today. It struck me as a bit odd.

In 1933, when we were attending the Deutsche Bank
course, people often said in passing, "Things are moving
forward!" or "Victory!" But it was all very vague, no one made
propaganda for one party or the other. Bob was there, too,
Lilly's brother, who was a Communist or a Social Democrat.

I always got the impression that Lilly's parents were conservative, what earlier was called German-national. The conservatives couldn't have been happier about the Nazi movement. The Nazi and Communist workers were beating each others' heads in, and they counted on that. As a rule it was the workers who were beating each others' heads in. But when I was together with Lilly I had other things on my mind than talking politics.

Elisabeth Wust noticed right away that Inge was an intelligent girl, quite different from the previous one who had worked for her, who then had left to get married before her year was up. Inge Wolf, for her part, found the red-haired lady of the house, with her translucent, freckled complexion and her high, sharp cheekbones, not exactly unattractive, but rather dense. She seldom found herself in the sticky situation of having to dodge a political discussion. Elisabeth Wust usually was preoccupied with other things, but now and then she would prattle on about something she had just read in the *Völkischer Beobachter*. And when the Hitler Youth marched by in their smart uniforms and their *ta-ra-ra-boom*, she would open the windows, lift up Eberhard and point down at them: "Look, Eberhard, Hitler Youth. When you're ten you can march with them."

Once a week Günther Wust was granted a day's leave from his guard company in order to visit his family. The slight, thirty-six-year-old with the little mustache was not bad-looking, and his pipe lent him the dreamy composure that pipe-smokers exude.

Things got political at home only when Lilly's parents, the Kapplers, visited. Barely did the door close behind Father Kappler than he was drawn to the likeness of Adolf, which soon was to be found lying face-down on the chest of drawers. Then his wife would fold her hands over her portly stomach and smile contentedly. This harmony was rare, however, for Günther and Margarethe Kappler were usually battling each other. Friends of the family report that each January a new vase of Bohemian crystal had to be ordered to replace the one shattered during the Christmas holiday fight. Mother Kappler smashed lightbulbs and Meissen porcelain now and then as well, not to mention the time she recklessly put them in debt for a pretty dress with a collar of Brussels lace, an act of irresponsibility that brought her rather miserly husband's blood to a boil. Lilly found it particularly irritating that her father—at home a pedantic tyrant and braggart who went around sticking little pieces of paper to the wall with the message "Do it right away"—was considered by outsiders to be an amusing entertainer and welcome guest. It was not uncommon for her parents' visits to Friedrichshaller Strasse to end in discord and leave Lilly in tears. Her father relished embarrassing his daughter by reciting risqué poems. *He's a windbag*, she would say to herself, her lips pressed together and her eyes on the floor in mortification.

Inge Wolf liked Father Kappler, with his little mustache, if only for his political beliefs. Like her father, he had been in the

German Communist Party, but had burned his membership book in 1933 to placate his fearful wife. He had a unique relationship with images of Hitler. Kappler had one at home, lying under the runner at the entryway to the apartment, and he took diabolical pleasure in watching everyone who entered his South End home step on Hitler first. He particularly savored it when it was his suave son-in-law, Günther, whose attempt to join the Nazi party (NSDAP) had failed due to the temporary freeze in new membership of May 1, 1933. That Günther Wust, out of injured pride, did not apply again did nothing to change his father-in-law's scathing view of him.

Bernd Wust, Lilly's eldest son:

I don't think we had a picture of Hitler at home, but perhaps we did; I wouldn't put it past my father, in retrospect. What we did have were those soldiers made out of papier-mâché or clay—and among them was the Führer in the pose of a military leader. I had a bunch of toy soldiers, a whole chest full: soldiers shooting, soldiers firing cannons, soldiers marching and little horses, too. Like tin soldiers, only a bit larger, and painted. We traded them as children—how many infantrymen do you have, and so on. And one boy had SS men in black uniforms; well, they were worth more, of course. So *that* Führer we did have. And whenever my grandfather came to visit I always found that Führer hung upside down somewhere. He stood in a broad-legged stance, an open space between his legs, so that he could be hung from a hook or a key. He was being hanged, that was clear. Vati also had a pile of other stuff, a lot of Nazi booklets, for example, booklets for functionaries, he had a subscription to them, but you could buy them too. Mutti didn't throw them away. And then when the Russians came—it was obvious what the booklets were, they had the eagle on them and such—we shoved them under the bed. And as we were sitting in the cellar and the Russians were searching the house, we were shaking with fear that they would find them.

In mid-November 1942, as the result of an embezzlement case involving the Berlin Gestapo, *SS-Hauptsturmführer* Alois Brunner, former head of the "Central Office for Jewish Emigration" in Vienna and personal secretary to Adolf Eichmann, arrived in Berlin. Brunner, an Austrian known as the "Butcher of Vienna," had rendered that city *Judenrein* ("Jew-free") as of mid-October. Small and bow-legged, he considered it his duty to "show these damned Prussian swine how to deal with Jew bastards." Brunner introduced to Berlin the moving van method he had tested in Vienna, by which Jews could be rounded up from their homes or work places without attracting a great deal of attention. Security police and Jewish police (so-called *Ordner*) systematically combed entire sections of the city, wandering the streets in the closed vans like dog catchers and shoving in anyone wearing the yellow star. Berlin had been teeming with rumors since Brunner's arrival. Gerd Ehrlich—who soon was to make the acquaintance of Inge Wolf and Elisabeth Wust—was the son of a prosperous Berlin lawyer who had died of a heart attack in 1940. At the end of the war Ehrlich, from his exile in Switzerland, recorded his account of

how he and his family experienced the "Brunner operation."
[Gerd W. Ehrlich, *Mein Leben in Nazideutschland* (My Life in
Nazi Germany), unpublished manuscript written in Geneva in
the winter of 1945]

Gerd Ehrlich:

> He arrived with a multitude of diabolical ideas. "Let the Jews
> exterminate themselves." From then on, the Jewish commu-
> nity itself was to take over the rounding up of victims for
> transport. Only in those extremely rare cases when the Jewish
> *Ordner* encountered resistance among their own was the Ge-
> stapo to step in. This obscene idea was brought before a special
> meeting of the Jewish Community Council on November 19.
> To the credit of our representatives it must be said that a good
> number of those executive members present refused to serve as
> executioners. Unfortunately, from the beginning the old gen-
> tlemen took the wrong path of resistance to those orders issued
> from Burgstrasse [Burgstrasse 26 was one of the addresses of
> the Reich Security Main Office]. They offered only passive
> resistance, not daring to call for an insurrection. As a result,
> decent people were arrested immediately and assigned to the
> next transport. It was in this way that the community leader-
> ship ended up in the hands of obsequious pawns of the Nazis.
>
> Among those council representatives arrested on Novem-
> ber 19, 1942, was my stepfather. He didn't return home from
> the meeting and I never saw him again. I myself was working
> the night shift on that dark day, and after lunch I went back
> to bed to get some sleep. Around four o'clock my mother,
> looking terribly pale, came into my room with the bad news:

"Benno has been arrested. The whole family has to go to the
collection camp this evening." Horrified. I jumped out of bed
and got dressed. The dreaded moment had arrived. According
to the agreement I had made with my parents, I now had to
separate from them, in order somehow to remain in Berlin
for as long as possible. I helped my poor mother and my little
sister pack the last of their things in rucksacks. I will never
forget this terrible afternoon. Thank God we were too busy
with preparations for the "trip" to see the whole tragedy of the
moment clearly. Neighbors helped us pack the paltry amount
of luggage that was allowed. By eight o'clock everything was
ready and we set off on the difficult path to the train station.
I accompanied my mother and sister to the collection camp,
located on Grosse Hamburger Strasse in the former Jewish
Home for the Aged. At the door of the building, which was
guarded by the police, I had to take leave forever of those
I hold dearest. A last kiss for my little sister Marion, a last
blessing from my good mother for my future, and the gate to
the prison closed behind them. A world had come to an end.
Despite its hardships my relatively sheltered youth ceased to
exist with the closing of that gate. From then on I had to stand
on my own two feet . . .

Several days after my family was transported, the Gestapo
came to seal off our rooms. Once again I had just returned
from the night shift, and personally opened the door to them.
They were somewhat amazed at the sight of the bare rooms
(I had sold all of our transportable items to neighbors), and
angrily asked who had removed everything. I played dumb
and said that I was merely a subtenant, worked my twelve-

hour shift at the factory, and was too tired to meddle in other people's affairs. I could state quite calmly that I had nothing to do with the "Walter family," for indeed I carry my father's name. So the rooms were sealed, and despite their threat that my presence in the empty rooms might cause trouble for me yet, I went back to bed. But the "friendly" advice of the two officials reinforced my decision to join the illegal underground soon.

In order not to arouse suspicion prematurely, I continued to report to work at the factory. I arranged with the man who relieved me that I would always work the night shift and he the day. I slept hardly at all during those first weeks of December. I had to take care of the final preparations concerning my uncertain future. I secretly carried from the apartment suitcases packed with the last of my belongings, quickly sold the remaining valuables, and burned any incriminating evidence. By mid-December I was finally ready. Not a moment too soon.

On November 24, 1942, Rabbi Stephen Wise of New York held a press conference in Washington. He told reporters that according to sources confirmed by the State Department two million Jews had been murdered in an "extermination campaign" aimed at wiping out all the Jews in Nazi Europe. This information was confirmed in Jerusalem that same day. A detailed report on the construction of gas chambers in Eastern Europe and on the transports of Jewish adults and children "to great crematoriums in Oswiecim, near Cracow," circled the globe. Though the mass murder of Jews had been going on at Auschwitz since mid-1942, this was the first reference to it to reach the outside world. BBC reports on the gassing and shooting of Jews were broadcast in Germany as well.

At the end of November, Roosevelt's "President's Third War Powers Bill" was defeated in Congress. The bill called for the repeal of laws that hindered "the free movement of persons, property and information into and out of the United States."

"As I read it," a Republican congressman said, summing up the majority opinion, "you throw the door wide open on immigration." The conservative press, the *Chicago Tribune* above all, expressed "shock" at finding politicians attempting to "flood this nation with refugee immigration from Europe and other nations."

"The ugly truth," *Newsweek* wrote on November 30, 1942, "is that anti-Semitism was a definite factor in the bitter opposition to the President's request for powers to suspend immigration laws for the duration."

TWO

On November 27 Elisabeth Wust and Inge Wolf had arranged to meet a friend of Inge's at three o'clock that afternoon at the Café Berlin, located next to the Ufa-Palast movie theater at the Bahnhof Zoo train station. Inge had been talking constantly about her women friends for some time now. Elisabeth's suspicion that these girls were "different" was strengthened when the two of them were making a bed one day and Inge began to stroke Elisabeth's arm and then asked her how she felt about it. It could be very nice with women too, Inge had said in a soft voice, looking at her employer in a bold way, her dark eyes shining. Oh yes, she could imagine that, Elisabeth said in embarrassment, and lowered her eyes. Without stopping to reflect on it, she accepted that Inge was "different." One of Elisabeth's qualities that Inge greatly respected was her discretion; she simply didn't ask questions. The disadvantage to this, on the other hand, was that newsworthy items sometimes had to be forced upon her.

The elegant brunette in the rust-red suit of fine English cloth whom Elisabeth met that day at the café introduced her-

self as Felice Schrader. Elisabeth was surprised, for she had expected someone named Elenai, of whom Inge had spoken often.
Felice Schrader, her long legs wrapped in shiny silk stockings,
was somewhat taller than Inge. She seemed determined to make
an impression on Elisabeth. What she said wasn't so important,
but *how* she said it was enchanting. She smiled constantly at
Elisabeth, a big smile that revealed perfect teeth.

When Inge murmured something about the furnished
room her girlfriend lived in, Elisabeth, as usual, had no comment. She simply stared in fascination at Felice Schrader's
delicate hands, with their impeccably polished nails, and
breathed in her perfume. It did not escape her notice when
Inge and Felice exchanged barely concealed glances. Elisabeth
felt herself being drawn into a magic circle, her senses in such
a heightened state that it seemed she had just awakened from
a deep sleep. Beside Felice she felt painfully provincial in her
dark blue rayon dress with its white and light blue embroidered roses, the fabric much too thin for this time of year.

After an hour that had passed all too quickly, she accompanied the two friends to the tram stop in front of the Ufa-
Palast, where she stood trembling in the cold. Then Felice
opened her briefcase and with an embarrassed little laugh gave
her an apple, which Elisabeth, shivering, accepted.

"Auf Wiedersehen," Felice said, and it seemed to Elisabeth
that she had winked at her.

Several days later Elisabeth Wust noticed that Inge was becoming more and more nervous as her workday neared its end,

and that she kept running to the living room window. Felice Schrader was waiting on the cobblestones of Friedrichshaller Strasse below, too timid to come upstairs.

"Come on up, you can't stand down there in the cold!" Elisabeth called down in her inimitable fashion, which brooked no contradiction. "Inge, go down for Felice at once. It's out of the question that she wait for you on the street."

After that, Felice appeared more and more often at five in the afternoon, climbing the stairs to "the lady of the house" on the fourth floor. She and Inge were frequently invited to stay for dinner.

"Call me Lilly, it makes me sound less old," Elisabeth said, playing up the eight-year age difference.

Sometimes they were joined by one or another of Lilly's gentlemen friends. Though Berlin housewives were complaining of food shortages and the lines of people waiting anxiously outside the shops were getting longer, Lilly always had enough to eat thanks to the rations she received for her four children. And at Christmas there was even a special bonus: fifty grams of real coffee and .7 liters of alcohol for the adults, in addition to meat, butter, wheat flour, sugar, peas, cheese and sweets.

Enjoying her role as lady of the house, Lilly looked on with pleasure as her home gradually filled with people. She was accustomed to gracious surroundings; her parents had enjoyed entertaining. Her mother would hire a woman to serve the table and clean up afterward, and her father would go down to the cellar for bottles of Koblenz white wine. Then he would

open the double doors between the living room and the study
and tune the piano, at which he would delight his guests late
in the evening with improvisations. To please the young men
present, Lilly would sometimes accompany her father's playing
with a spontaneous dance across the parquet floor. There was
a great deal of music in the Kappler home; in the summer her
father would sit by the open window and play Schubert *lieder*,
with Lilly's brother, Bob, accompanying him on the violin,
and Lilly and her mother singing a duet, and people would
applaud from the street.

The seemingly carefree young women who now met at
Lilly's several times a week were a colorful group. The prettiest
among them was Elenai Pollak, distractingly exotic-looking
with her deep blue eyes and thick, long, curly black hair.
Elenai would lapse into a brooding silence when Lilly blithely
chattered on about the interesting turn her life had taken. But
when trying to convince someone of her opinion Elenai could
become suddenly loud and forceful, her cheeks flushed and her
eyes sparkling with belligerence.

Lilly was only vaguely able to guess who was having a relationship with whom. Inge and Felice for certain, and Inge
and Elenai as well. The drab blonde, Nora, seemed stuck on
Elenai, who in turn had relationships with men. Someone
named Christine often turned up in conversation. And during
the day, if Inge didn't rush to the telephone fast enough to
answer Felice's call, Lilly had the pleasure of listening to Felice
whisper sweet nothings to her to beat the band. Lilly then
smiled so dreamily that Inge could not quite contain a certain

uneasiness. Inge felt that Felice should keep her hands off Lilly. Felice had recently arrived bearing a huge bouquet of red roses.

New Year's Eve, 1942, was a raucous affair. Felice had a portable record player, and Lilly an old-fashioned gramophone that had to be cranked by hand. Little by little Felice had brought over all of her records, so that Lilly's collection of hits ranging from Zarah Leander to Marika Röck to Hans Albers and back again to Leander now included banned French songs such as "La Mer" and "Germaine." "Can Love Be a Sin?" the girls roared in unison, followed by "There's a Stork's Nest on the Roof of the World," as Lilly happily served bread and cold cuts with eggs and chives.

Günther Wust was happy as well. During his visits to his family over Christmas he felt flattered by the presence of the charming young women in his home, and was pleased to see Lilly in better humor than she had been for a long time. They had quarreled often since the unhappy episode with Käthe Herrmann, and once he started seeing Liesl their estrangement was complete. Had Lilly met these friends earlier, perhaps the unfortunate affair with Erwin never would have happened.

On January 30, 1943, the tenth anniversary of Hitler's rise to power, the people of Berlin waited over two hours for a speech by Hermann Göring to commence: for the first time during daylight hours, English reconnaisance planes were circling over the city. Four days after Göring had declared his absolute confidence in a German victory, what was left of the German Wehrmacht in Stalingrad capitulated to the Soviets. The defeat was announced over the radio, and accompanied by funeral music.

On February 18 propaganda minister Joseph Goebbels incited the German people to even greater effort. In a "declaration of fanatic will" at Berlin's Sports Hall he proclaimed that "total war" would be the "salvation of Germany and of civilization." To honor those who had fallen in the Russian campaign, a three-minute traffic stoppage was ordered. At the Zoo tram stop people stood as if frozen, and avoided each other's eyes. Though it was clear to most that the war had been lost once and for all, no one dared say so.

The propaganda machine intensified its attacks on the "internal enemy." *Gauleiter* Goebbels promised to present a "Jew-free" Berlin to Hitler for his fifty-fourth birthday on April 20. The Gestapo stormed buildings and smashed locks, sawed through steel bolts, chopped down doors with axes and climbed through the windows of adjacent buildings. Many Jews went underground. Frightening rumors concerning the fate of those "evacuated" made the rounds.

On February 20 the Reich Security Main Office issued guidelines for the "technical enforcement" of deportations to Auschwitz. People were to take with them: food for a five-day march, one suitcase or rucksack, one pair of sturdy work boots, two pairs of socks, two shirts, two pairs of underwear, one work suit, two wool blankets, two sets of bed linens, one bowl, one cup, one spoon and one sweater.

At the end of February two new people joined Lilly's circle of friends. Ilse Ploog was a dark-haired woman who walked with a slight limp and had sad, dark eyes set in a broad face. It was she who had taught Felice photography; Felice owned a Leica and wanted to become a journalist. She commissioned Ilse, who was constantly worried about her soldier husband, to take pictures of Lilly and the children. The other newcomer was Georg Zivier, a forty-six-year-old writer whom everyone called Gregor. Gregor was married and was in no hurry to introduce his wife, Dörthe, to the housewife with the copper-colored hair and her female entourage.

Felice's wooing of Lilly was becoming more conspicuous. She called every day and appeared each time with flowers. Her compliments were becoming increasingly audacious, something that pleased Lilly, though it really shouldn't have. Perhaps the fact that Lilly was unconsciously pleased encouraged what was soon to transpire.

Günther Wust was home on a visit, and Felice and Inge had been invited to supper. Inge talked with Günther in the living room while Lilly washed the dishes, and Felice followed Lilly into the kitchen to help dry. When Lilly returned to the living room for something she had forgotten she was brought up short by the sight of her husband kissing Inge! "Oh, excuse me," Lilly stammered, and, covering with indifference her surprise that Inge had suddenly overcome her animosity toward the opposite sex, returned to the kitchen. As she reached over to place a clean coffee cup on a dish towel to dry, Felice suddenly pulled Lilly over to her and tried to kiss her. Lilly turned a deep red and pushed Felice away with a vengeance that surprised her, even going so far as to hit Felice with her fists.

"Are you angry?" Felice asked in a husky voice, equally as shocked as Lilly.

"No, why should I be? We can still be friends."

They finished washing the dishes in an embarrassed silence.

In the days that followed, the two women acted as if nothing had happened, but Lilly turned away when Felice looked at her with a questioning and somewhat amused expression in her gray-brown eyes.

Early on the morning of February 27, the tenth anniversary of the Reichstag fire, a "final clearance of the Jews," later referred to as the "Factory Operation," was undertaken in Berlin. It was contrived by Alois Brunner as one of his last acts in Berlin before leaving for France and Greece to devote himself to new duties. The Berlin Gestapo, which had totally appropriated the methods Brunner had initiated in Vienna, wanted to keep Goebbels's birthday promise to the Führer. Also, since Stalingrad even Nazi *Volksgenossen* (national comrades) were not holding back their criticism of internal affairs. Time was running out.

Already before dawn, columns of trucks loaded with soldiers of the Waffen SS were rolling through the streets. The SS armored infantrymen of the "Leibstandarte Adolf Hitler" regiment—soldiers in steel helmets and field-gray uniforms, their bayonets and machine guns drawn—swarmed out of the trucks to take out on the Jews their frustration at the defeat at Stalingrad. All remaining Jewish workers, men and women engaged in forced labor in Berlin, were to be arrested at their factories. The SS and the Gestapo attacked them as they sat at their workbenches, and herded them into the waiting trucks. Those who resisted were struck with rifle butts, and pregnant women and old people alike were thrown into the trucks like cattle. The roughly seven thousand Jewish women and men were then incarcerated in makeshift collection camps. It was a terrible scene: Those who had tried to defend themselves were covered in blood, their clothing torn. Mothers cried for the babies they had left behind at home, children who had been picked up from their homes screamed for their parents, married couples were separated. People pleaded to be released, pleaded for something to drink, for straw to sit on, shivering in the cold in their thin work clothes. There were no toilets. People threw themselves out of windows and under cars, or took poison.

At the predeportation "transfer site" on Levetzowstrasse, a member of the Gestapo stood in the middle of the large room on an overturned crate. The detainees lined up in front of him had to recite their names, family situation, and the Jewish category they had been assigned to on passage of the "racial laws." The man in the leather coat then gestured with his thumb to the right or to the left. Left meant Rosenstrasse, right meant the train station and camps. Persons belonging to various "privileged" classes of Jews were taken in trucks to Rosenstrasse 2–4 in the center of Berlin. Two thousand people already had been corralled there to await their uncertain fate.

In the days that followed, hundreds of women gathered before the building's gates to demand the release of their "Aryan-by-marriage" husbands. "Let our husbands and our children go!" and "Go to the front, where you belong!" they cried, hesitantly at first, and then more and more resolutely. Even as machine guns were being set up they screamed, "Murderers! Firing on women!" Traffic was rerouted away from Rosenstrasse to keep the public from witnessing all of this, and the nearby "Börse" station was closed. But many of the women remained overnight, and others were not deterred by the long detour on foot. When guards and SS men threatened to use their weapons the crowd retreated, only to reassemble a short time later.

On March 1 the "day of the Luftwaffe" was celebrated with much ado, and that same night the British staged a "terror attack" on Berlin that left over seven hundred people dead and almost sixty-five thousand homeless. Buildings burned in the western and southern sections of the city, the air turning the yellow color of sulfur. People carrying bundles, suitcases, and household belongings wandered the streets in a panic. Most of the bombs fell in the center of the city, but in the midst of the smoking ruins the four-story Jewish Welfare Agency on Rosenstrasse, which housed the defenseless captives, stood unharmed.

Eberhard, Reinhard, and Albrecht Wust spent the night in the children's bunker, as always. Streets, houses, and trees were covered in a layer of gray dust. A large new housing complex quite near Lilly's building had been hit, and the children, excited, related that a friend's mother had been killed that night by an aerial mine as she stepped out of the air raid shelter to smoke a cigarette in front of the building. The rumor circulated that the attack was in response to the deportation of the Jews, and the *Völkischer Beobachter* of March 3 railed against the "Jewish terror from the air." The next day the Berlin edition carried "our response": "Unyielding Will to Victory Over Enemy Bestiality." Every day the newspaper printed the hours when Berliners were to participate in a blackout. On March 3 it was from 6:42 p.m. to 6:10 a.m.

"We're finally clearing Berlin of the Jews," Goebbels noted with satisfaction in his diary on March 2. But on March 6, after 7,031 people were deported to Auschwitz and Theresienstadt as part of the "final action on the Jews," he gave the order to release the Jewish husbands and children of Aryan women. As he noted in his diary: "Unfortunately, a number of deplorable scenes took place in front of a Jewish old people's home, during which the population even sided with the Jews." It was a critical time for the "evacuation of Jews," he wrote. "We prefer to wait a few weeks; then we can carry it out much more thoroughly." The episode at the Jewish Welfare Agency was played down as an "error," a "violation," and the squad leader in charge was transferred.

While all of this took place outside the awareness of most Berliners, Felice went to visit friends in the Altvater (Jeseník) Mountains. She did not want to give Lilly the address, but she promised to write. In addition, they agreed to think of each other each evening at nine o'clock, when the radio stations changed their programs.

Felice kept her word. Her first news was an undated postcard:

My dearest Madam,

It is true that I am terribly lazy when it comes to writing, but not to the extent that I wouldn't prefer to substitute my daily calls for this card. But it will have to remain with "prefer," for what one is comfortable alluding to in passing doesn't appear half so good when written down. I'll make up for everything later!

I don't need to emphasize that it is beautiful here, but you will believe me, won't you, when I say that I was less happy to leave Berlin than expected? You not only believe it, you know it for sure! It's amazing, all that women know, isn't it?

What's new? Air raid sirens? Problems with Inge? A lot of love in general? As I want to find out about all of this, I'll send you my address tomorrow, after we go further up into the mountains. Will you answer?

I hope so, and I hope for much more besides, and until then I send you my most sincere greetings in friendship,

Yours, Felice

The card was followed by a letter written in black ink:

At the end of the world, March 12 or 13, 1943,
day of the week uncertain.

Dear Eve (always)-Dolorosa (sometimes),
   [Lilly is "Dolorosa" sometimes, if she is having problems with one of her lovers. When this happens her circle

of women friends might rush in to find the "lady of the house" in tears.]

I have just found a Hermes who has agreed to take my letter with him, for tomorrow he will be breathing the same Berlin air as you—the lucky man! (I place a certain value on having my letter arrive on a Sunday morning, perhaps somewhat less populated than usual.)

Following this preamble I am in the happy position of being able to relate that I had a wonderful dream about you this morning. I didn't know—oh, never mind. One thing I do want to ask, though: How does it stand with our moment of reverie at nine when the programs change? Don't forget!

Unfortunately, I've run out of my green ink, and because I can't switch my fountain pen to another color I'm writing with a borrowed pen. But unless I'm greatly mistaken and reading the signs wrong, I will have to, or will be permitted to, as it were, visit Vienna on this short trip. Once there I will buy ink, or a noose—both to the same end! Can you die of that? Surely more easily than of a broken heart. Are you smiling yet? Please, do so—I enjoy imagining it.

You probably will not be able to read my sublime handwriting. If I knew that for sure, I would be as daring as I am in broken phone booths—! But then you would struggle so hard to understand every word that I shall allay this by saying that these lines contain nothing more than a heartfelt greeting from

Your Felice

Felice's third correspondence is a picture postcard of Bad Karlsbrunn, "at the foot of the Altvater":

Back in Karlsbrunn, March 17, 1943

Dear Eve,

Hopefully you no longer will be Dolorosa when you hear that as of early Monday I once again will be available for anything—or rather, for telephoning, of course! When do you have time? I need someone to stroke my now deep gray hair—!

As you see, I have decided—I'm spontaneously changing the topic, as usual—to "discreet" this card by sticking it in an envelope; for in this godforsaken hole it is best to send the mail by messenger. I've already lined up one.

So I hope you'll keep a long evening open for me sometime in the next seven days—! I'm returning totally transformed, both morally and socially.

The card ended here. Felice only had room for, *How would Monday be? I'll call!* adding in tiny letters in the white margin on the front of the card: *I don't have any more stationery—reason enough to come back—and that's not the only one!*

On March 18, a Friday, Inge and Father Kappler took Lilly, sobbing in pain, to the St. Norbert Hospital near the Schöneberg Rathaus. For some time she had been suffering from a jaw infection that suddenly had become critical, and she was operated on the very next day. That Monday Felice returned to Berlin as promised and telephoned Friedrichshaller Strasse where Inge, who was caring for the children, answered the phone. Felice then immediately went to the hospital.

"Oh, Felice, I'm so sick," Lilly whispered as Felice, out of breath, rushed into the room grasping a bouquet of red roses. Felice did not say a word, simply put her arms around her. This time Lilly did not resist, and not merely due to her weakened condition. Felice's persistence had its effect.

From then on Felice appeared every day with red roses.

"*Aha!* The Rosenkavalier," joked Dr. Schuchardt, the ebullient chief of dental surgery and first-class "golden pheasant" [popular nickname for a high-ranking Nazi official, owing to the colors of the tan uniform and gold and red insignia], when he would see Felice's slender form hurrying down the corridor.

On Tuesday Lilly dared to make her first move toward Felice, slipping her a list of requests for the following day, written with a pencil stub on a small piece of paper torn from her pocket calendar:

skin cream
your handkerchief
correspondence cards
your love for me alone
needle and thread

On Thursday Felice presented Lilly with a poem written in pencil on a double sheet of paper torn from a school notebook:

DU [YOU]

There's so much I want to give
you, with only
one thing in mind:
You!
I want to find stars
for us up above—!
And do you know why?
It's you I love.

Lilly tore in half the sheet of paper with Felice's poem and on the other side she wrote:

Felice, when I think your name I see you before me. You are looking at me—Felice, you shouldn't look at me so—it makes me want to scream. But don't be afraid, I will scream very softly—and in that place where I can!!

Felice, when will we be alone, completely alone?—I am only as brave on paper as you are in busted telephone booths! And I'm wildly afraid of you. All the hairs on my arms are standing on end. . . . I just don't know. Felice, please be good to me. *Du!*

Lilly's time in the hospital passed in feverish dreams, and she tried to capture the confusion of her emotions in words:

St. Norbert Hospital, March 27, 1943

Du!

Felice, help me! Tell me what it is I'm thinking, you must know! Please tell me! Day and night I dream of summer, sun, flowers, blue skies, perfumed nights; I'm simply dreaming of—truly inexpressible—happiness. But I don't merely want to dream, I want to live, Felice—live—live with you. Tell me that you want to live with me, please tell me that. My heart beats for you, do you now know that?

I'm still sick—but afterward, finally—we will fall into each other's arms, and in the whole world there will be only you and me.

March 29 was Lilly's ninth wedding anniversary. Günther appeared at the hospital that afternoon bearing flowers.

"Do I need to worry about the children?" he asked in his usual stiff way.

"Not at all. Inge is at home and Mutti goes over every other day. I'll get over this soon. They're releasing me on April 2."

The minutes dragged by. Lilly was shocked at the distance that had grown between herself and Günther. Though their sexual relationship had died long before, she had never questioned their connection to one another, due to their mutual responsibility to the children.

Almighty God, please make him go, was the only thing Lilly could think of at this moment, *just go and leave me alone with my dreams.*

Felice wisely had arranged not to arrive until evening.

"Felice, finally! I've been longing for you so!"

"Aimée, my sweet, did you survive your anniversary? How is the honored husband? I hope you haven't disgraced me."

"Oh, Felice, I felt like screaming."

Lilly's knees turned to jelly as Felice bent over her and her hair brushed against Lilly's cheek. She felt a surge of heat in a place her gentlemen friends had failed to ignite, and was close to fainting.

"Felice," she whispered, so low that she could scarcely be heard.

Felice was bending down so close to her that Lilly's eyes began to swim. She felt her face turn as red as it had that evening in the kitchen when Felice had tried to kiss her. *Nothing can happen to me here,* ran through her head. The rush she felt in her head and body was as deafening as an avalanche; in order not to be crushed, Lilly closed her eyes and surrendered herself to Felice's soft lips. Suddenly everything stood still, as still as if their hearts had ceased to beat. When Lilly came to herself she looked up into Felice's eyes, which appeared strangely wise, and tears filled her eyes. Never had she experienced such tender feelings.

It has happened, she thought. The implicitness of this wordless exchange let her know that she had crossed an irrevocable line. Lilly would later realize that by this time she long since had crossed to the other side.

The young woman in the next bed was asleep. Who knows what Felice would have done had she noticed it earlier! Now and then a soft sigh floated over to them.

The next day Felice presented Lilly with a second poem:

YOUR MOUTH . . .

I promised myself solemnly,
That I would practice silent restraint—
But when I saw your mouth it confused me.
Did I cause you pain?
With plans I now must pass my time,
Heart pounding like a xylophone,
Plans for wonderful things, sublime,
More than mere illusion alone—
How could it have happened I no longer
want ever again to wander?
There is one thing, however, I ponder:
What would it be like, I only can wonder,
To lie at your breast and dream of your mouth?

In the days that followed Lilly wrote three love letters on the salmon-colored army issue postcards that Felice brought to her from home:

March 30, 1943

A storm is raging inside me—no, not a storm, much more than that. I will go to sleep now, and perhaps tomorrow will arrive more quickly, perhaps I can sleep—perhaps to dream: You are with me and . . .

Felice, if you knew how my heart is pounding at this moment! I would not wish it to be otherwise!—I hope that you can't read all of my thoughts, I don't dare think them to an end myself. Oh, these damned bandages, this miserable infirmity! Felice, I want to be alone with you. Stop, I must not think any further! And yet—do you wish the same? Please, you haven't yet answered any of my questions. Tomorrow I will be relentless, tomorrow. I want . . . no!—that is, yes, I want! Felice, remind me how old I am—only if I ask, of course. Tell me I should be reasonable. When is our wedding day to be? We've shown my own enough respect!! I sometimes feel totally paralyzed when I think of you. Forgive my outbursts, Felice, I am alone too much and confused. I love you too, Felice.

March 31, 1943

Felice, I love you! What a feeling it is to be able to say that! Oh, Felice, the nicest fate I could hope for is that of lasting happiness. I want to live with you for a long, a very long time, do you hear? And life is so beautiful, so wonderful. Felice, do you belong to me—without limit? To me only? Please say you do, at least for a very long time to come, please! Do you love me? I'm acting like a seventeen-year-old, aren't I?

Be good to me, Felice, please? And yet please don't hold back. I wanted to lure you out of your hiding place. I'm like a child playing with fire; will I get burned? A little? Totally? Felice, stop me! Isn't it just a little bit your fault that I'm so crazy, so totally crazy?

On the evening of April 1, Lilly called Felice from the hospital and tried to make clever conversation as Inge, Gregor, and, as she believed, her husband all listened in the background. Felice, for her part, knew better, and flirted so outrageously that it put Lilly in an awkward situation. Only at the end of the conversation did Lilly realize to her surprise that Günther wasn't there at all.

Du, someone really should—I don't exactly know what one should do with you, you're so terribly cheeky! And how that pleases me! Too bad my heart's delight really wasn't sitting around tonight in the background. Then things would have been even nicer!

God, Felice, the most horrible thought occurs to me now and then. But it can't happen, it cannot! If he doesn't come today, perhaps he will tomorrow, and then, Felice, I don't know what I'll do. I don't want to have anything to do with him, Felice, nothing at all. Please, please, don't be mad if I speak openly. But tell me, what does he want at home? Felice, you won't be receiving this note—I'm being too open. I'm giving away too much of myself, I love you too much, Felice, my beautiful dark girl. How pretty you've become of late! You don't know how your eyes shine. And when you look at me, Felice, I feel like I'm on fire. What have you done to me, I cannot forgive you. You've totally enchanted me; it's not air I breathe, but love!

On April 2 Felice took Lilly home. Inge believed that Felice stayed there with her because of Lilly's weakened condition. And Felice knew her way around the apartment because, after all, she had spent the last few nights there with Inge.

After reading Felice's poem with the lines, *What would it be like to lie at your breast and dream of your mouth?* Lilly had looked forward to their "wedding night" with a mixture of total impatience and absolute panic. Now she lay in bed in her long white nightgown with the blue embroidered collar, stiff as a board, butterflies in her stomach. *I have no idea what to do* was the thought that kept running through her head, while at the same time her body smoldered.

Felice, smiling uncertainly, emerged from the bathroom in yellow silk pajamas to lie down on Günther's side of the bed. They lay next to one another for a while in silence, each holding her breath.

"Can I come a little closer?" Felice finally asked, in a voice that was a bit too spirited, and in no time she had slipped under the blanket with Lilly.

Her temples pounding, Lilly stared at the ceiling, wound tight as a spring as Felice stroked the thick, rust-red hair she hadn't been able to take her eyes off at their first meeting at Café Berlin. Lilly couldn't breathe. In a weak attempt to prevent anything from happening, she grabbed Felice's hand as it moved under her nightgown. But then she closed her eyes and gave herself over to the heat wave that was engulfing her. She met the soft pressure of Felice's ample breasts with a welcome sigh. What was this unbelievable feeling, so fresh and innocent? This creature was so strange, and yet so very much like her. But as she touched the hard bones of Felice's hips with her fingers, and felt the downy skin of Felice's cheek against her own, it was as if she had never loved anyone else. The tastes and smells, how delicate and light it all was!

Felice was a good teacher, Lilly an eager pupil. There was not that unpleasant moment she always had to overcome with men, her fear of the throbbing penis, authoritarian and threatening, working quickly to spend itself. Her inhibitions fell away to be replaced by wholly new desires.

The next night it was Lilly's turn. Finally not to have to wait any longer, not to be the one to be satisfied, but to satisfy, not to take, but to give! Lilly traced the line of Felice's breast with her tongue, pausing with pleasure at the hard nipple nested in the center of the large brown aureole. Then she slipped down, further down, until her lips brushed against Felice's pubic hair. *Schamhaar* (literally, "shame hair"), what a strange word. Never in her life had Lilly felt so little shame. How good it made her feel! She wanted to do it all, to learn it all, make up for it all, all of it.

Felice made an uncertain sound, and now it was she who tried to push Lilly's head away. She was somehow uneasy with Lilly's eagerness to learn. Only yesterday Lilly had lain under the blanket stiff as a board! There ensued a power struggle.

"No," Lilly said, so decisively that Felice lifted her head, her gray-brown eyes looking at her in astonishment. "I don't want to be happy all by myself," Lilly blurted out. Had Felice underestimated Frau Wust? Lilly did not waste a moment reflecting on how this new relationship would affect the rest of her life. It was as if she had always been "this way." She could barely recollect the life she had led before meeting Felice.

Lilly:

I got nothing at all from my men. Men took their pleasure
with me and I felt used. With Felice it was just totally different. She was my counterpart, my complement, literally. I felt
I was both myself and Felice. We were a mirror image. She
needed only to touch me and I. . . . When she kissed me I
surrendered to her completely. Sex was pleasing for the first
time in my life. I had never found men attractive. I was built
wrong somehow, but I didn't know that. With men I was
always the inferior one. The men did it *to* me. *A woman always
has to wait*, that's how I was raised. With Felice, I myself
could be the one who loved. And then this sense of belonging
together unconditionally. It was complete: love and sexuality,
there simply was no separation. That's why, during those first
weeks, I always called her my "very first person," because she
truly was the first person for me on this entire earth. There
was nothing, absolutely nothing else for me at all. I felt as
if I had been reborn. Felice liberated me. I now knew who I
was, where I belonged, to whom I belonged; everything else
was totally unimportant to me. And Felice understood very
well what I meant by that. Of course, we also had our roles.
She always said, "I'm man enough for us both!" But with her
I played my role willingly, because that's how she wanted it.
That's why I was her little kitten, who now and then bared its
claws. Though I was older, I always had the feeling I was the
younger one. She controlled me completely, she did. But it was
wonderful! She also always wore pants. After all, it was she
who had seduced me!

Felice and Lilly got very little sleep in the nights that followed. "Do you love me?" Lilly would whisper in Felice's ear whenever Inge wasn't within hearing range. Lilly needed to hear the words "I love you" continuously. But Felice was plagued with doubt as well, asking Lilly, "Are you happy?" A mother of four, who would have imagined it? It was her dreaded recklessness, admittedly, that had given her the idea of seducing this unusual German housewife in the first place. She couldn't say that Inge hadn't warned her. But neither of them had for a moment seriously believed that Felice would succeed in bringing someone like Lilly over to the "other side." Felice vacillated between a feeling of surprise and pride at the unexpected success of her seductive skills, and the fear that she was in over her head.

Somehow the two women arranged it so that Felice spent most of her nights at Friedrichshaller Strasse. Only occasionally did she sleep elsewhere, and then Lilly assumed it was with Inge, but she said nothing. Felice remained silent on the topic as well, like Inge appreciating Lilly's discretion. To placate her after a night they had not spent together, Felice wrote a poem inspired by poetess Mascha Kaléko:

> *To you and to your hands*
> *On the sheet of night I send*
> *All the love I've ever conceived.*
> *All those who came before you, perceived*
> *Now in your light, I loved,*
> *Perhaps, because of you.*
> *Now night is ending*

Alone, alone, but I think of your hands,
And finally I sleep.

Eight days after Lilly's release from the hospital the two friends began going out together. Felice didn't want to miss the chance to promenade through the city with her new love. They made a date with Gregor Zivier at the Bristol on Kurfürstendamm. The writer enjoyed being seen in public kissing the hands of two such pretty and elegant young ladies, even if, to his regret, they only had eyes for each other. They went to the Café Reimann on Uhlandstrasse, and to the Hotel Fürstenhof at the Potsdam train station, where one could have an excellent meal for fewer ration coupons. And Felice once insisted on inviting Lilly to the Kaiserhof, one of Berlin's most expensive hotels. It was located directly across from the Reich Chancellery, which teemed with SS men strutting around in their studded boots. But it was precisely this that Felice seemed to enjoy.

Felice wanted Lilly to look as if she had just stepped out of a bandbox, so that she could be proud of her Aimée. From her extensive wardrobe Felice presented Lilly, one by one, with dresses of brightly patterned, soft foulard silk and fine linen. She herself preferred to wear trousers. Only once, one hot summer's day, did Felice pull out one of her light dresses. "Eek, a girl!" Lilly teased her.

Among the clothes that Felice gave Lilly was a lilac taffeta evening dress with shoulder straps, and a matching jacket. Lilly quickly disappeared into the bedroom to squeeze into this cloud of taffeta. Felice emitted a cry of delight as Lilly waltzed back into the living room encased in this feminine ensemble. With her light freckled skin, her dark eyes rimmed by pale lashes, and her red hair held back with a ribbon, Lilly, the older of the two, looked like a fancy doll, which aroused Felice's protective instincts.

"Careful, you'll crush the dress," Lilly said as Felice rushed over and took her in her arms, as if to kiss her good night.

For her part, Lilly relished introducing Felice to Käthe Herrmann, her friend of many years with whom Günther had betrayed her several years before. Käthe lived in Eichwalde, near Grünau at the eastern edge of Berlin in a section known as a Nazi stronghold. The trip, taken by steam locomotive, was a failure, however, for Felice found nothing at all engaging about the plump blonde in the dirndl. But Käthe's father, who lived in a little house in Königs Wusterhausen, was a retired tailor, and Felice placed an order with him for a royal blue ensemble in an elegant, barely discernible check pattern, to be made for Lilly. She accompanied Lilly several times to fittings, but had no wish ever to see Käthe again. In a photo taken by Käthe's husband, Ewald, Günther's colleague at the Deutsche Bank, Lilly, still recovering from her jaw operation, looks quite peaked, and Felice, sitting beside the "country bumpkin," has a grimly determined look on her face.

One sunny spring day, Hitler's birthday—with flags flying all over the city—Lilly and Felice traveled to Caputh, near Potsdam, to the idyllic surroundings of the club of the Deutsche Bank where Lilly first met her husband. Out of a desire unclear even to herself, Lilly was drawn back to the site of her first conquests, made just after she had left secondary school.

And they could enjoy a whole day away from Inge's probing looks!

Felice sneaked up behind Lilly. "Would the lady be so generous as to grant me a kiss?" she asked, putting her arms around Lilly's waist as they listened to the singing of the birds.

"'Touching objects with the paws is in violation of the laws!'" Lilly quoted.

As she pulled away from Felice, Lilly slipped on the forest floor and fell at Felice's feet, in the process losing her wedding ring, which she had put in the breast pocket of her new ensemble. She never wore the ring when she was out with her lover. Both women crawled around the forest floor in search of it, but the ring had disappeared. Lilly's right hand, the ring's impression still on her finger, looked strange without it.

"Your Rosenkavalier will give you a new one," Felice promised, kissing Lilly's hand.

Back at home with Inge, who kindly had looked after the children, they talked about what they had seen on their return: gardens blooming in the midst of piles of rubble, the only sign that a house had stood there once. When the air raid sirens weren't sounding and the sky was blue, one could almost forget they were in the middle of a war.

"It's all the fault of the Jews," Lilly blurted out.

Inge flew into a rage at Lilly on hearing this.

"Leave her alone, Inge! She doesn't know what she's saying!" Felice yelled in a strangely shrill voice as she threw herself between the two women.

Without a word Inge picked up her handbag and left, slamming the door behind her.

On April 30 German Jews were stripped of their citizenship. On May 2 there were roughly 5,000 U-boats—those who had gone underground—still living illegally in the city. Each month close to 150 of them were rounded up on the streets or taken from their hiding places and "relocated" to Auschwitz or Theresienstadt. On May 2 Felice officially, so to speak, moved in with Lilly, bringing with her a few of her things.

On May 3 Lilly brought up the issue of divorce for the first time to her husband: "It's useless. We don't understand each other anymore."

Günther Wust was thunderstruck: What had gotten into his wife? That Lilly was inclined to eccentric outbursts was nothing new, but divorce, with four children! It couldn't be jealousy of Liesl—Lilly had always been oddly open-minded about his occasional dalliances. And hadn't he, for his part, been the picture of tolerance when he found out that Albrecht wasn't his son? That had been an act of generosity bordering on weakness. Perhaps it was his fault, perhaps she simply needed a firmer hand. And how, if you please, did she intend to earn a living?

Their discussion ended before anything could be decided. Günther wanted to have nothing to do with a divorce, particularly as Lilly refused to take total responsibility for it herself. Lilly, however, didn't see it that way; in her eyes Günther's affairs were reason enough to divorce him. If Günther was so concerned about keeping up outward appearances, the only compromise she would consider was to remain married and have a separation of "bed and board," whereby she was prepared to share her table with him, but never again her bed.

Since Felice had entered her life Lilly lived in fear that Günther would claim his rights as a husband on one of his visits home. It must never again come to that!

Barely had Felice moved in than she went off again. She never revealed the destination of her "business trip," but called two days later. Lilly had waited anxiously for her call, but when she heard the honey tone of Felice's voice in her ear she couldn't utter a word. She then committed to paper what she had wanted to say:

> A few days alone. It's so terribly hard to say good-bye to you! Oh, Felice, my very first person, I love you. I'm sitting here sadly in the weak light of the 191 tram, with a feeling inside that I cannot describe. We're at the Ufa-Palast stop at the moment. It was at this stop that our fate was decided. You should never have given me that apple, never! Later tonight I'll go to bed and weep. I'll put your picture on my night table and look at you. You'll watch over me, won't you? And when you go to sleep, think of the fact that I want to kiss you, and then you won't be so sad. And tomorrow—! Tomorrow we no longer will be alone!!!

Felice returned as happy and charming as ever. Lilly, in contrast, was worried, troubled that Felice could go away for days without telling her where and with whom she was. What if something happened to her underway? What if Berlin were bombed and Lilly had no way of getting in touch with her?

The day that Felice returned was a busy one; Reinhard was especially fussy and it was nine in the evening before they could retire to their bedroom. But Lilly was upset and wouldn't come to bed. She stood at the foot of it in her blue pajamas with the white nap finish that Felice had given her, and clasped the bedpost of light-colored oak.

"Felice, there's something going on with you," she blurted out.

"What do you mean?"

"You go off and won't tell me where. You call and I still don't know where you are. What's wrong?"

"Everything's fine, darling, really. Come to bed and let me pamper you, you're going to catch cold."

"No, Felice, if we're going to stay together—you do want that, don't you?—then we must be honest with one another."

"Dearest, I am an open book. I love you, that's all there is to say."

"Felice, I'm serious. Either we're totally open with each other or we go our own way."

"Don't press me, Lilly, please. I can't tell you. You have enough to deal with as it is."

"Felice, I beg you. If we're going to spend our lives together, we must be totally truthful with each other. I love you, but this simply won't do."

Lilly didn't understand Felice's fear. It was distressing to her that she, who valued discretion above all else, had to pry in this way, but even more unbearable was the idea, now become certainty, that there was something between them which could not be spoken of. It took until midnight for Felice, by then totally exhausted, to look at Lilly, her eyes wide, and say, "Promise me that you'll still love me."

"Felice, you are everything to me. In the entire world there will never be anyone like you. It's because of you that I've finally found myself. You are my very first person. You know that!"

"All right, fine." Felice took a deep breath. "Lilly, I'm a Jew."

Lilly stared at her for a moment in astonishment. Suddenly she understood all the inconsistencies she had never asked about. Coming out of her stupor, she pulled Felice to her and held her tight.

"And now more than ever," she whispered.

"And my name is Schragenheim," Felice said, sobbing on Lilly's shoulder.

Lilly:

> We cried the whole night through. It was terrible to me, of course, that she had been so afraid to tell me. But then she surrendered to me completely. She didn't want to lose me. For a moment I froze, but then I took her in my arms, and that was that. I knew, of course, what it meant. At that moment a film of Felice's life during this whole period was running through my head. . . . Not for a moment did I think that I too could be in danger. On the contrary, all I wanted to do now was to save her. Someone in trouble—that's what she was! Let's say she had been a Communist—I would have felt exactly the same way, I can swear to that. I sometimes have to remind myself—Felice was a Jew! That's crazy, sheer

madness! It never would have occurred to me that she was Jewish. Nor did she look Jewish, only on those days when she had her period did she look Jewish. Inge wasn't Jewish either, but you might have guessed that Elenai was. Yes, and Gregor looked Jewish enough for ten people. He and I often went down to the cellar together when the air raid sirens went off, and it's amazing to me that not one of our dear neighbors said anything. I didn't think about the fact that Felice didn't have any food ration cards. I ran a hospitable home; if people came over, I fed them. Inge ate with me, so Felice ate with me too. She did have travel vouchers, which came at a high price. And I assume that she got vouchers from Inge and the others. Previously, at school, there had been several Jewish girls in my class with whom I was friends, but then we lost track of each other. Much later I found out from one of them that she had been able to emigrate in time. So there were no Jews left in my immediate surroundings. I simply wasn't confronted with that. That Gregor, for example, was a Jew, was something I found out for the first time that night. It had never occurred to me before. I know only that I felt incredibly comfortable in that circle from the beginning, the whole association pleased me, it was another world, a lovely world. I can only explain it by saying that I acted on my feelings alone. I spoke a great deal about it with my parents. I remember clearly how on November 9, 1938, my father came home with a piece of broken glass from a shop window . . . and we were horrified. He kept it for many years in a little box, a piece of the display window of the Wertheim department store. No, I was never an anti-Semite, that's not the way I was raised. But I didn't pay attention to what the Nazi ideology was causing. When I think back on that entire period—for years I lived with my head in the clouds and did only what my husband wished. What information I had at all, I had from my parents. My mother went through all kinds of terror because my father often couldn't keep his mouth shut, something I myself got a good dose of. I remember how terrible we felt on *Kristallnacht*, yes, I remember that quite clearly. We didn't discuss it with Günther. When we all got together for birthdays or such, we basically avoided politics.

Later I talked to Felice about the scene with Inge [when Lilly had blamed the war on the Jews]. "You dummy," she said, "it was a silly thing to say. You read the paper and then you said it, that's all." It was terribly embarrassing for me, of course—later—but Felice reacted wonderfully. I can remember that even after Inge's furious outburst I still didn't know what I had done wrong. . . . Though I should have considered my brother, of course, well . . . I knew, after all, that Bob had a Jewish father. When I told my parents who Felice was, my mother finally admitted to me that Bob was the son of the cantor at the synagogue on Levetzowstrasse. My father never found out about it, my mother made certain of that. And she only hinted at it to Bob; she never told him everything because she didn't want to give herself away. Nor did the Nazis know he was Jewish. But he looked Jewish. They punished him enough as it was. He was a Communist and there were a lot of street battles here in Berlin, of course. They always called him a damned Jew-boy. He and my father didn't get along at all, they were always fighting. I'll never forget how my brother came to me once in tears and said, "He can't be my father." But we knew already as children, because sometimes we would have to get all dressed up, and then we would go to meet a strange man. We always had to be especially good. It was him, Bob's father, and he wanted to see his child.

I tried to call him during the war, when my mother admitted to me that he stayed in contact with her until the end. He had rescued the synagogue's altar decorations, and wanted her to keep them for him. But she didn't dare. "I'm just a coward, that's all," she said to me. But he had been understanding. That's why I tried to reach the man. When I called I was told that there was no one there by that name. I was wrong to do that, but I meant well, I was thinking of the altar decorations. He sent his sons to America in time. He himself stayed here, married a second time, and went underground, in a laundry not far from the Wilmersdorf district city hall. "Further whereabouts unknown."

On May 11, 1943, Felice took another trip. On a green movie ticket from the Amor cinema on Uhlandstrasse, where a few days before she had seen a late showing of *Pheline* starring Käthe Dorsch, Lilly noted in Felice's green ink: "10:18 p.m. on the first evening without you! If they should do anything to any of you—then—I wouldn't live much longer."

THREE

Felice Rahel Schragenheim was born at the Jewish Hospital in Berlin on March 9, 1922, a year in which many people lost their entire life savings. It was said that the Jews got rich on the inflation, which wasn't true, but it offered those who had come down in the world a convenient excuse for anti-Semitism. Several months after Felice was born, Germany's Jewish Foreign Minister, Walther Rathenau, was murdered by right-wing radicals in the pay of nationalist "patriots" who were opposed to the Weimar Republic. Rathenau, who had proudly acknowledged that he was a Jew, was one of the most cultured men of his time, and more than likely served as a model to Felice's parents, who shared a dental practice on Flensburger Strasse in Berlin's Tiergarten district.

Felice's father, Dr. Albert Schragenheim, was born in Berlin in 1887, and served as a field dentist in Bulgaria during World War I. He married Erna Karewski, also a dentist, when he was on leave from the front in January 1917.

"Where did this blond child come from?" friends of the

family asked in astonishment. Felice's light-colored hair had gradually darkened to a mousy brown by the time she entered the Kleist School in April of 1928. Soon thereafter the family moved to Berlin-Schmargendorf, to Auguste Victoria Strasse, a quiet street lined with linden trees. Felice spent a secure and comfortable childhood there in a splendid home with lush gardens; the family also owned an automobile and a motorboat. She was called 'Lice, Fice, or Putz by her parents and her sister, Irene, and was the family favorite. Her parents were a handsome couple; her mother with her carefully marcelled bob, her father slender and narrow-shouldered, with prematurely gray hair at his temples. He wore round, nickel-frame glasses and the ubiquitous bow tie—the picture of casual elegance.

The Schragenheims' friends were liberal and socialist-oriented Jews who believed in assimilation and turned up their noses at the Yiddish-speaking "Galicians" who lived on Grenadierstrasse. Lawyers, doctors, and artists frequented the house, among them the writer Lion Feuchtwanger and his sister Henny, related to the family on Felice's father's side, and whom Felice called "Uncle" and "Aunt." A rabbi as well was counted among the family friends, for the Schragenheims, though not devout, observed tradition; each Sabbath, the candlesticks had their place on the elegantly set table. And on the evening before Passover, the children ran through the house looking for traces of leavened bread, a custom they pursued avidly due to the sweets their parents hid for them in remote corners of the house. The only thing missing from this perfect childhood was a Christmas tree. Their mother had nothing against it; for her, Jewish celebrations were an empty ritual, but their father stood firm.

Berlin Jews were well acquainted with the Schragenheims' dental practice. *I knew a dentist once . . .* many of them would recall when the name Schragenheim was mentioned, even a decade later, after they had emigrated to England. In Berlin in 1933 half of all physicians and dentists on the public health insurance rolls were Jews.

In 1930, when Felice was eight years old, her parents had a serious automobile accident while on vacation. Their Fiat convertible, with trailer in tow, overturned on a forest road, landing upside down. Putz and Irene lost their beautiful mother, who was thirty-eight. Felice would later recall that when their dazed father returned to Berlin his hair had turned snow white. But a mere two years later he married a stylish young woman with dark, almond-shaped eyes and a perfectly oval face. Käte Hammerschlag not only became Dr. Schragenheim's wife, she also worked as his office assistant. The daughters were less than enthusiastic about their nineteen-year-old stepmother, who came from a wealthy household, and they never quite forgave their father for betraying their mother. But Dr. Schragenheim soon had other things to worry about.

In 1930 he served as head of the Welfare and Insurance Office of the Reich Association of German Dentists, and at the same time was a member of the dental section of the Association of Socialist Physicians, a fact that caused some disquiet during the elections of the Prussian Chamber of Dentists in 1931. But Albert Schragenheim's days as a functionary were numbered. Following Hitler's "seizure of power," all Jewish executive members and their representatives, nineteen in all, were forced to resign their commissions. The "Decree on the Practice of Dentists and Dental Technicians Under the Health Insurance Plan" of June 2, 1933, removed Communists and Jews alike from the national health insurance plan. Former front soldiers like Dr. Albert Schragenheim were spared for the time being, according to the "Law on the Reinstatement of Permanent Civil Servants."

Between April 1, 1933, and the end of June 1934, six hundred Jewish dentists of the Reich were "shut out," the anti-Semitic propaganda of members of the medical profession surpassing even that of the Nazis. Previously, everybody who was anybody in Berlin went to a Jewish doctor. The growing number of professional bans on Jewish hospital staff doctors opened up positions for those of their Aryan colleagues who hadn't made the grade the first time around. On May 12 the *Gross-Berliner Ärzteblatt* [Journal of Greater Berlin Physicians] demanded the "banning of all Jews from the medical treatment of German *Volksgenossen,* because the Jew is the incarnation of lies and deceit."

In 1934 the "Aryanization of Private Insurance" was introduced. "Personally unreliable," "non-Aryan," and "politically unfit" physicians no longer had their bills reimbursed by private insurance companies. Lists of "non-reimbursable" physicians and dentists were made public. The Reich Agency for Jews established a relief organization for those dentists excluded from the insurance plans, which offered retraining as dental technicians and advice on emigration. England was the emigration country of choice, because foreign dentists were allowed to practice their professions there without being subjected to additional examinations. But requests for work permits far outnumbered demand.

Around this time, or perhaps even sooner, Dr. Schragenheim bought a house on Carmel Mountain in Palestine, but sold it again because the climate didn't agree with him. He *did* make provisions for his daughters, however: The Haavara Agreement of 1934 enabled him to buy Palestinian securities, which he deposited for Felice and Irene at two Tel Aviv banks. This agreement allowed cooperation between the Palestine Trust Company for the Export of German Industrial Goods—set up by the Reich Ministry of the Interior—and the Zionist Jewish Agency for Palestine.

On March 18, 1935—Felice and Irene were thirteen and fifteen years old, respectively—Albert Schragenheim died at the age of forty-eight. "I was at the grocer's around the corner," recalled Felice's former classmate Christa-Maria Friedrich. "A woman burst in and called out, "Dr. Schragenheim is dead! The doorbell rang and it startled him so that he fell over and died."

His death spared his being subjected to the Nuremberg Racial Laws issued the following September. He was buried at Weissensee Jewish cemetery. In 1937, on the occasion of the Führer's birthday, he was posthumously awarded the "War Veterans Cross of Honor" by the president of the Berlin police, "in the name of the Führer and Reich Chancellor."

The young widow, Käte Schragenheim, moved with her stepdaughters into an apartment on Sybelstrasse in the Charlottenburg district of Berlin. Käte, called "Mulle" by the girls, took her duties as stepmother seriously, to the great regret of Irene and 'Lice. Now they could only smoke at night in bed, when Käte's watchful eyes were turned elsewhere. The two girls considered the elegant woman rather silly and kept their contact with her to an absolute minimum.

Until 1932 Felice attended the Kleist School on Levetzowstrasse, right next to the synagogue that later was to serve as a "collection camp." When she was eleven she transferred to the Bismarck Lyceum, a secondary school for girls in a nineteenth-century building located in Grunewald, the elegant villa district not far from Königsallee, where Walther Rathenau had been murdered in 1922.

The first measures to be instated in education after Hitler seized power were the reintroduction of corporal punishment, which had been banned during the Weimar Republic, and the "German greeting" at the beginning of each class. Though the Bismarck Lyceum on Lassenstrasse was conservative, it was not Nazi. It was Queen Luise's portrait that hung in every classroom, not Hitler's, and the teachers only unwillingly obeyed the order to greet each class with "Heil Hitler" as they entered the classroom. The Lord's Prayer continued to be recited at school ceremonies, as it had been prior to 1933, and only then were the German national anthem and Horst Wessel song intoned.

In April 1933 the "Law Against the Overcrowding of German Schools and Universities" was issued. The percentage of non-Aryan pupils and students was not permitted to rise above that of the general population, and was set at no more than 1.5 percent of new enrollments and no more than

5 percent of the "rest." The law did not apply to students whose fathers had fought in World War I.

Christa-Maria Friedrich:

It's odd that I can so clearly remember the moment when I saw Felice for the first time. It was after the Easter holidays in 1933. We had just moved up to the Quarta, the seventh grade. The lawns next to the entrance to the school were not fenced in yet, and you could sit comfortably on the little wall if the school building hadn't opened yet. They didn't open the doors till around quarter to eight. Surprisingly, I once got there so early that I had to sit and wait on the wall. Pretty close to me a very young woman was standing, holding the hands of two girls. The woman looked too classy to be a nanny, but too young for a mother. When we were later all seated in our new class, I saw the younger of the two girls, Felice. It didn't take long for us to discover that we walked the same way to school. She lived diagonally across from me. On our many walks to and from school together I learned from her what the Social Democrats wanted and who the Zionists were. And when I had to play organ at the prayer meeting on Mondays, she held the handle of the broken motor for me. Felice was smart, well-read, very alert, athletic, sometimes boldly brazen and wonderfully happy—really a perfect buddy. With her broad shoulders and long legs she always seemed a bit masculine. She wasn't pretty in a conventional sense, but she had an inner charisma that radiated from her big, light brown and gray-green eyes. Although we weren't really close friends, we often saw each other in the afternoons, usually at my place.

On September 4, 1933, Felice received her certificate for endurance swimming, having swum for seventy-five minutes in the Lunapark pool in Berlin's Halensee district. It would not be long before she was forbidden to swim in public pools. In the summer of 1935 a sign appeared at the outdoor pool in Wannsee carrying the message: "Swimming and admission prohibited to Jews!" But at the urging of the Foreign Office it was removed in preparation for the Olympic Games to take place the following year. Felice joined *Bar Kochba*, the Jewish Sports Club.

Personal contact between Jewish and non-Jewish girls was made almost impossible with the passage of the Reich Citizens Law of November 1935. Pressure intensified following the breather that was created before and during the Summer Olympics. "At the present time Felice does not give the impression that she is in top form physically; that is one reason her responses are sometimes inadequate. Nonetheless, once again she has earned positive marks overall," wrote teacher Walther Gerhardt on Felice's class certificate dated October 8, 1936. Felice appears small and delicate in a class photo of June 1936. She was exempt from attending history classes, in which "World Judaism" was discussed, and perhaps had her skull measured in Ethnology class.

AND YET—

There are those who carry on today; they are
Poor and unsuccessful they say,
Who flirt continually with disaster,

Yet almost choose it as their master.
But this world, for my measure,
gives me much that grants me pleasure.
On sunny days I go into town
and see great personages of renown;
Records and books I look upon
with joy, and poems and scarves of chiffon.
I love the theater, Klabund I read,
and laughter is healthy and something I need.
Other people truly do
find my attitude taboo;
Whether or not it is their choice—
there is much in this world for which I rejoice.

[APRIL 6, 19——?]

But this school was a good choice for Felice nevertheless. Walther Gerhardt, who taught history and Latin, and whom the girls fondly called "Bubi," might have worn the gold party insignia on his lapel, but he was a good-hearted man who had probably long since turned away from National Socialism internally. And yet he dutifully registered in his class book the "race" of each of his students: "a." for "Aryan," "h.a." for "half-Aryan," and "n.a." for "non-Aryan."

Despite the large number of students who left the school in 1937, 58 Jewish girls still remained among a population of 343 at the Bismarck Lyceum, far more than the maximum quota allowed. This was perhaps due to the fact that the heads of many of the old Jewish families were war veterans. One student, who completed her studies in 1933, recalled that among her graduating class of 23 girls, only 7 were Aryan. The school's director, Dr. Friedrich Abée, was highly regarded by parents who wished to spare their child a Nazi education. When Berlin's schools were closed in the summer of 1943 there were still "half" and "quarter" Jews attending Felice's school. Ilse Kalden, who graduated in 1943, wrote in the school's chronicle:

> Each school year new students joined our class from other sections of Berlin, even from other central German cities. To us, they seemed shy and unsure at first, until they gained in confidence. Slowly we discovered that almost without exception they all had suffered because of their religious beliefs, and that they had been expelled from other schools because somewhere in their family tree was a Jewish forebear. They all fled to Dr. Abée and were accepted without reservation. He even housed some of them in his own home.

Officially, however, the school was "Jew-free" in 1939. The removal of the daughters of merchants, university professors, surgeons, bankers, industrialists, and theater directors "due to parents' relocation" had occurred in stages. On March 27, 1936, Felice's sister, Irene, received her school-leaving certificate "to attend school abroad." Five other girls in her class left at the same time, for the same reason. One year later at least eight other students withdrew, among them Felice's best friend, Hilli Frenkel. In the school newspaper of 1937 is printed a farewell poem written by Felice to Marie-Anne Hartog, a banker's daughter:

IN MARIE-ANNE'S ALBUM

"Just say a soft good-bye"—
The day after tomorrow,
Your schooldays' great sorrow
Belongs to days gone by.
What we attained, that for which we strived,
Is "once upon a time" now, but I feel
That though I have been left behind,
You shall yet achieve your "feminine ideal."

[MARCH 1937]

"What I Wish to Make of Myself—My Feminine Ideal" was the theme of an essay assigned to Felice's class in the 1936–37 school year. Compared with "Blood Is a Very Special Fluid," "Air Defense Is Necessary" and "The Heroic in Ancient Germanic Religion"—topics which students at other Berlin schools had been assigned since 1933—Felice's high school was conspicuous in its restraint. A test question in math is interesting as well:

A ship crossing the Mediterranean to Jaffa, at 32°5' long., 34°45' lat., has given its position as 34°45' long., 27°17' lat. What course must it take?

This question is difficult to interpret: Is it a veiled reference to the Jewish students' future prospects, cynicism, or a premature giving in to "Jews out and on to Palestine," the official "Jewish policy" of that period?

The "half-Aryan" Olga Selbach joined Felice's class at Easter 1937. Felice chose the plump Olga, who was always chewing her fingernails, to be her close confidante. When the school day ended in summer they would hurry to the swimming pool at the Reich sports field, and in the winter they visited each other at home, stretching out lazily on the couch, giggling, to talk about sex. As Olga, though almost two years older, was completely inexperienced, Felice could boast at will, always returning to the subject of lesbian love. When Olga appears deeply impressed, Felice lays it on even thicker. She had undergone an operation as a child, she said, something to do with her ovaries, and ever since then she had had these lesbian feelings. Olga was positively determined to be worthy of the friendship of a niece of Lion Feuchtwanger. Felice's dream was to become a writer like her "uncle," and the two girls polished their style by composing love letters. "Let's cultivate our feelings," Felice would say, and then they would think up imaginary people to whom they wrote passionate letters. Olga's were addressed to a Russian man she called "Vasja."

At Easter 1938 the Bismarck Lyceum was renamed the Johanna von Puttkamer High School, after Bismarck's wife. On July 22 Jews were issued identification cards marked with the letter *J*. That fall only one "full-Jew" remained in the class. Felice, in fact, was the last.

On October 11, 1938, Felice received her last regular school report: "Felice has been able to retain her favorable position in the class," her teacher, Walther Gerhardt, noted in his appraisal. The sole grade of "very good" that Felice earned was in English.

UNFORTUNATELY

True, we spoke of ancient sagas,
Of colonies far removed from here—
But how to ask the way in English
We haven't mastered yet, I fear.
I have no right to criticize,
I do not wish to make a fuss,
But "over there," I realize,
Is something else. What will become of us?
Just how are we to make it through?
Not even you yourself can say!
Dear Fräulein Dr. Merten, you
instructed us, now we must pay!

[AUGUST 9, 1938]

But Felice's chances of going "over there" appeared slim. As the situation grew even more critical for Jews with the annexation of Austria in March 1938, and it became increasingly clear that the League of Nations was unable to control the growing refugee problem, President Roosevelt called a conference for the establishment of a new international refugee relief organization. In July 1938 representatives from thirty-two nations traveled to the French spa of Evian-les-Bains. The conference opened with an offer from the United States to extend its quota for refugees from Germany and Austria to the maximum—increasing it to 27,370 people. Following this, one delegate after another apologized for his country's low immigration quota. The delegate from England would not allow debate on the issue of the British mandated territory of Palestine, and made it known that Great Britain, overpopulated and burdened by a large unemployment figure, was in no position to accept Jewish refugees.

On *Kristallnacht,* the pogrom night in November 1938, as synagogues burned throughout the German Reich and tens of thousands of Jews were dragged off to concentration camps, the world momentarily reacted with shock and sympathy. Holland, Belgium, France and Switzerland allowed thousands of Jews to cross their borders without passports or money; nor did they turn away illegal refugees after these borders were closed. "I cannot believe," President Roosevelt stated indignantly, "that such things can occur in a civilized land in the twentieth century." But when asked if he would support a loosening of immigration laws he cited national quotas that had been set by law in 1924.

After *Kristallnacht* even the most patriotic Jews realized that they would do well to abandon their homeland, at least for the present. Those who still were in a position to leave attempted to do so. But the Haavara Agreement, which had allowed some thirty thousand Jews to emigrate to Palestine, was annulled on November 9. And whereas in previous years Jews could pay a twenty-five percent "Reich refugee tax" and take the rest of their capital assets out of the country with them, any export of capital was banned as of June 1938.

In 1938, 140,000 people left the Third Reich. Those who stayed behind were, for the most part, the elderly, and single women. Half of the Jewish population remaining in Germany was over fifty years of age. While it was true that women exhibited a greater willingness than men to emigrate, more men actually left the country than women. A woman's presence was required where the need was greatest; women served as community workers, nurses and teachers in the social welfare institutions of the Jewish community, which more and more people were coming to depend on. In the communal kitchens women cooked for those who could not cook for themselves. And women remained behind because they felt responsible for their elderly parents. In 1933 women made up 52.3 percent of the Jewish population; by 1939 that figure had risen to 57.5 percent.

Felice's schooldays came to a sudden end as well, for on November 15, 1938, Jewish boys and girls were forbidden to attend public schools. "Following the heinous assassination in Paris, no German teacher can be expected to give instruction to Jewish schoolchildren," read the decree issued by the Reich Minister of Education. "It is also clear that it is intolerable for German pupils to sit in the same classroom with Jews. Over the past several years the segregation of the races within the educational system has been realized for the most part, it is true, but the remaining Jewish students attending German schools with German boys and girls can no longer be tolerated."

Felice, one of those remaining, received her school-leaving certificate "at the order of the Reich Minister of Education." It was signed by her teacher, Walter Gerhardt, and headmaster Dr. Friedrich Abée. Walter Gerhardt issued one last evaluation: "Felice was a quiet, friendly, gifted, and hardworking pupil."

The rest of Felice's report book remained empty. She was sixteen and a half years old. When she left she took with her the school library's German-English dictionary. "Stolen on

November 2, 1938," is written defiantly in green ink on the inside cover of the book.

OBITUARY

Certificate in hand, my school career
now finds its slow and certain end.
Last act, the iron curtain here
Closes on what I might have been.
One year more and I would have earned
my diploma, having played my part.
Instead this list of what I've learned,
States I was quiet, hardworking, smart.

Yes, gone those lovely days in time,
When once I dozed to Schiller's "Clock,"
Though much preferred was Scheffler's rhyme
Awakening me and signaling "stop."
Playing hooky, passing notes, my relinquished
School pass—all passé.
Only I remain, dismissed and hindered,
A ninth-grade student without a grade.

[SEPTEMBER 11, 1939]

On November 16, 1938, Felice's fellow students were curtly informed that she no longer would be attending the school. No one asked questions—they all knew what it meant. Even Olga went through a moment of shock that lasted for weeks. No one visited Felice. When Olga accidentally ran into her on the street one day Felice looked unhappy and lost. Olga invited her home, and Luise Selbach, seeing the suffering in Felice's eyes, opened her motherly heart to the teenager. Luise, who was Jewish, lived in a "privileged mixed marriage," ran a strict household, and soon accepted Felice into it as a fourth daughter. She was capricious, witty, and prone to theatrics. Her authority in the home rested not so much on her loud voice as it did on her capacity to inflict psychological suffering. And she was totally unpredictable. In the midst of laughter she suddenly would be reminded of some past transgression that no one else could even recall. But Mutti's apartment in Berlin-Friedenau was also a warm and hospitable refuge. Fice and Olga would hold serious discussions on the future of the world, in the company of their pretty classmate Liesl Ptok. They read Marx, Spinoza, Brecht and Tucholsky. Other times, sitting backwards on their chairs, they played "Going to Jerusalem," with Mutti accompanying them on the piano. Fice had found a family again.

Today, the Johanna von Puttkamer High School for Girls is called the Hildegard Wegscheider High School. Hildegard Wegscheider was a representative of the Social Democratic Party who served in Prussian parliament until 1933. On September 3, 1998, two plaques were unveiled, one in German and one in Hebrew, to commemorate the fifty-eight Jewish girls who attended the school in 1937.

MINOR INQUIRY

In deepest winter do you all
Still translate Latin, full of dread,
There in the niche by the art room wall,
Mathematics running through your head?

Are you still sneaking on the sly,
Up to the balcony's soothing sun?
And for this paean to the sky,
Must you pay with extra homework done?

Is Bubi still racing around on outings
Faster than a fast express?
Is Basche still threatening and shouting,
And wearing her sofa-cover dress?

Is Inge Matthie still always late?
Have you once again been apprised of the rules?
Is Fräulein Merten still so discreet
As to tear up the notes she finds at school?
Are you still writing—the past for me
Is still the present, of course, for you.
It is only memory that allows us to see
What is now past in a golden hue.

[FEBRUARY 1939]

The Schragenheims now too began to make concerted efforts to emigrate. On October 22, 1938, Irene was declared

of legal age by a ruling of the Municipal Court of Berlin-Charlottenburg, and she and Felice, still a minor, signed a "partition of inheritance agreement." Effective October 31, 1938, the following was recorded as property of their father's estate, to be divided equally between Irene and Felice:

1. Securities
   a. In the value of 94,448.75 Reichsmarks (RM), deposited at the Prussian State Bank of Berlin;
   b. one land deed Hanotaiah Ltd. Plantation and Settlement Company, Tel Aviv (5% land grant bond of 1934) at a face value of 814,522 Palestinian pounds. At a median rate of exchange for Palestinian pounds this comes to a total of RM 3,389.64;
   c. 162 Kerem-Kajemeth-Leisrael debentures at a face value of 6 Palestinian pounds each, on deposit in the name of the Schragenheim sisters at Haavara Limited in Tel Aviv, valued at 972 Palestinian pounds, or RM 7,916.90;
2. Jewelry at a total value of RM 745;
3. Claims in the total value of RM 2,339.09.
   The estate is valued at RM 108,823.08, therefore each sister is to receive RM 54,411.54.

It was agreed that the majority of the debentures on deposit at Haavara Limited were to go to Felice, in order to enable her to emigrate to Palestine. Should she succeed in leaving Germany, Irene's share would then be credited to her.

At this time, Irene had already returned to Berlin after a two-year stay with relatives in Stockholm. She attended a trade school in Berlin, presumably until the *Kristallnacht*. She had left the Bismarck Lyceum in 1936 "to attend a school abroad," as was noted on her school-leaving certificate. She emigrated to London in 1939, and was hired on a trial basis in February 1940 as a nurse in the St. Pancras Hospital. The earliest of her letters from England that survived, and which reached Felice through the Red Cross, is dated April 4, 1942.

On January 6, 1939, Felice's legal guardian, attorney Edgar von Fragstein und Niemsdorff, informed Käte Schragenheim that he anticipated that the Foreign Exchange Office and the Reichsbank would agree to the partition of inheritance between Irene and Felice, and listed the securities available to Felice should she and Käte emigrate.

On January 16 the Continental Illinois National Bank and Trust Company of Chicago confirmed to the American consul that physician Walter Karewski, Felice's uncle, the brother of her deceased mother, and his wife maintained a savings account in the amount of $2,091.04. Dr. Karewski, who called himself Walter Karsten in his new homeland, had lived in the United States since June 1936. On January 20 he signed an affidavit before a notary public applying for an immigration visa to the United States for Felice, a "housemaid" by profession, due to "conditions in Germany." An additional affidavit was signed by Jennie L. Brann, who had lived in the United States all of her life, and who listed herself on the yellow form as Felice's second cousin. On January 18 the Trustee and Transfer Office of Haavara Limited in Tel Aviv confirmed to the British Passport Office that the above-mentioned debentures on deposit at the Anglo-Palestine Bank Ltd, valued at RM 12,000, were being held in trust for the two daughters of the late Dr. Albert Schragenheim.

On December 6, 1938, Jews were no longer allowed to take certain streets in Berlin's inner city. Sections of Wilhelmstrasse and Unter den Linden were put under a "Jew ban."

Gerd Ehrlich:

Everything is transitory, and even the disturbances of November '38 came to an end. "Normal" life went on. A constant stream of people flooded the consulates, that's true, but it was not easy to emigrate. In addition to an entry permit to another country, difficult enough to obtain, one also needed an exit permit issued by the Gestapo. A passport office was set up on Kurfürstendamm, and one heard very little that was positive in connection with it. I personally always got hung up at the consulates. . . . The life we led was in no way desperate, however. We still had our relatively large apartments and for the most part could move about the streets in safety. But you had to take care not to jaywalk or commit some similar "crime," because then the game was up. The police had strict instructions to punish harshly any Jew who committed such a misdemeanor, which generally carried a fine of one Reichsmark. I knew of cases where Jews landed first in jail and then in a concentration camp because they disregarded some traffic rule. I myself once had my name taken down by a police officer because I was riding my bike on a prohibited street. For some inexplicable reason he didn't bring a charge against me; that was the end of the matter, at any rate.

As of January 1, 1939, Jews were ordered to add the name "Sara" or "Israel" to their family names on all pieces of identification. Felice became Felice Rahel Sara Schragenheim. Jews were forbidden to attend public theaters, movie houses, concert halls or cabarets. The theater run by the Jewish *Kulturbund,* and the Jewish movie houses were the only places where Jews could escape the bleakness of their everyday lives. The "New Reich Chancellery," designed by Albert Speer, was opened on January 9, and on January 24 the "Reich Central Office for Jewish Emigration."

Berliners were complaining that the supply of coffee was running low. "Germans, drink tea!" the coffee merchants urged. As regulations governing Jews soon were published only in the Jewish newspaper, the *Jüdisches Nachrichtenblatt,* it was made easier for Aryans to close their eyes to what was happening outside their front doors.

"Should Jews in international finance once again succeed, inside and outside Europe, in plunging the nations of the world into a world war," Hitler threatened in an address aimed at Washington on January 30, 1939, "then the result will be not a Bolshevization of the earth, and therewith the victory of Judaism, but the destruction of the Jewish race in Europe."

On February 4, 1939, Felice's grandmother, Hulda Karewski, presented to the American Consulate an affidavit signed by her son Walter, together with an additional affidavit signed by Sam Maling, an American citizen and merchant, whose wife, Hazel, was a friend of Hulda. Sam Maling attested before a notary that he resided in a five-room apartment at the

Chicago Beach Hotel, earned $1,500 a month, and had private assets valued at over fifty thousand dollars. He declared that he was a law-abiding citizen and had never been arrested for a crime or for any other misconduct. Nor did he belong to any group or organization whose goal was the overthrow of constitutional order. To the best of his knowledge and belief, the same held true for the applicant. Hulda Karewski, seventy years old, informed the American Consulate that in a registered letter of December 22, 1938, she had requested to be assigned a number on the waiting list, and asked that the matter be expedited, as her son was in possession of "first papers," and her presence was urgently required in his household.

As of February 21, 1939, Jews had to surrender all objects in their possession made of gold, silver, platinum, pearls, or gems, with the exception of wedding rings. At the end of April a "Rental Law for Jews" was passed. It was left to "residents of a building alone" to decide "as of which date the presence of Jewish tenants is felt to be burdensome." Jews who were forced to vacate their apartments were sent to "Jewish houses." The Schragenheims were forced to move out of the apartment on Sybelstrasse and went to live with Käte's parents, the Hammerschlags, whose ten-room apartment at Kurfürstendamm 102 was accommodating an ever-increasing number of Jews. "She moved to her step-grandparents on Kurfürstendamm," recalled Christa-Maria Friedrich. "She had a room there and lived among the white furniture with a rubbed-varnish finish, which were not hers and didn't match her taste at all."

THE MOVE

Ultimo, the flat stood strange
And empty, now mere storage room.
Paper and rags around us arranged
What long had been "home" into a tomb.
Shards bring luck—the Chinese vase
Now believes that too, praise
God. Burly moving men do race
Around with piano and bookcase.

Spots on the wall where pictures hung,
Crates our only chairs,
Dead black wires from the ceiling wrung
Not a single flashlight anywhere.

Once our things are on the street
The packers set off for a quaff,
At precisely that moment, nice and neat,
God chooses to send a rainstorm off.
But then the moment finally arrives,
And the moving van sways away.
In future when we speak of our lives,
"That's where we lived back then—" we'll say.

[JUNE 12, 1939]

In the second half of March 1939 Felice took the Cambridge Proficiency Test in English at the Jüdische Waldschule

Kaliski, a private Jewish school in the Dahlem district of Berlin, and waited for the day she would emigrate.

Refugees were permitted to take ten Reichsmarks in cash out of the country with them. Any violation of the foreign exchange regulation could result in being sent to a concentration camp or worse. Aryan Germans, who were permitted to travel abroad, increasingly departed elegantly attired in the furs and valuables of their Jewish friends, to get them out of the country. "Custodaryans" were storing Jewish possessions in their cellars and attics.

Until the late summer of 1941 the declared "Jewish policy" of the German Reich remained that of permitting the emigration of all Jews living in Germany. Of the 140,000 Jews who fled Germany in 1938, South America had taken in 20,000, and Palestine 12,000 legal, and an unknown but not insignificant number of illegal refugees. Perhaps 30,000 succeeded in being accepted by the United States. The rest were stuck in Western European lands of transit: France, Great Britain, the Netherlands, Belgium, and Switzerland. These countries began closing their borders when it became clear that the number of refugees being accepted abroad was shrinking. Foreign consulates were besieged by tens of thousands of people, but waiting lists were filled for years to come. By mid-May 1939 the British government had limited the number of refugees to Palestine to 10,000 a year until 1944, plus 25,000 refugees whose relatives would vouch for them.

Among those who made it to the United States was Felice's

best friend, Hilli Frenkel, who smuggled Felice's mother's jewels across the border in a package of sanitary napkins.

AUF WIEDERSEHEN!!

Earlier, when something funny occurred,
Whether humorous, wonderful, or absurd,
Touching little stories that ascertain
The continuing saga of Fraülein Merten,
Or Micha Nussbaum's splendid bass,
Or some dumb school affair, whatever the case;
When I did something foolish in this place or that,
Or got in a big fight or some big spat,
An inner voice would always insist,
You really must tell Hilli this!
No more!
I sit here all alone now,
No thunderous applause to soothe my brow,
Nor do I hear that silly laugh,
A friendship quarrel's aftermath.
Yet thrice a day, and often sorely,
When I pretend to be Evelyne Corley,
Or of lovely Chekhova catch a glance,
Or am struck by a hit song's sweet romance—
I have to tell her, occurs to me then,
I have to tell Hilli, tell my friend!—
But in a few years time, just you wait,
This no longer will be our fate.
Then we'll see each other again,

And everything that happened up 'til then,
All the little scandals, and what I've read,
What I've written, and what's in my head,
Whom I've contacted and whom I've provoked,
And the very best of all my jokes
Manna for our silly souls . . .
Hilli, I'll tell you in repose!

[MARCH 1939]

On March 15, 1939, the "Relief Organization for Jews in Germany" affirmed that in February 1937 Felice had appeared before the review board of the Bismarck Lyceum and successfully passed her home economics examination. She was therefore "totally suited to accept a position in a British household." Felice's little lined notebook from her cooking class has survived the decades, filled with recipes for chocolate soup with macaroons, breaded and unbreaded roast cutlet, hollandaise sauce, crumb cake, short pastry, semolina pudding, Kathreiner barley malt coffee, broth with egg, a ragout of game, apple bread soup . . .

THOUGHTS ON THE FUTURE

I like to dream of my career,
of cars and sun, of beauty and gold,
I think of blue seas far from here,
of journalism and worlds untold.

To far lands one can go, atlas in hand.
I do it gladly, well aware

That my life will change in some other land,
And my small star still is shining somewhere.

Yes, if only I were far away—
Once there I could continue my dreaming,
And then I would finally have my career,

If only in cooking and cleaning.
It's good that we were given hope,
And self-deception, so we cannot see
Our guest appearance in this life
For what it is—tragicomedy.

[MAY 1938]

On March 16, 1939, Dr. Israel Ernst Jacoby attested in English that Felice was "neither mentally nor physically defective," nor suffered from any contagious diseases. On April 1 she appeared at police headquarters on Alexanderplatz to have her fingerprints taken. The executive board of the Jewish Community on Oranienburger Strasse informed Felice Sara Schragenheim on April 18 that her emigration tax was set at 2,080 Reichsmarks, and requested that she deposit securities to cover this amount in the special depository of the Jewish Community at the Commerz und Privatbank AG.

A COMPLICATED INNER LIFE

The word "forbidden," today contains
Everything which to us remains,

Aimée and Jaguar—Lilly Wust (right) and Felice Schragenheim, taken with a self-timer at the Havel River, August 21, 1944.

Felice, in a photo taken by Lilly, at the Havel River, August 21, 1944.

Lilly, in a photo taken by Felice, during the summer of 1944 on the balcony of Lilly's apartment at Friedrichshaller Strasse 23.

Lilly's parents, Margarethe and Günther Kappler, Lilly's half brother, Bob, and Lilly, circa 1919.

(from left) Lilly's father, Lilly's husband (Günther Wust), Lilly's mother, Lilly with son Bernd, summer 1937.

Lilly with her sons, Bernd, Eberhard, Reinhard, and Albrecht in February 1943, taken by Felice's friend Ilse Ploog.

Felice (4) (left) and Irene (6) Schragenheim in 1926.

Felice's parents, Dr. Albert Schragenheim and Erna Schragenheim, née Karewski, in Berchtesgaden, 1921.

Käte Schragenheim, née Hammerschlag, Felice's stepmother.

Felice's grandmother Hulda Karewski, murdered in Theresienstadt.

Felice's school class in Berlin-Grunewald, with teacher Walther Gerhardt, in June 1936. Felice is seated in the second row, left, and Hilli Frenkel, Felice's best friend, is in the fourth row, left.

Medical Certificate of Health

Miss Felice Schragenheim, born on 9.3.1920, residing in Berlin-Charlottenburg, 27, Sybelstr., has this day been medically examined by me. I found her not to be mentally or physically defective in any way. I found exspecially that Miss Schragenheim is fre e from any infectious disease.

Berlin, den 16. März 1939

Jacoby.

A medical certificate prepared by Dr. Israel Ernst Jacoby, dated 1939, indicating that Felice was "free from any infectious diseases" and therefore fit for emigration.

Günther Wust, Lilly's husband, 1930.

Two notes. Top: from Aimée to Jaguar. Bottom: from Jaguar to Aimée.

Lilly with "bunker nurse" Herta, Reinhard, and Albrecht in front of Lilly's building on Friedrichshaller Strasse, taken by Felice in the fall of 1943.

Lilly, Felice, and Käthe Herrmann, Lilly's best friend, in Eichwalde,
taken by Käthe's husband, Ewald.

HANDGEPÄCK

X Umzugsgut Liste
x Reisegepäck x
(Nichtzutreffendes ist zu durchstreichen.)

Blatt 1

Zum Antrag vom 11.Mai

Name des Auswanderers Felice Sara Schragenheim

lfd. Nr.	Stück	Gegenstand genaue Bezeichnung	Zeitpunkt der Anschaffung
1	2	Handtücher	vor 1933
2	1	Doubléarmband	" "
3	1	Plätteisen	" "
4	1	kl.Plätteisen	1936-1938
5	2	Badetücher	" "
6	1	Hut	" "
7	1	Regenmantel	" "
8	1	Wollweste	" "
9	5	Kleiderbügel	" "
10	1	Kleid	" "
11	4	Blusen	" "
12	1 dtz	Taschentücher	" "
13	4	Pyjamas	" "
14	1	Regenschirm	" "
15	2	Kostüme	" "
16	2	Büstenhalter	" "
17	2	Höschen	" "
18	2	Hemdchen	" "
19	2 P.	Schuhe	" "
20	1 "	Hausschuhe	" "
21	1	Mantel	" "
22	1	Kleiderbürste	" "
23	1	Nagelnecessaire	" "
24	1	Weckeruhr	" "
25	1	lg.Hose	" "
26	1 P.	Handschuhe	" "
27	1	Kappe	" "
28	2	Blusenbinder	" "
29	1	Handspiegel	" "
30	2	Strumpfhaltergürtel	" "

Geprüft
Berlin, den ... Mai 193..
Sachverständiger der Devisenstelle

Vor Aufstellung Rückseite durchlesen

The list of belongings Felice wished to take with her when she emigrated, dated 1939.

FEE.—£1 (One Pound.) 38/271:90 Form No. 41.
COMMONWEALTH OF AUSTRALIA.

Permit N.° 32796

DEPARTMENT OF THE INTERIOR,
CANBERRA, A.C.T.,

13th June, 19₃₉

LANDING PERMIT.

To whom it may concern:

THIS IS TO CERTIFY that permission has been granted for the admission to
Australia of the undermentioned person or persons (one   in number), said
to be of   German   nationality, at present residing
in   Germany   ~~whose maintenance has been~~
~~in Australia has been guaranteed by Mr.~~
of

This authority has been granted subject to the conditions that such person
or persons shall be in sound health, of good character, and in possession
of a   German   Passport or Certificate of Identity,
bearing photograph of the holder, and duly visaed (if not issued) by a British
Consular or Passport Officer, and subject to any further conditions which may be
stated below.

This Permit is valid until   13th June, 1940.

NAME.	AGE.	RELATIONSHIP (if any) TO GUARANTOR.
SCHRAGENHEIM, Felice	17 years	—

NOTE:- This authority is also subject to the condition
that bearer will be accompanied to Australia by her
step-mother, Mrs. K. Schragenheim, holder of Landing
Permit No. 32795.

Transmitted per   The General Secretary,
Australian Jewish Welfare
Society,
SYDNEY.

By authority of the
Minister for the Interior.

NOTE.—This Permit should be forwarded to the person in whose favour it has been issued (or to
the chief member of the party if more than one person is included in the Permit) for production when
applying for passport facilities or steamer passage tickets, and for production and surrender to the
Examining Officer of Customs at the Australian port of disembarkation.
If an extension of this Permit is desired, application should be addressed to the Department of
the Interior. A fee of 10/- (ten shillings) is payable for each year's extension authorized.

The landing permit granted in 1939 to Felice by the Australian Jewish
Welfare Society.

Except yellow benches and future fears.
No swimming, dancing, or movie dreams,
Neither jewelry nor equal rights, it seems,
May we keep. At best our tears.

So it will be nice to go away,
I wanted to travel anyway.
And yet it is weeping that I roam,
Because this pace we understand,
Because as strangers we leave this land,
Because what is missing is the bridge leading home.

[JUNE 23, 1939]

On May 9, 1939, the American Consulate General on Hermann Göring Strasse informed Irene and Felice that they had been registered on the German waiting list under the numbers 43015-b and 43015-c. "It cannot be stated at present when your case will be considered, but you will be notified of this in due time."

In compliance with foreign exchange regulations, Felice applied on May 11 to the office of Berlin's chief financial president for permission to take with her two four-piece silver place settings, a small napkin ring, a bracelet, a salt shaker, and a cuticle remover. To her application she attached a list of objects she wished to carry into emigration in her hand luggage. The items were consecutively numbered and listed with their year of purchase:

2 hand towels, 1 rolled gold bracelet, 1 iron, 1 small
ironing board, 2 bath towels, 1 hat, 1 raincoat, 1 wool

vest, 5 clothes hangers, 1 dress, 4 blouses, 1 dozen
handkerchiefs, 4 pairs of pajamas, 1 umbrella, 2 suits, 2
brassieres, 2 pairs of underwear, 2 undershirts, 2 pairs of
shoes, 1 pair of house slippers, 1 coat, 1 clothes brush, 1
nail kit, 1 alarm clock, 1 pair trousers, 1 pair gloves, 1 cap,
2 shirt ties, 1 hand mirror, 2 garter belts, 2 tins of powder,
2 pocket combs, 1 sewing kit, 4 pocket mirrors, 4 coin
purses, 1 handbag, 1 pair overshoes, 1 watch pin, 2 belts,
1 bathrobe, 1 box gramophone needles, 1 pair walking
shoes, 1 writing case with accoutrements, 5 ribbons, 2
pairs shoe bags, 2 collars, 1 razor, 2 tweezers, 1 small photo
album, 3 lexicons, 6 books, 2 coupé cases, 1 suitcase, 1 hat
box, 1 briefcase, 1 bath towel, 1 hat, 1 first aid kit, 3 gauze
bandages, 6 pairs stockings, 3 bars soap, 2 pairs gloves, 1
cap, 4 wash pouches, 3 washcloths, 2 sponges, 2 combs, 4
brushes, 5 tubes lotion, 3 tubes toothpaste, 4 tins lotion,
4 packages sanitary pads, 4 packages laundry detergent,
2 veils, 4 packages absorbent cotton, 10 hair curlers, 3
bottles perfume, 1 bottle stain remover, 20 medications,
1 small box clip pins, 4 tins powder, 2 lipsticks, 2 pocket
combs, 4 packs bobby pins, 3 packs shampoo, 1 pocket
mirror, 1 wallet, 1 bottle ink, 1 pencil sharpener, 4 pencils,
4 boxes pencil lead, 2 boxes stationery, 2 fountain pens, 1
fountain pen case, 2 identification papers cases, 1 darner,
3 scissors, 3 belts, 2 boxes darning yarn, 12 pairs dress
shields, 2 pairs shoe bags, 5 ribbons, 4 boxes safety pins,
2 pocket calendars, 2 typewriter ribbons, 1 stocking bag,
1 ring, 1 fever thermometer, 1 pair sunglasses, 2 writing
pads, 1 shoe polish kit.

Following their father's death, each of the two sisters received a wardrobe trunk for their emigration, outfitted with
supplies to last for four years. On thinly lined paper Felice
made list after list of clothing and objects that seemed absolutely necessary to her new life. On her English typewriter
with its green ribbon she kept an account of the contents of
the "gray iron military trunk," one of three trunks packed
with possessions in anticipation of the great journey, which
was stored, for a fee of RM 4.20 a month, in the warehouse of
the Hamburg carrier Edmund Franzkowiak & Co.:

Monkey, bread sack, 1 pair socks, 1 pair ski boots, 2 pairs
ski gloves, ski suit, 1 pair galoshes, 7 sports shirts, 2 ski
bands, 1 devil's cap, 4 smocks, 1 apron, 3 gym shorts,
3 gym shirts, 2 bathing suits, 1 pair shorts, toy dogs, 1
wool blouse, 1 pair beach pants, 6 pairs socks, 5 pairs
knee socks, 10 pairs stockings, 4 boxes sanitary pads, 4
packages absorbent cotton, 8 clothes hangers, 1 linen
dress, 4 typewriter ribbons, 5 tubes toothpaste, 1 sanitary
belt, 6 bars soap, 4 packages laundry detergent, 2 rolls
film, 1 pair gloves, 1 pair wooden slippers, shoe travel
kit, 2 pads stationery, 25 envelopes, 1 bottle Eu-Med,
3 bath sponges, 6 gauze bandages, 1 bottle Spectrol, 1
bottle Inspirol, 1 nail brush, 3 packages absorbent cotton,
underwear, 1 dozen handkerchiefs, 1 dozen stockings, 1
iron, 1 Budko, 4 shampoos, 1 eyelash growth enhancer, 2
boxes badges, 1 evening bag, 1 tweezers, 1 white handbag,
5 pairs pajamas, 1 pair white shorts, 5 sets underwear, 2
brassieres, 2 garter belts, 1 brown winter ensemble, 2 pairs

stockings, 3 blouses, 1 cloth, 9 clothes hangers, 5 winter dresses, 1 evening dress.

On May 30, 1939, the British Passport Control office requested a meeting with Felice to discuss her immigration to Palestine. The outcome of this meeting is unknown. On June 3 the "pupil" without a school, Felice Rahel Sara Schragenheim, was issued a passport valid for one year, stamped with a large red *J*. On June 9 the J. L. Feuchtwanger General Commercial Bank in Tel Aviv verified to the British Consulate General that debentures had been deposited to Felice's credit. On June 13 Felice and her stepmother received a "landing permit" for Australia, valid for one year from issue.

THE TIMES ARE CHANGING—

Earlier our travel plans
Consisted of blue seas, palms, white sand.
Today our view is blocked by fate,
We no longer travel, we emigrate.

Those who once happily went away,
Now wish only that they could stay,
Without language classes, lists and such,
And if one must travel—then with the Baedecker touch.

Trunks that once to Biarritz went,
Now find that they are quite content
To travel to lands just recently found,

And therefore still as yet unbound
By polished manners, an overinsistence
On elegance, but for that, distance.

To find the promised land perchance,
One has to book far in advance.
And travel in the best of style,
On a luxury steamer—into exile.

[JUNE 16, 1939]

On August 7, 1939, an Australian visa was stamped in Felice's passport. On August 9 the Charlottenburg branch of the Reichsbank informed Felice's legal guardian, Edgar von Fragstein und Niemsdorff, that as many of Felice's Palestinian securities could be sold as needed to exchange for two hundred Australian pounds, "so that your charge may demonstrate to the Australian authorities that she is in possession of the funds needed to enter their country." On August 14 Felice was granted a two-year extension of the export permit for the belongings she had listed in May. Among Felice's effects was found a copy of a reservation from the Middle European Travel Agency, made out to Käte Schragenheim and valued at 1,268.45 Reichsmarks, for passage on the steamer *Australia Star*, to depart London December 20, 1939, for Melbourne.

At the end of August a number of events occurred in rapid succession: On August 23 the Hitler-Stalin Pact was signed, and on August 25 the British-Polish Alliance Agreement; August 26 was the first day of mobilization; the Reichstag assembly was summoned and children were sent home from school.

On Sunday, August 27, food ration cards were issued. Those distributed to the Schragenheims and the Hammerschlags by the concierge were stamped with a red *J*, which excluded them from all special provisions and from purchasing items of food that were not rationed. On September 1 German troops crossed the Polish border. France and England began to mobilize.

Gerd Ehrlich:

> In Germany the war was taken very seriously, but I never witnessed any of the fervent patriotism that is said to have been so dominant in August 1914. . . . The outbreak of the war had a decisive influence on my personal life. In the first months of the war, Jews were treated almost as fully human beings. They weren't totally trusted, of course, and once listening to foreign broadcasts was subject to severe penalties, their radios were taken away from them, for the sake of security. On the other hand, I was included in my building's air raid precautions and was given the honorable post of fireman for the building. Jewish schools continued to operate, but increasingly had to consolidate.

After war broke out, emigration to the United States became more and more difficult, as foreign shipping lines no longer accepted German currency. Once it became clear that very few refugees had relatives who could pay their passage, the American Consulate began to require confirmation of payment from the shipping lines before it would issue visas. In addition, Washington, citing "misuse," tightened the criteria required for an affidavit, so that only ten percent of those on

German waiting lists were able to produce the papers necessary to receive a visa when their number finally came up.

At the end of 1939 there were still close to eighty thousand
Jews living in Berlin. On September 1 an evening curfew was announced for Jews, from 9 p.m. to 5 a.m. in the summer months
and beginning at 8 p.m. in the winter. In October apartment
building residents were informed as part of their air raid instruction that "racial aliens" were not allowed in the cellar shelters.
As of December, coffee and sweets were made unavailable to
Jews. Large red signs were posted at all businesses and markets,
which read, "Purchases by Jews to be made only after 12." Aryans
seemed unaffected by this. Despite the rising cost of food and
beverages, the decline in the quality of beer, and the food substi-
tutes, cafés and restaurants were booming. Nor did the darkness
prevailing on Berlin's streets at night, allowing city-dwellers an
unusual view of the stars, keep people from swarming in droves
to movies, theaters, and concert halls. Everyone was seeking di-
version and a way to spend their money, for there was no sense in
saving it. Women were advised to seek the company of a man, for
since the outbreak of war the number of "crimes against moral-
ity" committed under the cover of darkness had risen drastically.

On January 24, 1940, Felice's sister celebrated her twentieth birthday.

THE WAY IT IS . . .
(For Irene)

When we were small, getting to know each other,
We tried, with gestures and with words,

To hurry and be like Father and Mother,
Like the so-called adults we saw and heard.
Nor could we avoid it, time went by,
We got older—each remained alone,
And finally, even without the disguise
We appeared as "people" in everyone's eyes.
But that's no reason to whine and moan!

The world is like a park in April,
Benches freshly painted, all in line.
You sit down more often, clueless and still,
And much too late you somehow feel
You look a bit funny from behind.

That is a bother, it is true,
But it would be mistaken to block
From mind the sun that is shining through,
When, from one too many benches, you
Have truly become a bit too blotched . . .

[JANUARY 24, 1940]

The war gradually began to interfere with daily life. Rationing was extended to include restaurants, the shops slowly began to empty of goods and the black market flourished. As of February 1940 Jews no longer were eligible for ration coupons for clothing. On February 28 Chicago surgeon Walter J. Karsten once again signed a notarized affidavit for his niece Felice: "We are anxious to welcome Fräulein F. Schragenheim into our home, so that she may help out in our residence and in our practice."

But the quota for Germans entering the United States had almost been filled. And German refugees from the transit countries of France, Belgium, the Netherlands and England were favored over others—a courtesy that America granted to its allies.

Gerd Ehrlich:

In the spring of 1940, Berlin was suffering a major housing shortage. Many people from the western regions whose presence wasn't exactly essential were coming to Berlin. An elderly aunt of ours arrived from Karlsruhe. Several minor air attacks, which at the time seemed major enough to us, destroyed a few buildings, and this resulted in "consolidation," which began with the Jews, of course. We had a seven-room apartment, which four of us shared with a girl. Slowly we had to take in more and more people, all of them Jews, naturally. By the time we were forced to move out, there were fourteen of us living in the same apartment. At first we were told that Jews could live only in so-called "Jew buildings," to be vacated by the Aryans living there. This plan was never carried out, however; instead, Jews had to vacate Jewish buildings if some party boss or other liked an apartment there.

In March Olga Selbach received her secondary school diploma.

GRADUATION CERTIFICATE
(For Olga)

For you the curtain has now rung down,
Complete with applause, critique, stage fright.

You've got your diploma and, in our view,
You've grown a good deal in our sight.

Student of medicine—quite a goal!
Requiring a strong dose of purpose, perhaps.
(The fact that you dropped your diploma today
We'll just let slide as a minor relapse.)

The family, Olga, expects something of you.
School was just the orals.
And between the two of us I'd advise,
Not to rest on your bed of laurels . . .

Equally matched we started the chase.
But then they checked the tangibles.
I had the misfortune to be erased,
But you're to cultivate the frangibles!
You've overcome so many obstacles—
Latin, and even your morning chores.
Now you've reached your first goal
We look at you and are proud.

[MARCH 1940]

Shortly thereafter, Olga found a position as a governess in Eastern Pomerania. "Are you crazy, why would you want to go there?" Felice scoffed.

On May 10 German troops crossed the Belgian border. "The battle that begins today shall decide the fate of the

German nation for the next one thousand years," Hitler declared.

Following a rather restrained reaction to the launching of the western offensive, a series of rapid victories quickly elevated the country's mood again. The press constantly urged Berliners to "return to theaters, movie houses, concert and music halls." The winter had been a hard one, with the flow of supplies so critically disrupted that schools had to be closed from January to March. Warmer temperatures brought on a mood of abandon that may even have had its effect on Felice. To compensate for the obstacles confronting her in life, she had a series of constantly shifting love affairs. Felice felt drawn to "prominent" people, those who enjoyed the spotlight she herself was denied. The actresses she fell for were usually quite a bit older than she, and had been introduced to her by her stepmother, who traveled in film circles.

At some point during the second half of 1940 Käte Schragenheim must have sailed for Palestine. It appears that Felice decided at the last minute not to accompany her stepmother. The prospect of traveling to Palestine with Mulle must not have appeared very enticing. And as her stepdaughter planned to go to her Uncle Walter's in America, Käte Schragenheim probably departed somewhat reassured. But it may have been the draw of Mutti that convinced Felice to stay. She spent a wonderful time with the Selbach family at "Forst," Mutti's summer cottage in the Altvater Mountains, with her white Scotch terrier, Fips, always in attendance. "Forst" was a perfect place to escape the Nazis, but above all it provided a feeling of security and warmth that she missed, having lost her own family at such an early age.

Mutti was an extremely important person to Felice at eighteen. She was part mother and part unattainable object of desire, whom Felice was obsessed with and in constant fear of losing. Felice's courtship went unreciprocated, though Mutti was flattered nevertheless when Felice arrived with flowers and hung on her every word. Each time Mutti took Felice tenderly in her arms, as she did her daughters, Felice believed that her dreams were finally coming true. But this moment inevitably was followed by a gruff rebuff: "What in the world are you thinking?"

"Must you be that way? Get it out of your head, you're crazy," Felice was warned often enough by Olga and her sisters. But Felice couldn't get it out of her head, and always started up again with the same thing.

Christa-Maria Friedrich:

One day a wood-carved Madonna was suddenly standing on Felice's desk. I asked her what that was supposed to mean. "It's pretty," she said, "a mother with child." I think there was a lot more sadness and sensitivity in her being, hidden behind her tomboyish cheerfulness, than one would at first presume. Her poems are evidence of that. They have the same tone as Erich Kästner's and also Mascha Kaléko's poetry. Such a mocking, satirical mask was evidently necessary in order to conceal the delicate, sadness-prone soul.

YOUR LETTER

Perhaps it was not at all fair
To read your letter lying there.

But I was destined to someday find it,
And as in some heavy and horrible dream
To see in black and white what seemed
Improbable. I didn't want to know it.

The higher you stand the farther you fall
Believe me, I fell after reading it all
I cannot escape your tone
Nor its refrain, no matter what.
It's all for naught.
And I am alone, alone, alone.

You said it quite clearly, and with it destroyed
My one slim chance at some small joy.
You must have felt it, this betrayal!
I was prepared to serve and love you,
But now I'm just a vagabond,
Who must stand outside the door . . .

[AUGUST 3, 1940]

Three days later everything appeared to have changed:

FALLING STARS

A shooting star lights up the sky.
It's meant to be, they tell the little ones,
Shooting stars carry their fate within,
That little one there has done much good.

Life gives and takes, and life falls mute.
One often stands at the window at night,
Asking and doubting and losing sight
Of the path. The little star showed me mine.

A bright star falls and lights up the night
And I feel, long hours having passed,
That I have found a way out of my plight
The little star has returned you to me!

[AUGUST 6, 1940]

Is this poem, which indicates a reconciliation with Mutti, a clue perhaps to Felice's foolish decision not to accept the "engagement" mentioned in a letter she wrote to her friend Fritz Sternberg? The journalist, whom many believed to be Felice's lover, answered her with concern on August 31: "What really displeased me was the way in which you handled the engagement that was so generously offered you. I very much would like to hear from you your true reaction to it. It is not something, after all, that one can disregard as easily as you did in your letter."

Is "engagement" a code word for Käte Schragenheim's departure for Palestine? "Käte cannot at all comprehend why Lice wanted to stay in Berlin and how it came to that," Felice's sister Irene would write from London in 1949.

The situation of Berlin's Jews worsened in the summer of 1940, once the "Battle of Britain" commenced on August 13 and people increasingly were wrenched from their beds to the sound of wailing sirens. As of July, Jews were permitted to buy food only from 4 to 5 p.m., and could sit only on those park benches marked "For Jews Only." In addition—the biggest blow—their telephone lines were disconnected and they were given until the end of the year to turn in their telephones. On September 15 Fritz Sternberg prepared Felice for her return to Berlin:

I imagine you joyfully rushing up the steps of your grand-father's house, greeting your dear relatives with a hammer-lock of an embrace [a pun on the Hammerschlag name] and then forgetting yourself and reaching for the tele-phone. Do not, oh do not do so, for you will find its be-loved place empty. It has been carried to its grave. You will hear that cherished sound no longer, nor will you be able to convoke it. It will be still, unsettlingly still. While there, where cows, goats, chickens, and the produce thereof de-light you despite the hail, snow, and rain, animal life here, minus the produce of course, will not do the same for your mood, because what is essential is missing: the telephone you reach for five times a day.

This situation has led to strange developments. I'll cite you an example from my own experience. The phone jangled recently at my workshop. An electric spark leaped toward me and sure enough, the call was for me. Lupus was on the line, inviting me to visit him and his wife. I accepted happily, mainly because an invitation by telephone is one of life's rarities today. So I hammered out a flat and ran off. Unfortunately I arrived fifteen minutes later than agreed upon in the heat of the moment. No Lupus, door locked.

I stood there and whistled to the point that I loosened my last remaining baby tooth, but nothing stirred above. Half an hour later I crept home, sad and contrite. The next morning I received—together with your letter, for which I thank you—a card with the following message:

Dear Fritz!

Yesterday, Thursday, I waited at the door from 9:15 until almost 9:40. My wife would have gone to bed had she not been anticipating your visit. Is it right to keep an old man standing at the door for so long? Is it chivalrous to keep a lady waiting? Get an appointment calendar, mend your ways, and then let us hear from you.

Best Wishes,

W.

In consideration of the actual circumstances, you must admit, in all fairness, that these reprimands turned things on their head somewhat. Wife not in bed, old man at the door, appointment calendar . . . I must say that's really taking it a bit far. But such things take place these days, and you shall now experience them for yourself. For I scarcely reckon that my introduction to the telephoneless age truly has been able to communicate to you such insight that you will be spared the emotional distress I myself am still experiencing.

Following this particularly difficult sentence, I shall close. You will be here at the end of the week, then you can write and tell me when we may see each other. Out of this will develop a lengthy correspondence, for it is not to be

assumed that our respective available appointment times
will be perfectly suited to one another. (Wife in bed, wife
not in bed, old man has no time, old man at the door, wife
back in bed again . . . there's no end to it.)

I will be happy to see you. But when, when??

At the probable urging of her uncle Walter, Felice continued her attempts to emigrate to the United States. But the
signing of the Franco-German cease-fire on June 22, 1940,
had made this even more difficult. U.S. ships were able to dock
only in British and Portuguese ports. Until the end of 1941
most emigrants would pass through the port at Lisbon, and
passage by ship from Lisbon had to be booked nine months
in advance. Still attempting to resolve the "Jewish problem"
through emigration, the Nazis shipped refugees to Lisbon and
to the Spanish seaports in closed trains. The greatest hurdle to
be overcome was the Americans' fear of a "fifth column," dis-
guised as refugees. Lacking a legal basis for the tightening of
controls over the issuance of visas, they resorted in June 1940
to foot-dragging:

"We temporarily can slow the number of immigrants to
the United States, and as good as bring that number to a
standstill. This will be possible if we instruct our consulates
to place all possible obstacles in the applicants' paths, to require additional information and establish various admin-
istrative measures, which will serve to delay and delay and
delay the approval of visas. At any rate, this will be possible
only for a short time."

On June 29 the State Department instructed its consular officials by telegraph to go over in the greatest detail all applications for lengthy stays in the United States, and to freeze the issuance of visas in the case of the "slightest doubt." "The telegrams bringing immigration to a virtual standstill have been sent," the State Department official in charge noted in his diary with satisfaction.

American historian David S. Wyman cites an example of this inhuman delay tactic, which Felice's grandmother, Hulda Karewski, may have experienced as well: Beginning in 1939 a Jewish refugee working as a physician in the United States attempted to bring his sixty-three-year-old mother from Vienna to the United States. After waiting a year and a half for her visa, her name finally appeared at the top of the list in March of 1940. But at that time her passport was in the possession of the German authorities. After it was returned to her she was informed by the American Consulate that new quota numbers would not be issued until the beginning of the next fiscal year, starting in July.

In August she was informed that everything was set, and that she needed only to undergo a medical examination, scheduled for the end of that month. To her son's horror she was notified in September that her visa had been denied, because the papers submitted by her sponsors were incomplete and her health left something to be desired. Finally, friends in the United States succeeded in getting her papers reexamined, and they were approved in March 1941, this time without mention of her health. She received her visa and joined her son, a positive turn of events that Hulda Karewski would never experience.

On January 15, 1941, from Chicago, Uncle Walter sent the American consul in Berlin a notarized copy of his 1940 tax return, and pressed for an answer as to when his niece would be issued a visa. Walter Karewski had no children of his own, and it was his greatest wish to bring both of his nieces to America. Karewski had had to repeat his medical exams in the United States, and was proud to have established himself as a gynecologist in so short a time. On January 17 he cabled Felice: DOLLARS 1000 BOND WIRELESS AT CONSULATE GO OVER IMMEDIATELY HOW ARE TRANSPORTATION TO AMERICA WHO PAYS TICKET = WALTER.

On February 11 American Express sent to the American Consulate General verification of passage booked on the *Marques de Comillas*, of the Compañia Transatlantica Española, to sail from Bilbao to New York on June 10. On February 19 Felice signed an application addressed to the district mayor of Berlin-Wilmersdorf and to the Finance Office in Charlottenburg-West for issue of certificates of fiscal nonobjection for persons who intended to emigrate. These were sent to her on February 22: "Valid until recalled!" On February 20 her guardian, Edgar von Fragstein und Niemsdorff, declared himself in agreement "that the passport issued to my charge for the purpose of emigration be handed over to her directly." Felice's passport was extended for one year on February 26. On February 28 (still Number 43015-c) she was to appear at the consular section of the American Embassy between 10 a.m. and 12 p.m., to receive her visa. "It lies in your own interests not to make any definite preparations, the dissolution of your household, etc., for example, before you are in possession of your immigration visa."

Felice was assigned Quota Immigration Visa Nr. 23989, valid until July 17, 1941. The inky impression of her ten fingerprints was attached to the visa, in addition to a declaration of consent signed by her guardian, a certificate of good conduct issued by the police, two notarized certificates of good conduct signed by Harry Israel Hammerschlag of Berlin-Halensee, sales representative, and Fritz Israel Hirschfeld of Berlin-Charlottenburg, photographer. Felice, whose "race" was given as "Hebrew," was 5 feet 3 inches tall and weighed 113 pounds. Her port of embarkation was Bilbao. On February 26 American Express certified that its New York office was holding three hundred dollars at Felice's disposal for purposes of passage.

Beginning in July 1941 the first Jews from the "Old Reich" were deported to Lodz, Kovno, Minsk, Riga and the Lublin district. On July 1 the Spanish Consulate in Berlin issued Felice a transit visa, valid until February 26 of the following year, for her trip to the United States on the *Navemar*, to depart July 15, 1941. Felice informed the American Consulate on July 12, "according to regulations,"

that my immigration visa to the USA will expire on the 18th of this month without my yet having been able to make use of it.

It was issued to me on the basis of my reservation of passage on the ship "Marques de Comillas," which I booked through the American Express Company. As this ship did not sail, I rebooked passage, and since then have made four further bookings through American Express, which were not met partly due to the temporary closing of Portugal's borders, and partly to a lack of ships.

I finally booked passage on the "Navemar," but it too postponed its departure date and still has not set a new one, so that I no longer may make use of my visa.

I would be very grateful to you if you would notify me of my chances for a possible extension of my visa.

An answer arrived posthaste: "Re your inquiry, we must inform you that the handling of matters concerning the issuance of visas has been suspended until further notice."

Diplomatic relations between Germany and America had ended. German consulates were closed on July 10, 1941. Three days later Germany responded with the demand that all American consular officials leave those areas of Europe under Nazi control, dashing the hopes of thousands of refugees. Of the thirteen thousand Germans who emigrated to the United States between July 1940 and July 1941, only four thousand arrived directly from Germany. This was an eighty-one percent decrease in the emigration quota compared to that of the previous fiscal year.

For Felice there was one last glimmer of hope on August 21. The "Emigration Department" of the Reich Association of Jews in Germany informed her that she would participate "in the twenty-second special transport of Jewish refugees, agreed upon by the agencies responsible," to leave Berlin for Barcelona on August 26. "We request that you obtain an emigration visa through Neuburg/Mosel." But by the next day the cancellation already had arrived: "We regret to inform you that your scheduled departure cannot take place, as the emigration of women and men between the ages of eighteen and forty-six is forbidden. We leave it to your discretion to contact us concerning this."

At this point Felice may not even have been in Berlin, for on August 24 Hans-Werner Mühsam, a friend, wrote to her at the "Forst":

My Dear 'Lice Fice,

I had come to the—for my part—depressing conclusion that, captivated by some babbling brook or some captivating babbler, you had forgotten me, when today—like the proverbial deus ex machina that leaps out at me from all the consulates where I proficiently go about my expulsion—your kind card arrived. I can only say that when it comes to you I am an outspoken individua-list (individua, envie, envy). How I would like to saw wood with you, and sleep with you, the former passion I seem to have inherited from our erstwhile Kaiser, to say nothing of blueberry-picking and enjoying a nip now and then! Don't you have a bit of room for me, even at the danger of it being at your vestal breast? In time of war one must tolerate everything, and I would be so happy with you far from civilization, forgetting the blessings of the Fontanepromenade [location of the Employment Office for Jews]. Aside from the fact that I have endured a house search and hours of interrogation (due to a denunciation), that all my preparations for emigration collapsed with the closing of the consulates of the duodecimo states of Central America, that Rosenstrasse [location of the Jewish Welfare Agency] has suddenly shown an interest in me (unrequited), and that my stomach is in revolt as a result of too many rationed fruits, I am faring splendidly, at any rate much better than I will be in the fourth year of war, 1943.

Fritz Sternberg wrote to Felice as well, addressing her as *Stift*, or "apprentice," a nickname her friends gave her when she was taking photography lessons from Ilse Ploog. The letter is undated and is apparently in answer to her question of whether or not she should remain at the "Forst":

Stift,

Knowing you as I do, you simply want a confirmation of a resolution/decision you have already come to. You want me to say: Stay there, keep drinking milk straight from the cow, laughing without civilization and sleeping without orthography. Am I right? You need nothing more than a little encouragement. If I knew for certain that a certain visit had not been paid to your grandparents on your stepmother's side, and if I knew for sure that they would not be receiving anyone in the foreseeable future, I would gladly grant you that favor. But unfortunately God did not bestow upon me the gift of prophecy, and so I can only say that there is, of course, a certain risk involved. I assume that you reported your change of address—then the risk would be slight, perhaps even nonexistent. (In that case I would then agree to an extension without the slightest hesitation.) But should that not be the case, and should they receive a visit—which could be anticipated, but then again is not certain; possible, but not probable—the situation could become unpleasant for both you and your foster parents. So I can respond to your precise question only with a highly imprecise answer: Hmm, well, let's see, well, then . . .

Now that I sufficiently have beat about the bush placed before me, I come to the second part of your letter. But first you must explain a few things. What, in good German, does it mean that you don't think much of worrying and thinking about yourself??? And in equally good German, what do you mean when you say that this year you are having thoughts similar to those of last year? What is the unpleasantness that awaits you in Berlin? Does all of this have some inner connection? What is it that is plaguing you and "clouding" your brain? It seems to me you've gotten hung up in some exceptionally dark thoughts. You know you can talk to me if you have something on your mind, or anywhere else. I often had the—perhaps false—impression here that there was something you wished to talk to me about. So, if you want to and are able—shoot. After all, I am—hopefully you will notice how my chest swells—at the mature age at which one either has or has not attained wisdom. I leave it to you to put that to the test.

In March 1941, twenty-one thousand Berlin Jews over the age of fourteen were assigned to forced labor. Following the June 21 offensive against the Soviet Union, Jews no longer received supplementary vouchers for soap, and ration cards were required for "fresh skim milk," which Berliners called "Aryan skim milk," because non-Aryans had to forgo this luxury.

In July the Nazi party leadership decided to prepare the "technical, material, and organizational" preconditions for a "comprehensive solution to the Jewish question." The *Reich Law Journal* published a decree stating that as of September 17, all Jews from the age of six years on must wear the "Jewish star."

Gerd Ehrlich:

We chuckled in disbelief at this piece of bad news, related one Sunday morning by my future stepfather. But when Benno then read the law aloud, my mother immediately began talking about "taking her life," and it took a great effort to calm her down again. And in fact, a classmate of mine poisoned himself that day, and he was not the only one driven to despair. Our distinguishing mark, which soon bore the sad epithet "pour le Semite," consisted of a yellow Star of David inscribed with the word *Jude* [Jew]. This "badge" had to be worn visibly on the left side of the chest, sewed securely onto the cloth.

In contrast to my friend Ernst, who only wore the star to work, I always wore it, up to the deportation of my parents, for anyone caught disobeying this law had to reckon with the "relocation" of the entire family. However, the star did not have the result the Nazis intended. I was not reviled because of it; to the contrary, it often happened that others would give up their seats to Jews on public transportation. The Gestapo later circumvented this show of sympathy by declaring a general ban on sitting down on public transportation. But it did make it much more difficult to get lost in the crowd. It was no longer possible to get around the lesser prohibitions and regulations without great risk. One could no longer shop in an unfamiliar district outside the proscribed times, no longer quickly slip into a telephone booth, and certainly no longer visit an Aryan friend.

Members of the Gestapo would stop people on the street and use a pencil to test whether the star was sewn on tightly enough. They waited in front of Jewish apartments to see if anyone would break the curfew; anyone arriving home five minutes late was arrested. This law, which was never committed to paper, was not taken seriously at first, especially since it was disavowed at police headquarters. A man who dared inquire about the "rumor" would find himself sentenced to fourteen days in jail for spreading "vicious lies."

As of September 13, Jews were permitted to use public transportation only to go to work. In April 1942 that too was denied them.

Soon after the star was introduced, Inge Wolf was visiting at Luise Selbach's. She was a friend of Mutti's daughter Renate, who was working as a secretary in the Collignon Bookshop in the heart of Berlin, where Inge also was employed. The doorbell rang and Felice came in. After a brief conversation she turned up the collar of her duster and with a small and uncertain smile showed Inge the yellow star.

"Pretty, isn't it?"

"What did you do last night?" Inge, feigning innocence, asked her friend Elenai.

Elenai burst into peals of laughter. "And you? The tip of your nose is such a funny color. Admit it! You've got a new sweetheart again."

Inge shrugged her shoulders contritely, her dark eyes round as saucers. "I admit it."

Felice was spending more and more of her nights on Kulmer Strasse in Berlin-Schöneberg, with Inge and her parents. When she ventured outside her own residential area Felice turned down the collar of her coat so that the yellow star would be concealed, or held an attaché case over it, neither of which was allowed. The feeling that she was an object of public spectacle made her anxious, even though she had decided to wear the star with pride. There were some who stared at her on the street, as if they had never been conscious of seeing a Jew before, but more often than not people looked away, shamefaced.

At the beginning of October the Employment Office for Jews, on Fontanepromenade in the Neukölln district, ordered Felice to report for work at C. Sommerfeld & Co., a factory that produced bottle caps and closures and was located at Stromstrasse 47, Berlin-Moabit. Employed as a wire worker, her job was to attach porcelain stoppers to bottles with a stiff wire, hard work which surely was not easy for someone un-accustomed to physical labor. But Inge never heard her com-plain. Unpleasantries of this sort were of minor importance when one's life was constantly in danger. The entries in Fe-lice's employment notebook began with the week of October 9, 1941, and ended exactly one year later. Week after week she noted in pencil her work hours, multiplying them by her salary of 46.5 pfennigs per hour. After deducting wage tax, medical insurance, and unemployment and disability insurance, she arrived at a sum of RM 16.13 for a forty-eight-hour week. On October 10 the firm certified that:

> For the purpose of purchasing foodstuffs, we attest that Felice Sara Schragenheim, born March 9, 1922, in Berlin, residing in Berlin-Halensee at Kurfürstendamm 102, is employed by us as a worker, and that same works for us from 7 a.m. to 4 p.m., and therefore is unable to make use of that time reserved for non-Aryans to do their shopping.
>
> An inspection of her residence revealed that no other persons were present who could make these purchases for her.
>
> We have established that the above-named may shop from 5 to 6 p.m.
>
> This attestation shall be revoked should conditions change, or should the above-named leave the firm.

At the end of September 1941 the Jewish Community was ordered by the Gestapo to convert the synagogue on Levet-zowstrasse, which had sustained only slight damage from the fires set on *Kristallnacht,* into a collection camp to hold one thousand persons. As more living space was needed for the Aryan population, the "relocation" of Berlin Jews was imminent, and the Jewish Community was to assist in this. Otherwise, the order continued, the evacuations would be directed by the SA and SS, and everyone knew "what that would lead to." There were roughly seventy-three thousand Jews living in Berlin, more than forty percent of all Jews in the "Old Reich."

On October 18 the first transport from Berlin, carrying more than one thousand Jews, left the Grunewald freight station in the direction of Lodz.

At first the deportations gave the impression of an orderly departure. Approximately two weeks before leaving, those persons who were to be transported received their "lists." A letter informed them of the date of their "exodus." The order to appear at the collection camp at a certain time was accompanied by a detailed instruction sheet, a list of objects they were permitted to take along with them and instructions for vacating their apartments. They were also instructed to make a list of all possessions left behind at their residences. People often had to wait for days at the collection camp until one thousand people had assembled there. Blankets, straw mattresses and a few real mattresses were distributed, and employees of the community passed out soup and bread. When the columns of trucks left Levetzowstrasse for Grunewald station, they found an empty train waiting for the human freight. At first old passenger cars were used, and later unheated freight cars or cattle cars. It often took hours for the train to depart. The change of address was officially recorded as "address unknown."

Gerd Ehrlich:

At the beginning of October I received a registered letter:
"Your apartment is scheduled to be vacated. Please report
immediately to Room 26 of the Jewish Community building."
Our subtenant, who had been arrested together with me, received a similar notice. As my mother was in the hospital following major stomach surgery, I went the following morning
to Oranienburger Strasse, where I was handed a questionnaire
of many pages to fill out. Every single object in our apartment
was to be inventoried, and there were a number of questions
to be answered presumably concerning the move. I told the
woman handling my case that, due to my mother's illness, I
was in no condition to fill out such an important document,
and asked to contact my legal representative, Benno W. Benno
worked in that same building as an executive member of the
Jewish Community Council, and I was taken to him. He was
terribly upset that we too had received this garbage in the
mail, and after he had sworn me to silence I heard for the first
time that this was a Gestapo measure that more than likely
meant being sent to the East immediately. He spoke with the
woman I had just dealt with and ascertained that our case
apparently was hopeless, as my name was on a list compiled
by Burgstrasse [the Reich Security Main Office address] with
the note that I was "asocial," that is, I was politically suspect.
After several terror-filled days during which I alternately hid
behind my mother's illness and my future stepfather's high
position, we managed to get our names struck from the transport list. One evening two officials came for Herr Schwalbe,
our subtenant, and his entire family, and took them away to

the collection camp at the Levetzowstrasse Synagogue. It was from there that roughly one thousand unfortunate souls were transported to Lodz, and it was from there that we received the final word. Packages addressed to the family were returned six weeks later, marked "deceased." I had escaped one more time, but as of October '41 every Jewish family in Germany lived in constant fear of receiving a "notice."

For a time following the first transport on October 18, a transport departed each week for an unknown destination in the East. Felice's friends, the Ziviers, lived on the top floor of a magnificent house on Trabener Strasse, with a direct view of the Grunewald train station.

Dörthe Zivier:

It must have been 11 or 12 o'clock in the morning. I was returning from the shop at the train station, and saw this procession of women and children coming toward me. It was very sad. They had to get out of the trucks on Erdener Strasse and walk down the middle of the street. They walked in rows of eight or ten, the women holding their children by the hand. Then they arrived at the Grunewald station and were put onto trains. That was the only time I saw this, usually they drove them directly into the train station. It was a very long procession. The people on the street who witnessed this were truly shamed. But you couldn't do anything, there were people standing there with guns. I went up to one woman, however, and pressed her hand. You looked around, and when the guards were off at a distance you could do that. Then I quickly

ran upstairs and looked down out of the window. And then I
saw how they were being shoved into the freight trains. They
had to move very quickly. I heard the guards screaming at
them. It wasn't pleasant.

Many tried in vain, with the help of their employers, to
be removed from the lists. Only at the end of January 1942
did a "reclamation" take effect. Businesses could certify that
their Jewish workers were engaged in labor vital to the war
effort, and were therefore to be exempted from "relocation"
for the time being. The Gestapo did not always agree to this,
and it happened that terrified workers would spend hours at
the collection camp before one or another company's director,
influential enough to reclaim his cheap labor, would arrive.

Felice, too, received such a certification from C. Sommerfeld & Co. on August 25, 1942:

We herewith certify that Fräulein Felice Sara Schragenheim, Berlin NW 87, Claudiusstrasse 14, is employed by
us as a wire worker.

Our product, "bottle closures," is recognized as essential to the war effort under Nr. F5 of the Regulations of
21 October 1940 of the Decree of the Executive Board of
the Reich Defense Council on the Urgency of Production
Programs. A loss of our labor force necessary to the manu-
facture of a guaranteed product should be avoided if at all
possible.

In addition to the direct demand for our product by

the army and for export to army services in Greece, we at this time also have a special order from the OKH [Army High Command].

The above-named worker is substantially employed in the production of bottle closures.

signed: R. Preiss

The above-listed grounds were recognized on the basis of agreements made on 25 August 1942 with the Employment Office of Berlin, Jewish Section, Berlin SW 29, Fontanepromenade 15, and should serve provisionally to defer from evacuation those Jewish workers in our employ.

signed: R. Preiss

As of December 21, 1941, Jews were not permitted to use public telephones; as of February 17, 1942, they were forbidden to buy newspapers and magazines. As of April 22 Jews could not frequent Aryan hair salons.

Gerd Ehrlich:

In addition to the continuing deportations, which were tearing apart our circle of friends, the Nazis also knew how to make life hard for us through small technicalities. A ban on visiting hairdressers, the withdrawal of ration cards for meat, pastries, etc., etc.; those kinds of irritating ordinances, the harshest being the ban on travel introduced in May '42. Jews were no longer permitted to use Berlin public transportation unless they had a special yellow ID card. These cards were issued only to armaments workers who lived more than seven kilometers from work, an hour-and-a-half by foot, that is. Pity the poor devil who was caught abusing this permission. Anyone who used this yellow card, which had to be shown to the conductor on purchasing a ticket, for any purpose other than going to work was threatened with immediate deportation, which was the same as a death sentence. On the Sundays I had free I would walk for hours to visit a friend or some nice girl or other.

Under these circumstances it is hardly surprising that life didn't appear worth living, even to a young person, and suicides increased at a frightening rate. No one could be sure that he would find his loved ones still there when he came home from work at night. Men who did hard labor, or women who stood at some machine for ten or twelve hours at a stretch, came home to a meal of cabbage and potatoes. Any other vegetable, and even meat and eggs, could be obtained only through friends or on the black market. Even a young, lively pup like myself longed for these everlasting horrors to end. I later asked myself why we looked on so passively for so long, as week after week a thousand or more people were loaded into cattle cars and taken to an unknown destination, and as our lives, which were spent in the heaviest of labor, were made even harder by all the little incidents of harassment. I am convinced that it was the unbelievably skillful tactics of the Gestapo brutes (consisting in a slow suffocation that prepared us to a certain degree for even worse things to come, so that each new regulation appeared as something we could still easily endure) that kept us from open revolt. Each of us held out the hope that he would be among the few to survive. On top of which, any opportunity to discuss things openly, which might perhaps have led to the organizing of some type of resistance movement, was denied us. And even within our ranks there were numerous traitors who hoped to save their own skins by denouncing others. In short, there was scarcely anyone at the time who dared to revolt.

After my class received our secondary school diplomas we boys immediately agreed to continue to meet once a week. Our former German professor offered to give us philosophy lessons every Sunday morning. That was the origin of our small resistance group, but it was not until mid-1942 that we actually came together for this purpose.

At some point during the summer of 1941 Felice left the Hammerschlags' Kurfürstendamm apartment, where she had never felt comfortable, and moved to the Moabit district, to the apartment of Dr. Kurt Hirschfeld, an orthopedist whose address offered the advantage of proximity to Sommerfeld & Co. Hirschfeld practiced as a "treater" of Jews in Berlin-Charlottenburg. Whenever she had the time, Inge waited outside the factory gate for Felice, to stroll with her to Claudiusstrasse. At the end of the year Felice registered herself at the address of her grandmother Hulda Karewski and her grandmother's brother, Julius Philipp, on Prager Strasse. And whenever she needed a room, there was still one available in the Selbachs' apartment in Berlin-Friedenau.

Among the possessions Felice left behind was a postcard

she wrote on January 3, 1942, to Frau Edith Blumenthal in the
Lodz (Litzmannstadt) ghetto:

> Dear Edith,
>
> I have tried for so long to find out your address, and
> am glad that I now have it and know how you are. I am
> sending you RM 15 by the same post, and hope to con-
> tinue to do so regularly. Please let me know, if you can,
> whether I should send the money directly to you, or if it
> would be better to send it to the municipal savings bank in
> Litzmannstadt, to be placed at your disposal.
>
> I am fine thus far. I have a very nice job and work with
> nice women colleagues.
>
> By the way, I have moved. I'm now living with my
> grandmother, but I'll continue to take my meals at the H's,
> and you can write to me there.

The postcard was returned, stamped: "Return. At this
time no postal delivery is being made to receiver's street."

Jews, who had to wear the yellow star in public, were given
until January 16, 1942, to hand over their furs and woolens.
As a result of the "Final Solution" decided upon on January 20
during the Wannsee Conference, all Jewish emigration from
the Reich was stopped.

On the occasion of Irene's birthday on January 24, Felice
penned a message of twenty-six words and sent it through the
German Red Cross to her sister, who was working as a nurse
in a children's hospital in England:

My Dear,

I think of you always, and most especially today, and hope that the Madonna will smile upon us!

> A thousand kisses from your PUTZ

An answer arrived dated April 4, 1942, written on the reverse side of the form:

My Beloved Putz,

My new job is just fine. Mulle [Käte] without word from you. Think often of you and Grandmother.

> A thousand kisses
> Your dear little girl
> Irene

In March the Royal Air Force began carpet bombing German cities.

> *When on heavy wings*
> *A little piece of death,*
> *From 'neath dark shadows sings,*
> *In its cold, cold breath,*
> *Words float off in space,*
> *Words that lack all sense.*
> *And when the shadows fade,*
> *We shake, and whisper, "Near miss."*
>
> *And thankfully, as in some parable,*
> *The burden is lifted at last—*

And only the heart beats hard and fast,
And one's hands tremble a little.

[MARCH 19, 1942]

The population of Berlin was appeased with the intimation that "fully furnished Jewish apartments" would be "quickly available." The residences of the "emigrated" were sealed, and their possessions auctioned off cheaply. As of April 15 Jews were ordered to mark their apartments with the "Jewish star."

At some point during the first half of 1942 Elenai Pollak met Inge's friend Felice. Though curious about each other, they were fearful as well.

Elenai Pollak:

The first time I met her, in that funny little café on Winter-feldplatz, we had an unintentionally odd and strangely sad conversation with each other. I had seen her from a distance before, and now got a good look at her face. She had beautiful eyes and a fascinating mouth, large and somewhat harsh. She was called Felice, or something like that. I didn't dare ask her name, because in this period of great uncertainty it was senseless to inquire after someone's name and address. And yet I noticed that she was waiting for me to. Our conversation began in a trifling fashion. She had gotten a newspaper from the rack, and it galled me that she was reading that stupid Goebbels page, with its lines of propaganda, always on the same "we've got to stick this out" theme, that she could think of nothing better to do that evening. And I would have left, had she not suddenly folded the paper and asked if I knew

Stella. I was truly astonished. Stella was the redhead whom everyone greatly feared. She informed on illegal Jews in exchange for her freedom. And Stella was known, actually, only to those who were illegal themselves. At that moment I didn't know whether Felice was testing me, or whether she herself was an informer. But then she made such a gentle gesture with her hand, almost tender, that all of my misgivings disappeared.

"I know Stella," I said, "but I don't know you." I simply addressed her using the familiar form. "And I don't know what you want, but, sister, if you're in the same situation as I, I have learned not to be afraid, and to reach out to people. You can trust me if you want." She trusted me. As long as we sat next to each other almost nothing separated us, and almost everything she said I, too, had experienced. After a while I wasn't listening to her words anymore, but only to the sound of her voice, which was wonderfully even and melodious and quite deep. Her voice took me away from reality and strangely enough, it now and then reminded me of Altvorden, and suddenly I saw Andreas and Ursula before me. They were sitting there with their Bible and their children, as comfortably as always, such that I wondered if the war hadn't already ended. And then suddenly I came to myself again and noticed that Felice's voice no longer sounded so good. That is, it didn't sound at all, she had stopped talking. It goes totally without saying, of course, that her story was a familiar one. It was the story of all of us then. But she had fallen silent for another reason. It wasn't because she wanted to know what I had to say, nor had she finished her story. It was this "I don't know why we don't tell each other everything." It was that life-threatening. Or perhaps she found our story tiring by then. It didn't move me anymore, either. It's like dying—when you know it's coming, it's as matter-of-fact as living. I wasn't sure whether she wanted comfort or just conversation, nor did I feel like asking. I found it better to simply suggest we walk a ways together on Hohenstaufen Strasse. Things come to me sometimes when I walk. She nodded, and we paid and left, silent at first, and with no particular destination in mind. Then it started to rain, and that gave flight to my fantasy. Suddenly I felt very lighthearted and relaxed, and was ready to forget everything else. But there was something else as well: I knew that I might never see her again, that this day would end as it had begun. Just as undiscernibly. Without my wanting to take notice of it [written in the late 1950s].

Because she had three Jewish grandparents Elenai was a "full-Jew" according to the Nuremberg Laws. Her half-Jewish mother had remarried and assumed her husband's "Aryan" name, therefore Elenai was spared having to wear the yellow star. After being expelled from public school she attended a private Jewish school where she could complete her high school education. Her encounter with Felice in the café on Winterfeldplatz was the beginning of a close friendship between the two girls, which vacillated between erotic attraction and sisterly trust. Together with Inge they were always underway somewhere, "organizing" one thing or another. Everyone Inge met was immediately checked out in terms of whether or not he or she could be of help in making the survival of

Felice and others in her same situation a bit easier: a place to stay for a few nights, food ration coupons, medicines, identification papers, possibilities for escape. And Inge was continually meeting people who were in need of her help. Elenai was impressed by Felice's talent when it came to procuring things, and by her iron will to survive. Turning on the charm, Felice seized what she could whenever she could, but at the same time gave the impression of wandering about without purpose, of being quite lonely and withdrawn.

That spring there were once again problems with Mutti. A long letter written by a furious Felice to Mutti's daughter Olga, dated March 20, 1942, imparted that Felice's friend Fritz Sternberg had been deported: "We have received two receipts for cash from Fritz. So he is alive, even though we don't know under what conditions." But the letter also revealed that Luise Selbach was trying desperately to conceal her Jewish heritage:

Monday was the seventh anniversary of my father's death, and as the train connection from work is good I went to the cemetery, reluctantly as always. The H.'s asked me to check on the grave of a tenant of theirs, as they pay for the upkeep. So once I had taken care of my visit, I went over and discovered that nothing had been done for the other grave, naturally, and made my way to the exit. That was when I accidentally came across your grandmother's grave, and it made a sad impression, something that could be remedied, of course. So I mentioned it in passing to Renate, figuring that that at least had become semi-official to some degree. The next day Mutti called, quite perturbed.

My conscience, God knows, is seldom clear. That evening as I was making my bed it started all over again. Mutti appeared unexpectedly and stood in the doorway to my little room until almost midnight while I, lying in my bed, had to listen to her tell me that I had been spying on her! There were things I didn't know, she said, and that I shouldn't ask about, and there were things that she had heard, and did not wish to speak of, and I should watch out. Bam! I still had no idea what it was all about. But I had that night and nine hours of work the next day to think about it, and I decided, Olga, to clear up the matter. I could no longer tolerate this eternal fear of having committed some offense, if you know what I mean, this eternal worry that I had said something wrong. On top of which, I took it that Mutti really did mean that I didn't know anything about it, and it seemed to me that I would be lying if I continued this farce any longer. Do you know that feeling of having been lied to, like you're standing in a dark room, afraid to take even one step forward because you might stumble over something? Or of being afraid to ask a question, because if you don't then no one can lie to you? That feeling that you're going to climb the walls or do something crazy because someone you'd do anything for tells you you better watch out, and says that you're spying on her?

I tried to talk to Mutti about all of this. I wanted calmly to explain everything yesterday, to put my cards on the table, act chivalrously. Well—so at first she started talking faster than I've ever heard her talk before, throwing out words like "half," and "none at all," and "quarter," and "responsibility" and "designation" and "not applicable," until my head was spinning. Then all of a sudden something occurred to her, and she asked whether perhaps she was obligated to tell me everything. Bam! I brought up trust, and that I surely could expect, after all that we . . . I tried to explain to her this feeling of being lied to. And that was a mistake, for all Mutti heard was that I was saying that she had lied to me, and then she wanted to throw me out. . . .

I tried to explain to her what it is like to be afraid for someone who doesn't want you to be. She replied somewhat haughtily that that wasn't at all necessary. At any rate, we ended on the note that Mutti "seriously would have to consider, under the circumstances," and after what I had "accused" her of, "how things were to continue."

So, Olga, that's the way things stand, and the fact is, it's the last thing I needed. The very last. For then my whole life, with all its ups and downs and bottle closures will have been for naught. A terrible word, naught. And for that reason—I'm not a rational person, after all—I won't draw any consequences. I'll go over this evening and not mention any of this until—the next clash. Do you remember March 1940? That was the first time, and I had the feeling it wouldn't be the last. And that was true.

On June 2 the first transport left Berlin for Theresienstadt, a "ghetto for the elderly," reserved for persons over sixty-five years of age. Located on the road between Dresden and Prague, the former garrison of Terezín was founded by Austrian Kaiser

Joseph II in 1780, to honor his mother, Maria Theresa. Its "great fortress" was separated from the world by high walls and moats; but the "little fortress," designed by the Hapsburgs to serve as a first-rate prison and torture chamber, stood ready for further use. The 7,000 people who had occupied it before the war were forced to move, and at the end of September 1942, 58,500 people were crowded into Theresienstadt. "From there the Jews will be sent to the East," the minutes of an internal meeting of the SS revealed in October 1941. "Minsk and Riga have already agreed to take fifty thousand Jews each. After the Jews have been totally evacuated, Theresienstadt will be settled by Germans according to a plan already completed, and become a center of German life. Its location is well suited for this purpose."

As notification of their deportation, the elderly received a letter from the Reich Association of Jews in Germany, in which they were informed of the day on which their "exodus to the Protectorate" was to take place. As luggage they were permitted to take one travel bag and one rucksack, which could extend "at the most from the hip to the shoulder." Only one piece of hand luggage was allowed, and it was to contain sleepwear, a blanket, dish, spoon, drinking cup and food. Travel and hand luggage together were not to weigh more than fifty kilograms. "Anyone who does not observe these stipulations must reckon with the loss of his luggage."

Beginning at 8 a.m. on . . . , an official will seal your apartment. You must be ready at that time. Hand apartment and room keys over to the official. You will then be taken by truck, as arranged by us, to the collection shelter at Grosse Hamburger Strasse 26.

All savings bank books, bank books, etc., securities (unless they are being held by a bank), mortgage bonds, bank documents, etc.; in short, all credentials that give information on your assets, and any safe-deposit box keys in your possession are to be placed in a thick, unsealed but sealable envelope, to be handed over at the collection shelter at Grosse Hamburger Strasse 26. Write your full name, exact address and transport number on the envelope.

Homes for the elderly, and for the deaf and dumb and blind, were emptied. Patients of the Jewish Hospital on Iranische Strasse could postpone their "relocation" only if they were scheduled for surgery, or "in the final stages" of an illness. Pregnant women had to show proof that the "birth is in progress"; any newborn child six weeks or older was "evacuated" with its parents.

In July 1942 Jews were forbidden to use the waiting rooms of public transportation. On July 11 the first transport of Berlin Jews departed for Auschwitz. As of July 13 blind Jews were no longer permitted to wear armbands for the blind. Criminal statistics for the year 1942 revealed only one single case of a Jew receiving a sentence for an act of resistance against the state. Many chose suicide as the only possible escape from being picked up. "Do you want to kill yourself or be evacuated?" was a stock question among the Jewish population of Berlin.

On August 6 Felice's seventy-four-year-old grandmother

Hulda Karewski and her seventy-eight-year-old brother, Julius Philipp, were deported, on the thirty-eighth transport of the elderly to Theresienstadt. On the day before their deportation Felice took Elenai with her to say good-bye to "Oma" and to pick up her remaining possessions from the apartment. Elenai couldn't find the courage to address the elegant old lady, who was amazingly calm. And despite their close friendship Felice did not comment on the leave-taking, nor did Elenai dare ask her about it. They all knew that this farewell was final, yet Felice held out the desperate hope that her beloved grandmother would have a chance of surviving Theresienstadt. After all, a "ghetto for the elderly" had the ring of a home for the elderly.

In the second half of 1942 the number of illnesses recorded in Theresienstadt reached a record high: The old people succumbed to scarlet fever, measles, jaundice, typhus and enteritis. In September there were over thirty thousand of the "elderly, ill, and invalid" housed in Theresienstadt. The crematorium began operation on September 7. In September 3,941 people died, among them Hulda Karewski, on September 14, 1942.

At the beginning of October Felice, too, received notice of her deportation, the so-called list, and Dr. Hirschfeld, at whose address she resided, was picked up. Felice and Inge rode their bikes over to Claudiusstrasse to break the seal on the apartment and remove Felice's belongings. On the kitchen table, Felice left behind a farewell letter she stained with water, in which she announced her plans to commit suicide. She then removed the yellow star from her coat and went underground.

From then on she lived illegally as a "U-boat," with Inge's parents on Kulmer Strasse, at the home of Elenai's stepfather on Nollendorfplatz, and with others. What remained of her family's valuables—a fur coat of her grandmother's, jewelry, silverware, linens—she stored with friends. She kept her head above water by selling off these possessions piece by piece.

At the beginning of October Inge Wolf began her year of compulsory service at the home of Elisabeth Wust.

Inge's father was a Communist, her mother a Social Democrat and both parents were book dealers. Hiding someone who had "bolted" was a dangerous affair, particularly for a Communist. Inge's father preferred for Felice never to leave the house, especially as "red Stella," the Jewish "catcher" with the encyclopedic memory, was on the loose.

Made notorious by the "Jewish *Mundfunk*" ["mouth radio"], Stella Kübler-Isaaksohn, née Goldschlag, was known in Berlin as the "Jewish Lorelei," the "blond phantom." To save her own skin and that of her parents she and her second husband, Rolf Isaaksohn, made an agreement with the Nazis to hunt down underground Jews and deliver them to the Gestapo. This, however, did not keep Felice, girl of the Ku'damm, from going out onto the city streets.

While Felice was gathering her first experiences as a "U-boat," Gerd Ehrlich, a few years older, was preparing to become an "illegal." It is probable that the two met casually around this time through a group of ten young people who regularly got together in Berlin.

Gerd Ehrlich:

The Gestapo introduced new regulations concerning deportations in August of 1942. In the weeks preceding it often
happened that persons ordered to prepare themselves for
victimization decided not to await their executioners. So the
Gestapo simply began surrounding apartment buildings that
held a large number of Jews, and forcing their way into any
residence that displayed the Jewish star. Those unfortunate
residents then had ten minutes to prepare for their journey
into the unknown. Only through a great effort could companies succeed in freeing at least their skilled workers from the
collection camps. Many people no longer dared to sleep in
their own homes, and others spent their nights lying on their
beds fully clothed, ready to flee at any moment. Of course
there was no one who didn't have a rucksack packed and
ready. I think this uncertainty was the worst thing I experienced. Each time I came home from the night shift I breathed
a sigh of relief when my loved ones were still there and in one
piece. I took count of my friends and acquaintances each day
at the factory, and considered myself lucky when no one was
missing.

Our preparations for illegality had continued in the
meantime, and the first two comrades had already set off
down that thorny path. The initial difficulties had been
overcome. We were no longer passive victims, we even had
weapons and were organizing our own defense. Though our
means were more than limited, our solidarity gave us strong
moral support. I, personally, was prepared to leave home on

any given day. I had taken my belongings—suits, underwear, books, etc.—in small trips to friends I could trust, and I continued living at home only in order not to endanger my family. It was clear to me that even the strongest nerves would not tolerate this constant strain over the long run, and deep within me I longed for the day of decision to arrive. It was to arrive more quickly than I had imagined.

Felice, in the meantime, was brooding over love, reading her way through the wealth of literature to be found in a household of book dealers, and chatting with Frau Wolf, who kept Felice's occasional forays into the city a secret from her husband. Felice also spent her time penning poems in green ink and listening each evening as Inge related what was going on in the Wust household.

At the end of October Inge returned home from work furious. "Damn, she's one of them after all! Do you know what she said to me today? 'Jews? I can smell them!' I can't take it any longer."

"Oh yeah? She said she can smell Jews, did she? I'd like to test that out!"

Felice, her interest already piqued by Inge's colorful descriptions of her work as a housemaid, and craving a change in her monotonous and static life, could not let go of the thought of having Elisabeth Wust take a whiff of her. From that time on she pressured Inge to arrange a meeting.

Inge found none of this very amusing, particularly since her father was constantly telling her not to allow Felice to leave the house. Inge herself was inexplicably afraid of such a meeting, which was silly, of course, for Frau Wust could not really smell Jews!

"Will you set it up? I'd like it sooo much. . . ." Felice giggled, paraphrasing Tucholsky in an effort to make the idea more palatable to her reluctant friend.

FOUR

On April 2, 1943, when Felice asked if Inge would object to her spending the coming nights with Lilly, who was still weak from her visit to the hospital and didn't want to be alone with her four children, Inge found this an excellent idea. Felice had lived for six months as a "U-boat" in Inge's parents' apartment, a situation that was in no way safe, and Inge felt it was high time that Felice found somewhere else to stay. Nor was she safe any longer at Elenai's, whose half-Jewish mother had been sentenced to ten months in jail for railing at Hitler, and was in the Moabit prison. With bombing attacks on Berlin on the rise, the situation was becoming increasingly precarious. Inge usually stayed in the apartment with Felice when the alarm sounded, but once going down to the cellar became imperative they would be forced to come up with a credible identity for Felice, for their building was full of Nazis. If it were discovered that Father Wolf was hiding someone who had gone underground, he would be sent to a concentration camp for sure. Felice would be much safer in the apartment of a respectable soldier's wife; she couldn't do better, in fact. Inge knew nothing yet of the feelings that Lilly and Felice had developed for each other.

"So how shall we manage this?" Inge asked. "You don't have food coupons." One could not exist in this fourth year of the war without food coupons. "Just tell her you have a neighborhood grocery in Friedenau, near the Selbachs', where you always buy your rations, and that you don't want to give it up. Say, 'I go there often,' or something like that. And then when I have to shop for the Wusts, I'll just set aside for you some of what I buy. Wust gets an amazing amount of food for her four children, she won't even notice it. They can't eat all of it as it is."

And that is how it went. Inge got hold of some suitable packing paper and after she bought groceries she would stop on the landing between the fourth and fifth floors and repack some of the rations for Felice. If there was a half-pound of butter for the children she put aside a quarter-pound for Felice.

"I went shopping today," Felice would say, and everything, literally, went smooth as butter.

Felice, too, was pleased with the new arrangement. She would tell Lilly that she had to go to Babelsberg, and then spend the day at Elenai's, or at Mutti's in Friedenau, or would wander back and forth from one to the other, always in search of new information that would tell her whether her situation was getting better or worse. Elenai recalls one day when Felice made fourteen visits. But Felice also enjoyed the security provided by living in the apartment of a Nazi woman. It was wonderful not to have to hide, to live with a real family, and in Schmargendorf to boot, close to Auguste Victoria Strasse where she had spent her childhood. This could also, of course, be a source of new danger, for it was possible that she would be recognized and denounced here. Moreover, it was clear that mothers held a special attraction for Felice—especially if they had a charming freckled face like Lilly's. Under Lilly's care Felice was able to forget for a while that she was not even supposed to be alive. Lilly's devotion and the children's affection made up in part for the indignities she had been subjected to for a decade now. When Albrecht ran toward her crying, "Hice, Hice," in his high little voice, her eyes filled with tears of joy. She had not felt this at home and secure since last summer, at the "Forst."

Christa-Maria Friedrich:

I don't know when it was that I ran into Felice on the 176 bus. When I had seen her earlier she had been wearing the yellow star, but now she wasn't. She noticed my questioning glance to her left breast. In her characteristic happy, mocking way she said, "You're looking for the star, aren't you? I'm not Jewish anymore." "What?" "Yes, I'm an Italian guest worker. I learned Italian in six weeks. I'm now working in a factory." "And what if you run into N.?" (N. was the only Nazi girl in our class.) "I did recently, in the subway." "And what happened?" "She didn't see me and at the next stop I changed cars." Sometime around then she got her visa. I was with her and the rubbed-varnish furniture one more time. We wanted to say goodbye but she simply did not let herself be sad. About four weeks later I ran into her again somewhere on the street.

I was truly shocked. What had gone wrong? Felice was more contemplative than usually. And then she told me that she was on the ship but she simply couldn't leave. She said she just had to stay in Germany. "And what'll you do now?" I asked, concerned. "Now I'm staying near Roseneck and I take care of four children." I didn't ask for her address.

At the beginning of the year Felice, with the help of her underground friends, paid two thousand Reichsmarks to secure a chaperone ID issued by the Reich Central Office of the "Country Stays for City Children, Inc." This rather simple document, without photo, identified Felice—under the name Barbara F. Schrader—as a "chaperone for children on domestic outings," valid until April 1, 1944. The clumsily filled-out pink authorization never would have passed close inspection, for Felice had filled in the date in her own hand, whereas the name "Barbara F. Schrader" had been written by Inge. But if one were picked up it was better to have some kind of ID than none at all.

Gerd Ehrlich:

My group consisted of Walter, Ernst, Lutz, Herbert, Gerdchen, Günter, Halu, Jo, Fice (the only girl), and myself. In addition to this core group there were other friends who met with us on an irregular basis, and with whom we exchanged experiences.

We had successfully overcome the initial difficulties, but the more experience we gathered in our new life the more we realized that major problems were to come. And we encountered difficulties finding housing soon enough. It was not always possible to stay with good friends who were Aryans, for though they meant well there was almost always some member of the family who opposed the plan of hiding one of us. Halu was the first to come up with the brilliant idea of renting a furnished room by the day. There were various "accommodations agencies" in Berlin, so one day Halu went into one of them and paid the prescribed fee, saying that he had had a fight with his family and wanted to spend a few days away from home. He was given a list of addresses where there were rooms to let, and so he rented one of these furnished rooms and told the landlady the same story. When the good woman mentioned that he would need to register with the police, he said he was registered as it was in Berlin anyway, and didn't want to change his address due to the enormous difficulties with ration cards and ministry of defense forms.

Once Lutz went underground our organization arranged for him to go to a branch of the German Red Cross as an unpaid volunteer. With his usual aplomb, he soon gained the confidence of his superiors, and using the name "Fred Werner," he was left to work independently. As his job was to take care of correspondence, it was not long before he had a collection of official stamps on his desk, and one day Lutz also came into possession of a large block of blank DRK [German Red Cross] identification forms. He quickly added to this a set of stamps and a few pieces of letterhead stationery, and that was the last the DRK saw of him. We found out that a warrant was even being circulated for his arrest. So he was the first of us forced to make his way to Switzerland.

But we had what we needed for the time being. All of a sudden we all had advanced to the position of consultant, or sub-department head or interpreter. Each of us was in possession of an impressive ID, identifying us as good Germans. The documents would never have passed a serious check by the Gestapo, of course, but they served splendidly in the case of a street roundup or for the eyes of a curious landlady.

Gerd Ehrlich was one of the few Jews living underground who had no financial worries. There was always someone willing to buy one of his deceased father's valuable rugs, stored at friends' homes, and so he found himself in the fortunate financial situation of being able to assist those of his friends who were less favored. And if one had money and connections it was not at all difficult to buy food coupons. Once in a while someone would turn off the counter of the food coupon machine and let it run, and the group suddenly would have an entire stack of coupons they would have to use up in a very short period of time.

Whenever Gerd left the house he carried a forged military photo ID made out to Gerhard Kramer in one pocket of his jacket and—as a passable speaker of French—a Belgian foreign worker's permit in the other pocket. Foreign workers were checked by the Gestapo but not by the army, so he simply had to remember not to get his pockets mixed up.

The forging of identification papers was achieved in the following manner: First, a future ID holder was located whose outward appearance—hair and eye color, height, age and identifying marks—matched as closely as possible the description on the ID. A new photo was then attached using a special device, and half of the official stamp was copied onto the photo, a piece of specialty work that came at a high price unless a sympathetic colleague could be found to do it. Gerd Ehrlich's circle finally came in contact with a "half-Aryan" graphic artist who was a master in the field, but he unfortunately lived far outside the city.

Identification papers had to be located first, of course. One method particularly favored in the summer was to go to the Wannsee, where pieces of clothing left carelessly in the grass and sand could be searched while their owners were swimming. In a desperate attempt to match the personal description on one such document, someone once actually chopped off his own finger. Then the documents had to be taken to the graphic artist and picked up again. Among Felice's responsibilities in the "organization" was to carry out this sort of task. She was always asking Lilly to accompany her to various places where she met with people she did not introduce Lilly to. Sometimes it was at the *Haus Vaterland* on Potsdamer Platz, at other times they took the Number 51 tram from Roseneck to Pankow, to the Schmidt Photo Shop, or they would ride the *S-Bahn*, the suburban train, to Babelsberg, where Lilly would wait for Felice in a café. Once, Lilly watched from a safe distance as Felice whispered with a pretty young woman in a gun shop on Taubenstrasse and then slipped a piece of paper into her pocket. Lilly didn't ask questions.

"This has nothing to do with you. These are things you shouldn't be seeing," Felice said, after Lilly discovered a picture of Elenai stepping out of the bathtub nude, drops of water glistening on her skin. "We make these things for soldiers."

Lilly had no further comment, merely noting that the girls were having pornographic pictures taken by Schmidt the photographer. It was more likely, however, that he too was involved in forging documents for them.

Elenai Pollak:

> I met Schmidt one day, I no longer recall where. He thought I was interesting and good-looking, and asked if he could take some nude pictures of me. He wanted to enter them in a photography contest, and with my looks he had a good chance of winning, he said. This didn't surprise me greatly; I found it quite understandable, actually, and so I said, well then, if you wish, take them. He absolutely insisted on shooting me in the bathtub under the shower. And because our bathtub at home was dreadful, he invited me to his place. There was another man there when I arrived, he seemed a clever sort. So I said to him, tell me, who are you, actually, and what do you do for a living? I'm a pastor, he said. To which I replied, well, I'm certainly in strange company, when pastors start taking nude photos of girls. Very well, then, whatever. I was adventuresome and had a surplus of energy. Life and my imagination went on. It was a diversion, something different for a change. Inge still has the photos of me.

In one of the portraits that Schmidt made, Elenai is wearing her long black hair loose and flowing, and staring dramatically into the distance. Otherwise she never wore her hair down. On the contrary, she did her utmost to appear less exotic and striking. Her mother was obsessed by the thought that Elenai was recognizable as a Jew even from a distance, and constantly afraid that something would happen to her. Felice and Elenai tried to figure out how they could "Germanize" her appearance, and arrived at the grandiose idea of fixing Elenai's hair in the "Gretchen" style, with a braid wrapped around her head and fastened into a knot at the back.

Lilly continued to write monologues to Felice on the yellow- and salmon-colored army-issue postcards—the only afford-able stationery—even when the lovers were separated for only a short period. Inge's presence during the day, and the flurry of activity necessary to maintain a household with four children, with rations becoming ever scarcer, left the two women little time for any prolonged communication. A few quickly penned lines, an "I love you" on a scrap of paper discovered in one's purse when shopping, in the toothbrush glass or under a pillow, helped to compensate for hours spent in longing. Felice continued to disappear, even overnight, as she did at the end of May, after Lilly already knew Felice's true identity:

Another night alone!
And what a night I had! I want you so, it hurts. It hurts terribly. I love you! I fell asleep, but then I had such lovely dreams that on waking I was terribly disappointed that you weren't lying next to me. I had to bite into my pillow so that no one would hear me. All I can think of is: Felice! I'm so afraid that one day soon you will love someone else.

Please don't be sad when I say this, but you have changed me totally. I am no longer myself.

I have your picture here in front of me! When I think of the years I have wasted! Felice, please don't leave me alone, please take me with you! I know that would mean that I would leave everything and everyone behind, but what does that matter if you love me! We belong together. You know that you've brought my world crashing down around me (nor, God knows, am I sorry)—my whole world. And now you must protect me. Will you be able to do that? Do you love me? I want to live in your world, even at the cost of great pain. Your love alone will help me through. It's a great responsibility! Are you anxious? Are you afraid? Can you answer me?—I'm waiting for you . . .

But the moments Lilly spent in the agony of love and fear for the future were more than compensated for by the joy of everyday life lived with her beloved. She felt like a window had been thrown wide open and there was so much sun streaming into her life that she was almost blinded. As long as Inge remained in the dark about what was going on, it was fun to run the household together. Felice and Lilly had to try terribly hard not to give themselves away, for they had decided not to cause Inge hurt. Neither Inge nor Felice were model housewives, it was true, despite the marvelous cooking course that Felice had taken in her sixth year at school. But when the two of them washed dishes and sang "Little Marie sat in the garden weeping, her slumbering child in her lap . . . ," one more off-key than the other, Lilly, who was raised on Schubert and Brahms *lieder*, got a knot in her stomach. She then had to stop and take a deep breath, amazed at the miracle that this girl, Felice, hounded as she was, had brought to her life. Inge fell silent at the sight of Lilly smiling at them indulgently. If she envied Lilly anything it was the clear and strong singing voice with which she sweetened her daily chores.

Elenai Pollak:

Naturally we found it amusing that Lilly perked up so much in our circle. We had our own missionary tic, of course. A woman like that can indeed become "different," we thought, maybe we'll do it. And there was empathy involved as well, on Inge's part at least. We, too, had entered a world we had never known before—a petty-bourgeois Nazi milieu, with a woman who suddenly wanted to come over to our side. That was a challenge, of course. We were all watching to see how she would react. We had adventuresome natures and found what was happening exciting: to us and to her, alternately.

It was in May 1943 that Inge made the acquaintance of Gerd Ehrlich.

Gerd Ehrlich:

One evening Ernst and I were to meet Felice in a pub on Nollendorfplatz. She arrived in the company of another young girl, who had stunningly beautiful brown eyes. Her name was Inge W. and she knew all about us and our situation from Fice. After I had taken care of "business" with Fice, I turned my attention to the lovely Inge. By the time the evening was over we already were good friends, and had arranged a rendezvous. Inge was my only love during the time I spent as an illegal. . . .

The following Saturday Inge and Fice invited my friend Ernst and me to the Wust residence. This Saturday was the first in a long line of Saturdays I spent in the apartment near Roseneck. I passed many a pleasant evening there in the company of the women and my friends; we even stored some of our materials there. [Frau] Wust was known in her neighborhood as a true Nazi. It was our (positive) influence that converted her. Of course, in order to be of even greater help to us she remained a loyal follower of the Führer on the outside.

Gerd Ehrlich, Walter Johlson, nicknamed "Jolle," and Ernst Schwerin soon became welcome guests in Lilly's home. Gerd was living at that time in "Aunt Ilse's" groundfloor apartment, which could be seen from the street, and so he had to leave the apartment early each morning and not appear on the weekends at all. The question of where he was to spend Saturday nights often arose. Despite Inge's warnings about Lilly, the couch in the Friedrichshaller Strasse study served nicely.

"Great," Gerd had responded to Inge's argument that Lilly was a "good Nazi." "We couldn't do better. We're that much safer here. If she has no idea of who we really are, and anything happens, she'll act totally innocent."

Gerd and Inge, for their part, had no idea that Lilly had known what was going on for a long time, for, as was her habit, she had betrayed nothing. But she never found out about the things they hid in her apartment.

Nor did Gerd have any inkling of the household's romantic entanglements. The first night he spent on the couch he heard sounds coming from one of the rooms, which even he, in his innocence, could hardly misinterpret.

"Man, what was that?" he asked Ernst the next day. "Frau Wust's husband must have shown up last night."

Ernst stared at him in disbelief and shook with laughter. "How old are you anyway? Don't you know that our charming Fice has crossed over, and turned our good Lilly's head hopelessly?"

It had occurred to Gerd Ehrlich that Fice reacted with indifference to the charm he exerted so successfully over the other young women he knew, and for that reason he had dropped his usual flirtatious banter with her. Nevertheless, this explanation appeared highly unlikely to him. *Not with a woman with four children, and the Führer hanging on the wall,* he pondered, until finally he arrived at an explanation that suited his world view: Men were a scarce commodity in wartime, and this was probably a makeshift solution. He himself had masturbated with a friend as a young boy, and was a long way from being homosexual.

The far-reaching changes in her life were almost too much for Lilly, who had suffered from a weak heart condition since birth and was still recuperating from her jaw operation. But she was the kind of person who pursued with enthusiasm anything she undertook, and so she added another item to her list: She wanted to divorce her husband as quickly as possible.

Felice became greatly upset on hearing this news, and ran to Inge to discuss it.

"She's *meshuggah!* Think of what would happen if my name came up in court!"

"You must be out of your mind," Inge said to Lilly, trying to discourage her from her plan, "thinking of getting divorced with four children!"

"Don't you think you owe your children a stable home?" her parents-in-law commented in their Prussian mode, feeling vindicated in having instinctively rejected this redhead as a daughter-in-law.

"For God's sake, child," Lilly's mother pleaded, clapping her hands over her head, "have you gone mad? You're totally vulnerable! Who will take care of you in your old age?"

"First four children, and now divorce! Couldn't you have thought about this sooner?" Father Kappler growled in exasperation.

"Don't worry, I won't be coming to you for money," Lilly countered harshly.

Günther objected as well, of course, and behaved in the customary fashion of husbands in such a situation. *What would he do if he knew the real reason*, Lilly mused, and relished the thought. Too bad he could never find out! Günther employed the usual threats to keep the mother of his children tied to him. He wanted the apartment, he told her, and two of the children, and Lilly was to assume entire responsibility

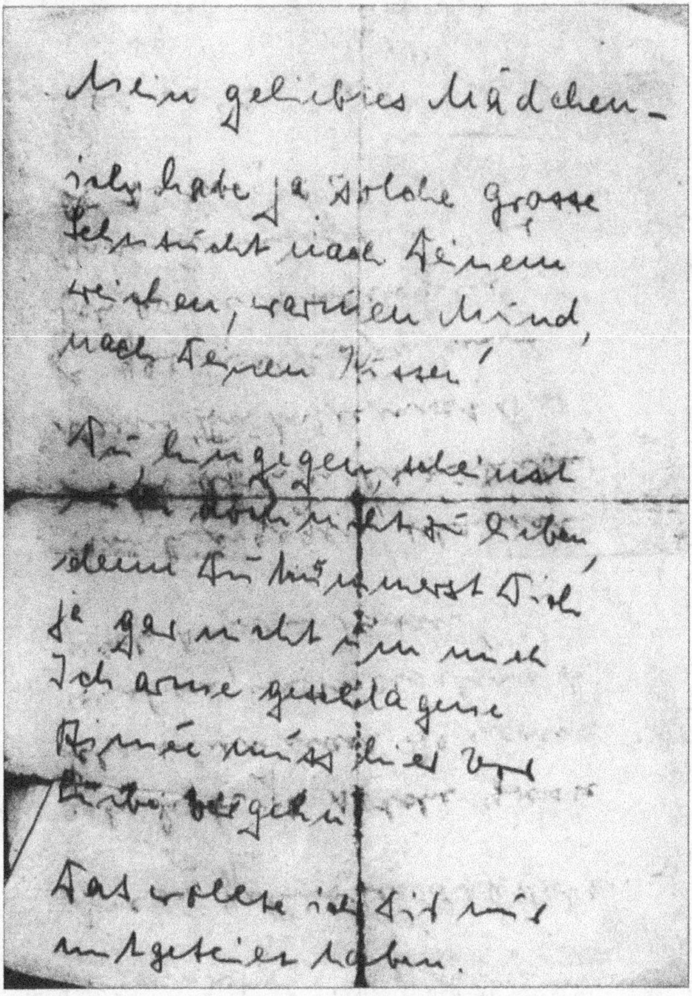
Mein geliebtes Mädchen –

ich habe ja solche grosse
Sehnsucht nach Deinem
weichen, warmen Mund,
nach Deinen Küssen!

Du hingegen scheinst
mich doch nicht zu lieben,
denn Du kümmerst Dich
ja gar nicht um mich
Ich arme geschlagene
Aimée muss hier vor
Liebe vergehn

Das wollte ich Dir mal
mitgeteilt haben.

A note from Aimée to Jaguar.

Felice in 1941 on the Selbachs' balcony at Bornstrasse 4 in Berlin-Stieglitz. The Gestapo was in possession of this photograph when Felice was picked up on August 21, 1944.

Lilly shortly after their "wedding night," in Grunewald, April 1943. It is the first photo Felice took of her.

Meine Aimée!

Ich liebe Dich so sehr, dass ich Dir gar nichts schreiben kann. Und ich brauche Dir ja eigentlich auch gar nicht zu schreiben, denn alles so enorm wichtige, werde ich Dir - wenn es Dir recht ist - nachher im Bett - sagen.

Und wenn Du einmal davon sprichst, dass ich Dir einen Mann suchen soll, oder dass Du heiraten willst, dann verlasse ich nach Strich und Faden

Dein

treuer, mutiger, edler, wilder

Jaguar

Dated September 1942, a letter from Jaguar to Aimée.

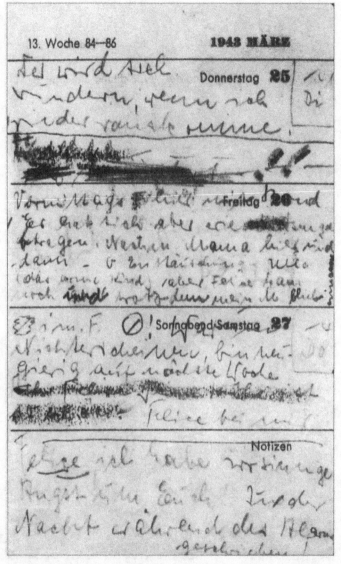

A page from Lilly's calendar during the time she was in the hospital.
March 25, 1943, was their "engagement day."

Taken earlier on the day of Felice's arrest by the Gestapo, August 21, 1944, at the Havel River. Taken with a self-timer and developed after the war.

A letter from Felice written in the "Jewish collection camp" at Schulstrasse 78 in Berlin.

Lilly's "book of tears": a copy of a page from Lilly's diary, and all the letters and poems that Aimée and Jaguar wrote to each other, copied by Lilly in the winter of 1945.

Top: Felice's passport. Bottom: Lilly's train ticket to Theresienstadt.

A postcard from Felice, written at the Theresienstadt concentration camp.

Felice's last letter from the Gross-Rosen concentration camp, written on December 26, 1944.

Dr. Grünberger's letter to Lilly: "Fraulein Schragenheim took the same path as my daughter . . ."

Lilly in the spring of 1947.

Felice in a photo taken by Ilse Ploog in January 1944.

Lilly Wust and the author in February 1991.

Lilly Wust in February 1991.

Lilly Wust in the spring of 1993.

for the breakup of the marriage. His extramarital escapades of course carried less weight than hers.

Lilly felt pressured from all sides.

"I have a difficult time ahead of me. You must help me to get through it," she wrote on the back of a shortening ration voucher issued for children between the ages of six and fourteen. Each time she purchased butter, margarine or cheese, her shop on Breite Strasse stamped "canceled" on a coupon on the pale yellow ration sheet. The constantly tipsy shopkeeper who sold groceries, canned goods, butter, fruit and vegetables was called Adolf Hoch ["Adolf Hurrah"] of all things, a name Felice found hilarious.

Lilly was also beginning to feel pressure from within the household, for gradually Inge was coming to realize that in arranging the encounter at the Café Berlin, she not only had found a splendid home for Felice, she also found herself losing her lover. Felice's other affairs were insignificant to her, there would always be time for monogamy later, but a Nazi! On top of which, Inge harbored a deep distrust of Lilly. In her opinion Felice had made a big mistake in telling Lilly the truth about herself. But Felice was relieved not to have to hide things from Lilly. And now Inge was reproaching herself for setting up a situation in which Felice was delivered, for better or worse, into the hands of this Nazi woman who was in love with her. Lilly and Inge quarreled more and more often.

I'm terribly depressed again, of course. I truly do not understand Inge. She knows she's tilting against windmills. If this is her great love—well—I would have felt the same way too, at first, if the tables were turned. But then, precisely because I love you, I would have given you up, even if it had broken my heart. I would much prefer for the other person to be happy. And what good does that attitude do her? What does it change? She can't seriously ask us not to love each other. Or do you think that would be better? But I'll tell you one thing outright: I will not consider losing even a small part of you, I will hold on to you as fast as I can! I can do that—and most important of all: I don't want it any other way!

Lilly was impressed on the one hand by the sexual freedom exhibited by the *ménage à trois* of Inge, Nora, and Elenai—she preferred not to know what Felice was up to—for after all, Lilly herself had not passed up any opportunity. On the other hand, the girls carried on a bit too much; why were they always quarreling with one another? She once again used a postcard to express her thoughts: "I will tell you where your dissatisfaction lies," she primly admonished Felice. "All of you take things a bit too far, and in the process you destroy the intimacy that needs to exist between people. You think only of yourselves, all of you, and of whatever suits you."

Sunday was the one day Lilly and Felice could sleep late. On Sunday there was no Inge arriving at the door at eight in the morning. Lilly looked forward to Sunday all week. The children, too, knew that once their mother had given them their Sunday breakfast, they were to look after themselves all morning, and were more than happy to run around their room and be able to do what they wanted. Each Saturday evening Lilly prepared a second, late-morning Sunday breakfast, for Felice and herself. She then had only to reheat the fried potatoes and pour the barley malt coffee. The morning would pass quickly between dozing, eating, reading, and making love. Their friends knew not to put in an appearance before 4 p.m.

The doorbell rang on one such Sunday in June. Eberhard opened the door to let in Elenai, whom he knew. In higher spirits than she had been in a long time, she stormed into the balcony room where Lilly and Felice were lounging about in bed. On Lilly's sewing table across the sundrenched room from the balcony lay two yards of gold lace with which Lilly intended to trim one of her dresses. Delighted, Elenai wrapped the glittering lace around her mop of curly black hair and then around the waist of her summer dress. Thus attired she played dancing girl for the couple. Suddenly the large double doors to the study opened and there stood Lilly's mother, frozen to the spot. Lilly froze in place as well, for neither she nor Felice had anything on under the covers.

The situation could not be hidden after that, and Lilly decided to take her parents into her confidence. Perhaps then they would better understand why she wanted a divorce. Everything spilled out one afternoon when she paid them a visit. Lilly not only informed them that Felice was Jewish, she told them the truth about Felice and herself as well.

"We're lovers, and want to stay together."

After a moment of shock that seemed to Lilly to go on forever, her father was the first to regain his composure.

"And what will you do later?"

"Oh, seduce young girls," Lilly said impudently, to cover her embarrassment.

Lilly:

Actually, my parents weren't surprised at all. At that moment they probably thought back to my youth, when they had done everything in their power to suppress that. They sent me to dancing lessons and brought young men over to the house. Horrible! I was always being introduced to some suitor or other. It was dreadful!

When I was seventeen my father wrote a poem: "Every crush on some young man begins with a girlfriend and from afar/and Lilly too, was carried away by a teacher on the horizontal bar." In my seventh year of secondary school I got a terrible crush on my gym teacher. She was small and wiry, and had black curly hair and dark, sparkling eyes. In a word, I found her wonderful. Out of sheer desire I became the best gymnast in my class. And then I found out where she lived. She had a room in Spandau, and I would lie in wait for her there; sometimes I would almost freeze, I can still remember that. I would just walk back and forth, and once I even dared to show up at her door. I lied the blue right out of the sky, saying I had an aunt who lived in Spandau. She was very embarrassed, of course. She was really in fear for her life, the poor girl. Carola Fuss was her name, and she was Jewish. (Just as Jews showed a liking for me, I showed a liking for them, that's the way it was.) The others were always making fun of me: Ha, there she is again, they would say, or: Hey, she just went

that way. Girls are so spiteful. And then the whole thing came
out, someone probably squealed. The faculty was in an uproar
about it. They called a meeting at school because of it, which I
had to attend with my parents, and they almost expelled me.
But then I told them my side of the story, and they realized
that I was totally oblivious and innocent. Even then I didn't
know what it was all about. And my parents never discussed it
with me, people just didn't talk about things like that. Everything was so vague: You don't do that, you don't feel that, that
doesn't exist. Somehow, in their subconscious, they already
knew, yes well, she's, you know . . .

Today I know why it's so easy for me to put my arms
around women. I do it automatically, I always could. After I
graduated, for example, and before I began my compulsory
service, I attended a school for housework, in Saarow-Piskow
in 1933. By that time I was already engaged to be married,
but I had a girlfriend. Everyone was always whispering about
us behind our backs because we went around holding hands.
We liked each other an awful lot, but neither of us knew what
was going on. Our beds were next to each other and we didn't
do anything, but the other girls got all riled up about us. Had
we known at the time what was going on, I never in my life
would have. . . . And then she got married too. I still have
pictures of her daughter; Felice took them. I made an extra
trip with Felice to see her, and when we went into the kitchen
together she began complaining about her husband. Our
friendship waned during the war. If we had stayed together
everything would have been different. Her name was Lotti
Radecke.

I always said it was a good thing that there was an "e" at the end of her name, because there was a scandal at school once involving me and a girl named Gerda Radek. The teacher who instigated the whole thing was our professor. It all began on a class outing, and Gerda Radek's mother was there too. We did nothing more than hold hands. I only remember that they said I had acted in an immoral way toward her, and that is absolute nonsense. Her mother said something to the teacher and the teacher called my parents. Something like that couldn't be allowed, it was outrageous, and so on. My parents were shocked, but they saw that I was totally without a clue. We were forbidden to sit next to each other after that. One of us had always sat behind the other in class, so that we could pass notes. They forbade us to be friends, really, and we obeyed. Gerda withdrew completely. And after that we became somewhat enemies.

I always had girlfriends, bosom buddies, so to speak. For years I had a friend named Lotti Thiede. Her parents were always giving house parties, and I could stay overnight because it would get too late to go home. One time three of us were sleeping in two beds pushed together. I was in the middle and suddenly Lotti moved over closer to me. And I said to her, quite gruffly, "What do you want from me?" I was terribly sorry for that later. She had one leg that was shorter than the other, and was a very dear person. That was terrible of me, I'll never forget it. I didn't understand anything then.

So finally, when I started up with boys, my parents heaved a sigh of relief: Thank God, she has boyfriends!

The fact that Felice was Jewish was frightening enough to Lilly's anxious mother, but her parents were much more concerned about the other thing. At the same time they could not help but notice how happy their daughter was, and how Felice was spoiling her. Father Kappler would happily have given his Nazi son-in-law the boot were there no children involved. Yet despite their misgivings they accepted Felice into the family with astonishing magnanimity.

Felice took Papa to her heart the first time she met him, which was at Christmas. As he stood before her, tall and thin in his nickel frame glasses, she turned pale and had to sit down: The resemblance to her own deceased father was amazing.

Lilly was preparing for a long life together with Felice, and bravely battled the fear of an unknown future. War, four children, no experience other than cooking, changing diapers, and cleaning, and with a Jew hiding in the house—what she had taken on was no small thing.

Felice, please don't make the mistake my husband made. If for some reason I get irritated or furious, don't add to it by arguing with me. Just say nothing, and be very good to me later. It's not that I'm insensitive, but just let me rage, it will pass just as quickly if you do. When will we ever be able to be alone (Inge!)? I think it will only get worse in the future (our dear friends!). Let's hope for the best. After all, there are two sides to everything. Who knows how much time we'll have to be alone together!

Say, I just had a great idea! How about a marriage

contract? For my part, for example, I could pledge to be faithful and lovingly patient with all your manifold responsibilities ...

At the moment I'm so eternally—it's not that I'm despondent or disheartened, just eternally sad. Never make me any promises you can't keep, never! I truly believe you will never leave me, a woman like me doesn't get left. The best thing would be for us to really be in the world, to build a whole new future. But thinking this, I feel sorry that you're so young and burdened with such an old woman as I. But you will be, won't you? And gladly? For me!

Do you know what? I want something of yours, so that I will truly know you belong to me. We can't wear rings, unfortunately. I don't know what it will be, but there must be something. Felice, my girl, I am thinking about your eyes. Felice, I love you, the more so the longer we're together. I'll make a list of the things I wish to keep. It will be nice at our place, you can depend on that. Will you be able to get me a couch, too?

I get a little worried when I think about my future. But it's not that I'm afraid. I've thought carefully about what I want to do. Carefully! I want to live with you— and be happy. To pull myself out of my routine—I don't belong there. I would rather experience great unhappiness and be destroyed by it than live in moderate happiness to a moderate end. Felice, I have never loved anyone with so little consideration of everyone and everything else. Don't leave me alone!

By June 1943 only two Jewish institutions remained in
Berlin: the Jewish Hospital and the Weissensee Cemetery.
Over six thousand Jews still lived in the city, in mixed marriages and in the underground. On June 10 the total assets
of the Nazi-instituted "Reich Agency of Jews in Germany"
were seized—a total of eight million Reichsmarks. Dr. Walter
Lustig, director of the Jewish Hospital, was entrusted with the
founding and management of the "New Reich Agency," to be
housed in the administration building of the Jewish Hospital.
The agency was barely given the opportunity to do anything
for its compulsory members. Under the eyes of the Gestapo,
its few Jewish employees, partners of mixed marriages, admin-
istered to the city's last Jews, until April of 1945. The ill were
treated, those underground were hunted, widowed partners of
"mixed marriages" were picked up and deported, burials were
performed and statistics kept.

Lilly and Günther Wust were bickering constantly. He absolutely refused to give her a divorce, though he had been living
with his girlfriend, Liesl, for a long time by then. Surprisingly,
Liesl came to Lilly's aid by putting pressure on Günther to
marry her. Lilly and Günther finally thrashed out a compromise on the children: Günther would take the two oldest boys,
Bernd and Eberhard, and Lilly would keep Reinhard and Albrecht. Lilly's female friends were horrified that she had agreed
to this with such relative nonchalance, but Lilly was almost
certain that, due to his situation, Günther would not hold up
his end of the bargain. Once Günther finally agreed to a sep-

aration, the next stage was the battle over money and who would get to keep what from their apartment.

I'm going to see my husband again. But I've decided that this will be our last conversation. I don't want to do this anymore. He'll just have to figure things out somehow. I'm finished with it, and won't discuss it with anyone except you and Inge. He imagines everything will be so easy: He's in for a surprise. At any rate, things aren't going to happen as quickly as he would like. By the way, about your typewriter? It would be very nice if I could have it. I'd like to get something accomplished finally. I'm so afraid of everything, but I'm always like that. And then once I get into it I feel better immediately. I absolutely want to make it on my own, to stand on my own two feet.

And you will help me, won't you? You do love me! And I really will have only you—nor do I wish it any other way. Forget about everyone else: I love you more than my life! I so want for everything to turn out all right—and then— then the world will be ours. (But I won't take care of your suits!!!)

"And I don't like your circle of friends, by the way," Günther said, as if in passing, during one their arguments.

Lilly stared at him in disbelief, and her expression hardened. Did he realize that he had found the key to keeping her under control? Feeling stung, words he once had spoken suddenly pushed their way forth from her memory: "Save me the child, at least." She had almost died giving birth to Reinhard. "Save me the child, at least." Anyone who could utter a sentence like that was capable of anything.

From then on Lilly agreed to everything Günther asked.

And as if she didn't have enough problems with Günther, Inge was adding to her anxiety. "Please don't leave me alone tomorrow night," Lilly pleaded with Felice, after Inge told her that Elenai suddenly had announced a visit.

"What is love, torturous happiness, glorious pain?" she noted at the end of June on the back of four expired pink food coupons:

God knows, everything from before is extinguished for me, Felice. It simply no longer exists—everything is today, everything is tomorrow, it shines no matter what. I love you so immensely. And you love me! My girl, my beloved, beautiful girl. I don't think we could get along without each other. Without each other it just doesn't work. And that's how it should be from now on. A lifetime long. There is nothing I wish more fervently than that. One should never say never, and never say forever, but I want to say it and have it be true: We shall remain together forever, never leave one another unless it were for the best. I don't see why two women cannot make their way alone together, completely happy and in harmony with one another. What do we need men for! I'm not at all afraid. After all, you're "man enough" for me, isn't that so? You know that you must always protect me, and also that you want to. I know from experience that one doesn't need a man in order to be happy; in the end they simply are different creatures, living on another star and seldom letting us poor women in. I have experienced this not once, but many times. And you, my dearest, you are something unutterably familiar to me, you are really I myself! We are truly a wonderful idea. My life up until now was not lacking in love, God knows, but was empty of life, real life. I have spent years living for nothing, have wasted my life. And that is not what life is for. I want to live, to love with all the fire in my heart, to savor life and love to the fullest. I will never stand before you empty-handed. I will look after you, be your homeland, your home and family. I will give you everything you lack, and I know that my call in life is to make you happy—my Felice.

As of the end of 1942 Felice and her sister Irene had succeeded in finding a way to correspond with one another, through an Emmi-Luise Kummer in Geneva, Switzerland. Frau Kummer had been the governess of Alix Rosenthal, one of Irene's schoolfriends, back in Berlin. Frau Kummer would copy sections of their letters to each other and forward them to London or to Berlin. It sometimes took a letter from London fourteen days or even a month to pass both the English and the Wehrmacht High Command censors, and to arrive in Geneva bearing its blue mark. Many letters never arrived at all. On July 6 Irene thanked Felice, whom she called Putz, for a photo she had sent. "I really can merely clap my hands above my head," she wrote, "and say girl, girl, how you have changed. But that's because I keep thinking: Putz is seventeen and not twenty-one."

Felice began calling Lilly "Aimée" at the first sign of their fondness for one another. *Aimée, or Good Common Sense,* was a play by Heinz Coubier, and actress Olga Chekhova had presented a copy of it to Felice in January 1940, "in memory of a play that gave so many people and me joy." It was a simple comedy, set in the period following the French Revolution, and it premiered on April 30, 1938, at the Schauspielhaus in Bremen. The character Aimée is introduced as a young woman "whose irrationality hides a good deal of intelligence." Lilly liked the name Aimée—Beloved—yes, that was what she wanted to be, beyond measure, forever. And didn't the description of the character fit her as well? Everyone told her she was irrational, but wasn't it a sign of intelligence to abandon the suffocating narrowness of her previous life and throw herself into adventure before it was too late? Was there anything more unreasonable than to grow old, like her mother, at the side of a man she did not love?

On June 26, 1943, Aimée used Felice's green ink to record her part of a "marriage contract":

> *I will* love *you beyond measure,*
> *Be* true *to you unconditionally,*
> *attend to* order *and* cleanliness,
> work hard *for you and the children and myself,*
> *be* frugal, *when it is called for,*
> generous *in* all *things,*
> *trust you!*
> *What is mine shall be yours;*
> *I will always be there for you.*
> *Elisabeth Wust, née Kappler*

"And you?" she wrote on the back side of the postcard. On June 29, using a double sheet of real stationery, Felice answered the challenge:

In the name of all responsible gods, saints and mascots I pledge to obey the following ten points and hope that all responsible gods, saints and mascots will be merciful and help me to keep my word:

1. I will always love you.
2. I will never leave you.
3. I will do everything to make you happy.
4. I will take care of you and the children, as far as circumstances allow.
5. I will not object to you taking care of me.
6. I will no longer look at pretty girls, or at least only to ascertain that you are prettier.
7. I will not come home late very often.
8. I will try to grind my teeth quietly at night.
9. I will always love you.
10. I will always love you.

Until further notice,
Felice

"It is strange," Lilly wrote during a train ride once, "that when I think of the future, I never think of the children, it is always as if we will be alone together."

Bernd Wust:

Mutti fed and diapered us, of course, but she did not enjoy being a housewife, for sure. She was always carrying on about how, when the war was over, we would all be able to eat out of cans, thank God, and she wouldn't have to clean any more vegetables. I always experienced the opposite: When we were invited to Grandma's, I noticed that Grandma had a completely different attitude toward the household and cooking and so on. She cooked like they do in the Rhineland. I didn't like the way things tasted, but because Grandpa wanted me to I had to compliment the food. Sweet and sour veal fricassee, for instance—maybe that wasn't a Rhineland recipe at all— but Grandma was the only one who cooked it. Grandpa was a very funny man, but he became an absolute and obstinate grouch later. That's how he was all the time, it was his way of getting through life. Not exactly courageous and brave, but he knew how to hide that behind a lot of nonsense. But he was an excellent grandfather to us children. He could get all four of us on his bicycle. There was a wide pedestrian promenade with benches in the middle of Hohenzollerndamm, and he would take us there, small as we were, and joke that we should watch out for the policeman.

One morning Inge appeared ready for work to find Lilly and Felice still in bed in their darkened room.

"Inge, open the window, please," Felice purred lazily, as she wound a strand of Lilly's tousled hair around her finger.

"I'm not your servant," Inge growled, and with a furious,

"This is really too much!" slammed the bedroom door behind her and went to work in the apartment. There followed a loud and furious battle of words between Lilly and Inge, and Inge's career as a domestic was over. Her bag was waiting for her at the door.

But her departure was not unanticipated. Some time before, Inge's boss at Collignon had told her that he wanted her back at the bookshop. In the end they went together to the Labor Office, and he succeeded in getting Inge released from her job by proving that she was indispensable at the shop. On June 21, 1943, Inge finally returned to being a bookseller, relieved to have escaped the tension at Friedrichshaller Strasse. For Felice and Lilly, this marked the beginning of a period of freedom.

> My Felice-girl,
>
> I'm sitting on the train to Grünau. Can you tell that I'm thinking of you? Whenever my heart moves or aches for some reason, I believe you are thinking of me! Why does love hurt so? As a result of a few love affairs I once had, I thought perhaps I didn't truly know how to love. Now I know that I can. I love you. You really are my "first person"! Before, I would sometimes get the strangest feeling of guilt, that something wasn't right. I was ashamed— and now—now my feelings spill over without end.

On July 13, 1943, the Central Office of the Gestapo in Berlin sent a letter to the presiding president of the Berlin-Brandenburg Revenue Office, Department of Property Holdings. The letter requested the confiscation of the assets of "the Jewess" Felice Sara Schragenheim, stating that as of June 15, 1943, she had been registered as a fugitive. The request was quickly filled. On July 1, 1943, the correspondence section of the Prussian State Bank of Berlin reported to the president of the Revenue Office that assets belonging to "Felicie Sara Schragenheim," account number J 361 224, had been seized following an announcement appearing in issue number 144 of the *Deutsche Reichsanzeiger* of June 24, 1943.

Sometime between July 14 and July 26, 1943, Felice sent a letter via Emmi-Luise Kummer to Irene in London. Irene passed it on to Felice's friend Hilli Frenkel in New York:

Of course I think your Fritz is delightful, since he likes you and because that makes you happy. Hopefully I'll get to meet him soon. Give Ludwig my regards a thousand times; sometimes I feel longing, but I think it would be good if it stayed at that, without the necessary disappointment that would come if we saw each other again. Or doesn't he think so? I really know nothing whatsoever anymore about slim, dark-haired young men. And at seventeen I had thought I knew so much about them! Wherever love falls—that's what we used to say, and would you find it very bad if my love fell elsewhere? You don't understand entirely, do you? Doesn't matter, we'll talk about it sometime. . . . Lilly is entirely delightful; you must meet her. Not an outstanding personality, not at all intellectual, just average intelligence, she makes an endearing effort to get involved in my world, my books, my interests, and to live with me the way I want to. Of course I thus have a lot of responsibility, but I gladly take it on, considering that I have someone who unconditionally belongs to me and sticks by me. Living together is simply wonderful. Each of us makes such an effort to offer the other a hundred little joys and to be considerate. Sometimes we don't say a word to each other an entire evening, but we know that the other one is there, and that's a lovely feeling. Our primary principle is not to get on each other's nerves and not to bore each other. I'm mostly in charge of the latter, since I constantly keep her in suspense, as she always assures me. The children are delightful and very well-bred, especially the little ones, "ours," who we will keep after the divorce. They are two and four years old, simply darlings. Just now the divorced spouse has arrived—Lilly has gone to visit someone. He's a nice guy, but the two of them just don't get along. He gets along fine with me.

Somewhat later: It was really delightful. Five minutes after her husband arrived, her charming father came. I have to call him "Papa" and he just loves to kiss young girls. The third one who showed up was Gregor, a writer, for whom I occasionally type. He is often at our place or goes out to eat with us. He is in his mid-forties and aside from having a wife and child he also has total understanding for Lilly and me. He is six-and-a-half-feet tall and everyone calls him "Good Gregor."

And I am the housewife caught between these three worlds. Everyone complimented me afterwards for how well I managed to avoid any pitfalls.

I'm still at Mutti's. But of course she notices that I'm
not particularly enjoying it. Talk it over, argue, make up—
that's how it always goes. Yet she still has a strange power
over me. If only I didn't have the feeling that she takes
ample advantage of that. Next week she'll be going to the
"Forst" and I'll probably drive up on the weekend. Unfortunately Lilly can't find out—it's difficult with women.

Under the Damocles' sword of Günther's threats, Lilly agreed
to assume partial responsibility for the failure of their marriage. This meant that she was eligible for only one year of
alimony payments. In July, in preparation for her life as a di-
vorcée, Lilly enrolled at the Rackow Language School on Wit-
tenbergplatz, signing up for a course for beginning interpreters
of English, but she first had to learn German shorthand and
how to type. When her morning class ended, Felice would be
standing at the school gate in her white linen shorts. Side by
side they would then bicycle through Wilmersdorf, to sit chatting for a while on a bench in Hindenburg Park before it was
time to go home to the children.

The population of Berlin still believed that the city's air
defense would be able to ward off any major attack on the
Reich capital. They had become accustomed to the minor
destruction caused by "mosquito attacks," and listened with
sympathy, though somewhat incredulously, as refugees from
the Ruhr District talked about whole streets on fire and cities
that had been totally destroyed. But Berliners' composure gave
way to growing anguish when in nearby Hamburg, between

July 24 and 30, roughly fifty thousand people were killed by
British fire bombs and high explosives as part of "Operation
Gomorrah." On August 1 a handbill was distributed to all
Berlin households ordering all women and children, and the
sick and elderly, to leave the capital. With the temperature
hovering around ninety-five degrees, masses of the population
stormed the train stations and ticket agencies. Thousands left
the city to camp at night in the surrounding forests. Thousands
more went to visit friends and relatives in the country, taking
their possessions with them for safekeeping. The *Völkischer
Beobachter* quoted Frederick the Great: "In times of storm and
distress, one must have insides of iron and a heart of brass in
order to rid oneself of all emotions."

Newspapers reported that "well-prepared" Germans would
"defy the terror of the bombing." Valuables should be taken to
friends in less-endangered areas for safekeeping. Pieces of paper
bearing the exact name and address of the owner were to be
attached to furniture, rugs and household possessions. "Once
and for all, women and children belong in the cellar," warned
the *Hakenkreuzbanner* (Swastika Banner), the National Socialist newspaper of Mannheim and North Baden that soon was
to play a part in Felice's life story. As there was a danger with
high explosives of being buried in the debris or of burning to
death, Berliners were instructed to memorize the escape route
they would take out of their air raid shelters. It was forbidden
to obstruct shelters with crates, equipment or air raid shelter
bags. Openings in walls had to be blocked off, otherwise they
might function as a chimney in the case of fire and imperil an
otherwise secure building. People were to take with them to

the cellar only what was necessary for the most basic survival. "A few hand towels are more important than silverware, rugs, paintings, or a hundred volumes of classical literature," according to the *Hakenkreuzbanner*. Above all, candles, matches, gas masks, blankets and water were needed. If cellar exits were buried in rubble, and burning embers on the basement ceiling raised temperatures to a dangerous degree, shelter inhabitants could survive by soaking blankets and coats with water. They were then to dash through the burning building with their mouths and noses covered with the damp cloth. Each resident was to keep an air raid shelter bag packed with savings book, food coupons, drinking water, and "provisions" ready-at-hand. Clothing worn in the shelter was to contain as little rayon and cotton as possible, as these materials were flammable. Heavy leather gloves and coats and vests of leather were preferable, as well as glasses that offered protection to the sides of the face, like skiers' or welders' glasses. Women could tie a scarf around their heads.

"Do men belong in the air raid shelters?" the newspaper asked rhetorically, to answer: "Their responsibility is not to protect themselves, but to protect the community from harm." Fire was best fought with sand and water; stick type incendiary bombs looked like white fireworks, phosphorous bombs spit and smoked, sparks could be put out with firebeaters but phosphorous fires could not be, as the firebeaters would cause sparks to fly in all directions.

The city was greatly uneasy; each evening Berliners waited for the major air offensive to commence that was constantly being announced by the BBC. Each night city-dwellers vanished into their cellars at the first sound of the sirens. People stormed the train stations; anyone who didn't have to remain in the city headed east or south. The pavement was stripped from the city's squares and every patch of green was dug up to make way for air raid shelters. Any male pedestrian who happened to be strolling by was stopped by the block supervisor and put to work with a shovel. Maintaining a rapid pace was advisable. Not until August 27, after Berliners had regained confidence in their air defense system, did the long-awaited event occur. In the event of a bomb attack, "U-boats" like Gerd Ehrlich had to hurry to reach the public shelters in time.

Gerd Ehrlich:

The Berlin radio broadcast went off the air at 9 p.m., which was customary when enemy planes were approaching. I hurriedly put on boots and jacket and strapped on my Hitler Youth belt. I waited at the door, my briefcase packed, and then the sirens went off. So I left the house quickly and walked along the street for a bit. For the last few times I had gone to a wonderfully large cellar in a building on Bismarck-strasse. A former classmate of mine lived there, Klaus H., a half-Aryan who, as such, was left more or less alone in an acceptable job. That day I barely reached the building before the flak let loose and began firing. The lights went out and dust floated down from the ceiling. The cellar swayed like a ship at sea; women began to scream and it seemed as if the whole building was going to collapse. After a few minutes of confusion we began to collect ourselves. The air raid warden ordered all young men to the doors. Klaus and I were elected to check the property.

So we put on our steel helmets and set off. We had a stunning view from the roof. For one moment we forgot the danger we were in. The night sky was blood-red as far as you could see, and above us things that looked like multicolored Christmas trees were being fired on by German antiaircraft planes using tracer ammunition. Searchlights singled out individual planes, but they were undaunted by the furious attack and kept flying, to fearlessly swoop down on some industrial or rail target and thus escape the line of fire. Then we hurried out onto the street. A strong wind had blown up, sending smoke, ashes and leaflets all over the place. We quickly gathered up several copies of the "Appeal to the German People" that the planes had scattered, and stuck them in our pockets. The attack had lasted only an hour perhaps, but the damage was rather considerable. Two days later I walked through streets that still were on fire. That night I had to wander around until about 3 a.m., as my building was too stirred up for anyone to enter unnoticed. I helped put out fires in various buildings and carry out furniture.

Felice, known and loved by the neighbors as Lilly's charming friend, accompanied Lilly and Bernd to the cellar at the sound of the sirens, while the three youngest children spent the night in the children's bunker nearby, a privilege not all mothers enjoyed. At first Lilly had delivered them to Herta, the shelter attendant, personally, but later they walked over on their own. The boys thought themselves very grown-up when, at a quarter to six, they held hands and crossed Kolberger Platz to Reichenhaller Strasse. Eberhard, thoughtful and considerate, was responsible for seeing that "Chubby" was handed over to Sister Herta's care. Albrecht, not yet two years old and still in diapers, was too young for the bunker, actually, but Sister Herta had taken a fancy to him and turned a blind eye to his presence. As the other children climbed into their bunk beds with their teddy bears, "Chubby" was allowed to snuggle up against Herta's ample bosom. "Fold your hands/bow your head/Think of Adolf Hitler only./He gives us our daily bread/And leads us out of worry" the children would murmur in chorus, their eyes on the picture of the Führer. Then lights-out was called and those on the lower bunks would begin kicking those above them in the small of their backs. "Quiet!" Sister Herta roared, pressing "Chubby" to her and thinking wistfully of her Hans, from whom she had heard nothing for more than two months, since the capitulation of German and Italian troops in Tunisia.

At home, a stressful time began for Lilly with the wailing of the sirens.

"Come on, hurry up!" she would moan, running nervously back and forth with her air defense bag between the front door and the bathroom. But Felice would stand at the mirror, combing and combing her straight and brittle dark brown hair. It would have been unsightly were it not for the fact that her hairdresser kept it elegantly waved. It required constant care and had to be in perfect order before she would proceed to the cellar. The more presentable Felice was to the other residents the safer she felt.

After the all-clear siren, the tables were turned.

"Don't fall asleep, please don't fall asleep," Felice would plead, as Lilly sank down on the stairs in exhaustion and had to be dragged back up to the apartment. With Lilly stretched out motionless across the bed Felice then had to undress her, not infrequently leading to Lilly's suddenly being very wide awake. When the children returned the next day, ringing the bell at 8 a.m., they both were dead tired.

It was around this time that Ernst, Jolle and Gerd asked Felice if she wished to attempt an escape with them. Lutz, wanted for arrest following his heroic forging of identification papers created from supplies stolen from the German Red Cross, had succeeded at the end of May in fleeing to Switzerland—with the help of a female "escape helper" and an ID from the Reich Armaments Ministry, permitting the bearer to travel in the vicinity of the border.

Felice and Lilly despondently debated the issue: to flee or to stay? And—unnoticed by Lilly—Felice, Inge, and Elenai were also holding vehement debates. An unlawful escape across the border to Switzerland was by all means dangerous. And there were more than a few incidents of Swiss border guards sending fleeing Jews right back across the border into Nazi Germany.

Lilly weighed leaving the children behind and following Felice into exile. There were a number of children's homes in southern Germany; after the war they could come for them again. Lilly was sure there would be an "after." Felice, for her part, was skeptical. The rumors she had heard and quickly suppressed were too horrible for her to be able to imagine an "after." But she did entertain the idea. As it was a well-known fact that escape-helpers were not interested in money but in things, Felice wrote to Luise Selbach in the Altvater (Jeseník)

Mountains and asked her to return her possessions. Mutti, to whom Felice's relationship with Lilly was an unforgivable breach of loyalty, had crated Felice's things—carpet runners, linens from several apartments and, above all, her grandmother's expensive Persian lamb coat—and shipped them to the "Forst" and to Olga in Eastern Pomerania for safekeeping. She was irritated by Felice's request, and always came up with new excuses. She had always admonished Felice that someone "on the run" could not stay in any one place for long. Lilly dutifully tried to talk Felice into leaving without her.

An unsigned letter from August 1943 was found describing the weeks of torment. It was written in green ink and the handwriting could easily have been Felice's.

My Dear Beloved,

    I cannot imagine life without you. Does such a thing exist? Doesn't one change, doesn't one become a stranger to oneself during every moment of separation, and discover oneself anew at each reunion? Am I to do without you for days, weeks, months, do without your voice and hands and mouth? Do without the certainty that all of your thoughts are with me, and mine with you? Must I give up everything I love? Am I never to be permitted to be unconditionally happy? Distance, time, custom—must we be threatened as well by these mortal enemies of love? Or is our love so weak that longing, that slowly fading fire, will only do it good? Why am I writing all of this—I love you so much, in a way I have never felt, never known before. Now I am

tormenting you and me. Why does one torment that which
one loves? Because one loves.

Elenai was amazed when one such letter written by Lilly
came into her hands.

"Tell me, why are you always imitating Felice's handwriting?"

"That's love," Lilly answered.

Elenai, Inge and Felice decided that, in view of the uncertainty of escape, Felice was safer remaining in Berlin. Felice
knew that this was her last chance to leave Germany, and drew
nearer to Lilly.

NIGHTS

I love to bend above you there,
To gaze into your sleeping face.
Your gentle breath disturbs the air,
And fills the twilight's still, gray space.
When my eyes across your clear
And oh so familiar features glide,
I comprehend at once, my dear,
The wonderful gentleness you provide.
As with some masterwork of art,
I sink into you like a stone,
Respond to the silent call of your heart,
But suddenly I feel alone!
You are so distant, and stricken with fright,
I suddenly know just where you are.

I lift you up. You sit upright
Return to my world from afar.

My Aimée!

I love you so much that I can't even put anything down on paper to you. But it's not really necessary to write you at all, for I can tell you all of the enormously important things I have to say later—if it's all right with you—in bed.

And should you even once mention that I should help you find a husband, or that you wish to marry, then you are off-base—right, left and center.

Your loyal, brave, noble, wild
Jaguar

It was the first time that Felice called herself Jaguar.

On August 10, 1943, Felice wrote to her sister Irene in London:

What does Fritz look like? When I read the name I always think of my Fritz, the best friend I had, and then I get very, very sad. And still it is possible to forget everything and to assert that I am completely happy. How long that will last—I fear, based on my experience, that it won't last, but that might be because today, after an absolutely wonderful Sunday at home, we got some bad news. At the moment I am sitting in almost pristine white shorts with an almost perfect crease (due to Lilly's devoted ironing services) on our balcony, from where I can look out over the allotment gardens, and she is sitting across from me, pensively filing her nails. I really have to describe to you sometime how she looks, so you'll recognize her if it gets to that point. Now she has switched to crossword puzzles, and occasionally demands erudite words from me. So: Charlotte-Elisabeth, 29 years old (but the cigarettes that she is thus authorized to obtain are all smoked by me), with a figure like the one I had at seventeen. Consequently, she wears all my summer dresses that don't fit me anymore, with my broad shoulders and otherwise rather athletic figure. She is a bit shorter than me and anyway looks like she's eighteen, so that no one believes she has four children, or a husband, since she doesn't wear a wedding ring. Due to her French family background, according to my friend Gregor, she has prominent Celtic cheekbones in a narrow face, a very high, rounded forehead, a narrow, delicate mouth and dark brown eyes, which are very unusual with her copper-red hair. She is in part—with good reason—proud of her hair, but in part she also has a complex because of it, just like with the rimless glasses that she has to wear, and with which I think she is prettier than without—and that is what matters! Michael Arlen wrote a novel *Lilly-Christine*—and that's her! My small watch from Käte looks outstanding on her narrow hands. It is virtually reprehensible how much fun I have making her blush and when she squints a little then I am ready to give her all my assets without a thought. No, I should find another comparison, since they are a thing of the past. When she turns red she also reproachfully calls out my name, which she never shortens on principle. These are all superficial things, you'll find them overstated and maybe hard to believe coming from me. But those are the facts! If I didn't have her—well, you could not even imagine. But you must, and you must promise me that you'll make good for it all someday if I cannot. She's getting divorced, now I'm responsible for her. You shouldn't consider that impetuous; I am fully aware of my accepting it all, since it is nothing compared to what she is always prepared to do. This is not meant to be a "last will and testament," but you have to understand that I want to know that I have taken care of it. My things, the linens and silverware that I have, are mostly stored at Mutti's so that I can't get to them now. As far as possible, Lilly should have that; at least it is something. You cannot imagine how hard it is for bachelors to get all their things back that have been left in their various more or less furnished abodes. People who are otherwise decent then have either a very short memory all of sudden or else they just misplaced the key to the basement.

Mutti is at the "Forst." Considering I got her a fantastic seat on the train and up to now have been cooking and vacuuming every other day for her husband and oldest daughter, she hasn't even written to me at all or passed on her regards to me. I don't know what's the matter with her. She's also miffed that I want my things back. And that I don't really want to keep playing the cleaning lady for nothing. By the way, that doesn't keep her from asking her daughter if I took care of this or that, or got something for her. I don't understand it at all, and I'm not doing anything for her. That she made great demands on me, without standing by me in the least when I loved her so much, doesn't really entitle her to utterly exploit me now that that is long past and I have another person who stands by me. Maybe that sounds ungrateful now, but even when it was wonderful to adore Mutti, I was always aware that it was an illusion that cost me a lot of time, money, and headaches. . . .

Lilly has meanwhile finished the puzzle to our general satisfaction. She even found a city in Arabia, which I really marveled at. But if it was the very last word to be filled in then it wasn't all that hard anyway. It's getting to be bedtime; just a little more of Dostoyevsky's *Crime and Punishment* and then to sleep. . . . Tomorrow Lilly will start learning office skills at a commercial school. Recently we have often ridden out to the old canoe stomping ground to swim, but generally we enjoy ourselves the best at home. I also have a lot of retouching to do. Now and then a movie—that's all.

On the second day of each month Aimée and Jaguar celebrated the second of April, the day that Felice first crawled into bed with Lilly. On September 2, 1943, Jaguar and Aimée exchanged rings. Aimée's was a gold wedding ring with "F.S."

and the date "2.4.43" engraved on the inside. She gave Jaguar her silver ring with the green stone. Felice's hand was so small that she was only able to wear it on her right middle finger.

> My Most Beloved Girl!
>
> On our wedding day—a long and yet thrilling half-year—I wish you, and myself as well, the very best. Above all—a happy future! And along with that, a little money, a nice apartment, and nice friends. The latter we shall certainly never lack, and we'll have the apartment as well. But money? Well, we'll see! What can happen to us, right? With our love! And what more do we want!
>
> I love you without end and will never leave you.
>
> Your Aimée

At the end of September Felice had an appointment to meet Ernst Schwerin and Gerd Ehrlich at a café on Savignyplatz.

Gerd Ehrlich:

We had planned to meet the girl there at three-thirty, but we arrived somewhat early. Ernst sat down at a table and I, dressed in my uniform, went to the buffet to pick out a few pieces of pastry for us. There were several people in line in front of me, and directly before me stood a member of the secret service. I hadn't been standing there for five minutes, the secret service agent had just been served, when suddenly I felt a hand on my shoulder. Turning, I recognized a Jewish colleague from E & G, who had gone underground with her parents, but who had been picked up by the Gestapo a short time later. We knew that since her arrest this girl—her name was Stella Goldschlag, and her beautiful blond hair had earned her the nickname "the Jewish Lorelei"—had been working for the police as an informer. She had managed to turn over a number of Jews to the officials.

"Hello, Gerd, how are you?"

"I'm sorry, Fräulein, I don't know you. You must be confusing me with someone else!"

"But no, you're Gerd Ehrlich, don't you remember me, we worked together at Erich & Getz!"

"You're surely mistaken, that's not my name!"

At this moment the official in front of me picked up his order and turned around. He probably was working together with the informer; she would finger illegal Jews and he would then arrest them. If I were taken to a police station my lovely identification papers would do me little good at all; I couldn't let it come to that. I gave the girl, her hand still stretching out for me, a shove on the chest. Then I whistled to Ernst to alert him to the danger, and at this moment the secret service man reached out to grab me. Ernst, who saw that I was in danger, jumped him from the side and the tall guy fell across the buffet table. All of this happened within the space of a few seconds. Before anyone had the chance to recover from their surprise, we were on the street. We raced around the corner and up the streetcar platform, down the other side, and then jumped on a passing streetcar. When we reached the Bahnhof Zoo station two stops farther on and were sure we weren't being followed, we got off and took the streetcar one stop back to Savignyplatz. We had to get back to the café in time to warn Felice before she fell into the trap. We kept an eye on the café entrance from the corridor of a building across the street. Finally our friend arrived. We were able to get her attention before she went in, and took her to another restaurant, where we told her what had happened.

For the first time I had experienced something that made me truly nervous. Even more disquieting was the news we received from a comrade who worked for the Gestapo. Stella had given them my name and description, and now I was on a list of wanted persons, complete with picture. It was time for me to fold up my tent in Berlin.

Two weeks later everything had been prepared. The escape helper wanted a bicycle and a typewriter, perhaps some money, and these had to be found somewhere. Hedwig Meyer, who lived in a villa in Grunewald and dressed only in black after she lost two sons on the eastern front, took care of everything else. She sent an encoded telegram to farmers in Singen, Baden, who would take care of preparations for the refugees' escape into Switzerland and show them a safe border crossing. At ten on the evening of October 7, 1943, their friends gave Gerd, Ernst, and Ernst's fiancée, known only as "Chubby," a small farewell party in celebration of their "vacation." Earlier that evening Gerd had picked up Inge from Collignon's to take her to dinner with what remained of his food vouchers.

Once on the train the three travelers passed two ID checks by the Gestapo without incident. After spending the night in a Stuttgart hotel, they took a local train to Tutlingen, and after a brief stay there went on to Sigmaringen. After a stop midday the three then took the next local to Radolfszell on Lake Constance, and there changed to a train that took them to the border town of Singen, where they arrived as scheduled at 5 p.m. They had been warned to avoid the closely guarded express train that ran from Stuttgart to Singen in favor of the branch line. The "lady in black with bicycle" was waiting for them at the station, and they had been instructed to follow her as inconspicuously as possible. Their adventure ended in the Swiss village of Ramsen, after a night spent in woods where they almost took a wrong turn and headed back into what would have been sure death. A young Swiss border guard picked them up on a country lane and took them to his customs house. The Berliners couldn't understand the Swiss German of the Berne sergeant on duty.

"Parlez-vous français?"

Sergeant Fisch wanted to send them back to Germany posthaste.

"Do you have a gun?" Gerd asked.

"Yes."

"Can you shoot it?"

"Yes."

"Then shoot. That's the only way you'll get me to go back."

Gerd Ehrlich then asked to be permitted to call Washington.

FIVE

Lilly was granted a divorce at the regional court on Alexanderplatz on October 12, 1943. Sergeant Günther Wust, army post number 14 063 B, could not attend his own divorce proceedings, as he had been stationed in Hungary since August. Felice sat shivering on a bench outside the courtroom and used the time to write a poem:

REGIONAL COURT

I promised you, once and forever,
To stand beside you in your need.
And yet at this first difficult endeavor,
It is alone that you proceed.

Dearest! Hopefully they'll go easy
On you in their gloomy hall.
The dentist's chair can make me queasy,
But divorce must be worst of all.

You're still such a small one,
And your hair like copper wire glows.
Later I will not leave you alone
Has Fräulein Schulz perhaps a rose?

In hopefully not too long you'll be
Here again. Are courtrooms always so cold?
And from then on you'll belong only to me.
And later—you want the same I see,
Together we will both grow old!

"Am I really divorced?" Aimée stammered in a daze when Jaguar went to meet her after the hearing.

"You're completely under my control now," Felice beamed as she presented Lilly with a bouquet of red roses from Fräulein Schulz's at the Schmargendorf station on Heidelberger Platz. That evening they rearranged the apartment. The bed was moved from the balcony room to the study; the study's light gray tile stove wasn't working, so in winter the room was suitable only to sleep in.

Lilly's divorce decree, dated October 18, was issued "in the name of the German people." It stated that Lilly had filed for divorce and named Günther as the guilty party, on the grounds that he had broken their marriage vow. Günther, for his part, asserted that Lilly did not wish to have any more children and "for this reason had obstinately refused conjugal relations since December 1942." Günther Wust's counterclaim was recognized, with the court ruling that both parties were culpable, because "the reason given by her [Lilly], that they already have four children, is not justifiable."

At almost the same time in London, a wedding was being celebrated: On October 23, with a large number from the refugee scene in attendance, Irene Schragenheim married Fritz Cahn, from Berlin. The groom was soon to drop his embarrassing first name, thereafter to be known as "Derek." As coincidence would have it, his sister had gone to school with Käte Schragenheim, née Hammerschlag. Käte in turn, as Felice was to hear through Madame Kummer, had spent the last few years in Palestine, going through Irene's inheritance. "Our relationship has ceased to exist," Irene wrote at the beginning of October, and in the same letter responded to Felice's question of whether she had read Radclyffe Hall's *Well of Loneliness*, the classic of lesbian literature: No, she hadn't read the book, but had been trying to find a copy of it for years. "Personally, things of that nature are foreign to me," she pointedly added, "as I hope they are to my Putz as well."

"You will by now have received word of the court's decision. Your attorney has surely notified you," Lilly wrote to Günther Wust at the front on October 29:

Nothing out of the ordinary is going on here, except that I can no longer go to my English class. It was taking up too much of my time. If I didn't have children I could better devote myself to it. Now to the issue of the apartment. It was mentioned at the court session that you would keep it, but it was also stated that it would be very difficult for me to find another, and that you, of course, cannot simply put me and the children on the street.

Soon after this, Lilly was notified that she was to retain custody of all four children. But she remained willing to turn over the two oldest sons to Günther and his nineteen-year-old fiancée, Liesl Reichler, once they married. In October only the two youngest boys were in Berlin; under the threat of bombing attacks an increasing number of city schoolchildren were being removed to the country. Bernd was sent to Grünrode in East Prussia, not far from the Lithuanian border, and Eberhard provisionally went to stay with Liesl in Silesia.

Bernd Wust:

It was a simple country school: first grade—first row, second grade—second row, third and fourth grades—third row, and the fourth-graders sat in the back. In the room adjoining were the fifth- through eighth-graders. They spoke German with a very harsh East Prussian accent. The people I first stayed with were named Skat. In the beginning we were thrashed indiscriminately by teacher and fellow students alike. We had been in a big school in Berlin, and a weak student could always hide behind the rest of the class, but that didn't work in East Prussia. And in the country they had everything drilled into them by rote. That you could recite your multiplication tables in your sleep was the alpha and the omega of instruction, and we Berliners couldn't do that. Once we got boxed on the ears for this by the village schoolteacher, and our fellow students,

boys to the left, girls to the right, would set us up unmerci-
fully: "Teacher, didn't you want to run the Berliners through
their multiplication tables?" The boy I was with at the Skats',
Knut was his name, was a year older than I and a big bull of a
fellow, and he beat up the others for us. In time we all adjusted. We filched apples with the peasant boys, and we had to
help out at work. When it was time to harvest potatoes anyone
who could crawl on all fours went over to Farmer A's first, and
two days later to Farmer B's. When the women retired for
lunch we played in the barnyard, slinging mud at each other,
torturing the mutts, playing hide-and-seek. If one of the men
came home on leave and had the Iron Cross, first or second
class, then to us he was a big hero.

Those were exciting times. The Führer was going to
triumph, the teachers taught us that. Once a month we had
a class where some women would show up and tell us some
wonderful thing or other. I still remember how one of them
said, in a voice thick with emotion, "An assassination attempt
has been made on the Führer." And then there was the Battle
of Normandy, and the old men who were left in the town took
their guns left over from World War I out of the cabinet and
set out for the woods looking for some escaped prisoner of
war, or I don't know what—usually it was Russians. We were
discouraged from going too far into the woods by ourselves.
The forests that ran along the Lithuanian border began in our
area, in northeast Prussia, and went all the way to Leningrad,
you mustn't forget that.

Mutti visited twice during the year I was in East Prussia.
A visit entailed a great number of difficulties; there weren't

many trains. I can remember that people laughed when Mutti arrived wearing pants. They were women's pants, but the provincial women of East Prussia weren't used to that, their mouths dropped open! And later they said, well, all right, they might come in handy if you ever had to climb through the window of a train. I didn't feel at home at the Skats', I was still too much of a city boy. I must have come across as arrogant and unreliable, a fibber. I broke a window once and told them that a tramp had done it. Perhaps it was due to the way Mutti raised us; we were never really punished for anything. If Mutti lost her temper, whoever was standing close by got the brunt of it, and in most cases it was the wrong person. That was the way she was, and I took that behavior with me to East Prussia. But I always got caught when I fibbed, and was punished for it. Then I went to live with another family, the Rimkuses. They weren't farmers, but agronomists—to the Nazis this was a major distinction. They had two daughters, and I could play with the twelve-year-old. And the wife took a little better care of me. And then when Eberhard arrived my troubles were over. I turned into a real East Prussian yokel. The others always said, yeah, the one from Berlin can work his mouth, but real work is something else entirely. We Berliners weren't used to it. In the time it took for one of the village boys to harvest a whole row of potatoes, we could only gather about ten percent of what he did, either because we were being too careful or because we got clods of dirt confused with potatoes. Or if we were bringing the cows in from the meadow and one of them put its head down and came at me, I would let go and she would run off into the clover field . . .

The children were removed from Berlin just in time; the "Battle of Berlin" commenced during the third week of November.

Sirens began to wail at 7:30 p.m. on November 22, and around 9:00 the "carpet bombing" began. Reinhard was sick and therefore not allowed to go to the children's bunker. A deadly silence fell once the lights went out in the cellar on Friedrichshaller Strasse, the only sound was that of mortar trickling down from the walls. In the darkness Lilly held on to Felice's arm with both hands. She was always afraid they were going to be separated from one another.

"Our building's made of iron, isn't that true, Mutti?" Reinhard's thin voice broke through the all-pervasive fear. One woman gave a shaky laugh, and people came out of their dazed state. "That must have been a bull's-eye," someone joked. In the shelter everyone sat shoulder to shoulder and had to deal close-up with the other residents. Frau Kluge, wife of the building custodian, who lived in the basement apartment with their ten-year-old daughter, was a good person. Lilly and Felice would go to her place to listen to Radio London, the radio wrapped in blankets to muffle the sound. "Aunt" Grasenick from the fourth floor was also nice. Lilly always gave her the key to the apartment when she had to leave the children at home alone. "We know you're listening to enemy broadcasts," the Eichmanns on the top floor had said threateningly more than once. Lilly and Felice had to be careful as well in front of their neighbor Frau Schmidt, whose enthusiasm for the Führer knew no bounds. "It's not over yet," she intoned in the din of the bombing. But whenever the political mood in Berlin changed, her party badge disappeared as if by magic.

After things had calmed down and Lilly and Felice had long since gone to bed, the doorbell rang. Father Selbach arrived in the company of a young woman with Marlene Dietrich cheeks, carrying a large suitcase. Their faces were covered in soot and both were totally disheveled.

"All hell has broken loose out there. Half of Steglitz is on fire and we got caught in it. I'm leaving for the 'Forst' tomorrow. Can Lola stay here with you?"

Lola could. Lola Sturm was no stranger to Lilly and Felice. For some time now she had been living in the small room at the Selbachs', which earlier had served as Felice's hiding place. And Mutti's daughter Renate had brought her along for a visit in the past.

"Jessissmaria!" was the only thing she could manage to say.

Lola worked as a secretary at the Berlin subsidiary of the Böhler Works of the "Ostmark," as Austria was referred to after the Anschluss (Annexation). Böhler Berlin served as intermediary between the OKH, or Army High Command, the OKW (Wehrmacht High Command), and the Ministry of Aviation. Every day the piece numbers of items manufactured south of Vienna in Enzesfeld were sent by teletype to Berlin, which passed them on to the OKH and Ministry of Aviation. The firm had its own plane that flew between Enzesfeld and Berlin. Lola enjoyed a position of trust at the company. The Selbachs had first become acquainted with the twenty-one-year-old Sudeten as she was traveling by train from her native village of Freiwaldau in the Altvater Mountains to Berlin, her important work contract in her pocket. Luise Selbach offered her the empty room, and Lola Sturm appreciated the connection to "Mutti" Selbach and her three daughters, for Berliners did not exactly make it easy for the newcomer. In the streetcar, people made fun of her as soon as she opened her mouth.

But she liked it better at Aimée and Jaguar's.

Lola Sturmova:

I felt at home there, which was not the case at the Selbachs'. They were strange somehow. I don't know, it was as if the Selbachs trimmed their sails to the wind, the daughters too. After all, with officers they . . .

They tested me, Lilly and Felice, on my political views. Yes, and discovered that we had always helped people when we could, even here in Jesenik, which used to be called Freiwaldau. And here, too, I had—there was a girl at the high school with me, Marianne Stuckart, she was Jewish, and then there was the Gessler firm, they had the quarry works here, and the Schwalmburgs, who owned the sanatorium in Zuckmantl. People didn't hate them, it was nothing out of the ordinary, but then in '38 . . . I knew Felice was Jewish, and Lilly and Felice told me anyway. So I said to myself, we'll have to help them. People knew about it, but they didn't say anything. We were always afraid there was a bug hidden somewhere.

Felice was very cooperative, a nice soul, intelligent above all, yes, and the fact that she and Lilly had a lesbian love, so to speak—they were all afraid that they'd get sick somehow, catch something if they went with soldiers. And there were a lot of half-Jewish women who met at Lilly's, and the couples got together there. Felice always dressed as a man, always, in pants, blouse, tie, and Lilly dressed normal, as a woman. She was in such good shape, despite the four children. But I noticed it. One time I was in the bathroom and was getting ready to take a bath, and Felice wanted to come in. She started grabbing at me, and I said, "Are you crazy!" Yes, and then I knew what was what. But Lilly needed love, and what she probably didn't get from her husband she just turned around. She was happy with Felice, believe me when I say that. I saw nothing wrong with it.

Two days after Lola moved in Lilly celebrated her thirtieth birthday. Though she felt that she had reached an advanced age, her circle of friends could only carry on about how she had blossomed during the last six months. Felice gave Lilly a Turkish espresso machine made of Jena glass. Only with effort could Lilly hide her disappointment. Günther, too, was always dragging home some appliance or other, absolutely convinced that his wife had only one thing on her mind day and night. And then something as superfluous as an espresso machine! Felice, on the other hand, was delighted by her unique choice. Real coffee could be had only on the black market, and not inexpensively—if that wasn't a luxury, then nothing was!

As Bernd was in East Prussia, Eberhard in Silesia, and Albrecht and Reinhard were spending nights in the children's bunker, a cot was set up for Lola in the children's room, and she easily adjusted to the intricate comings and goings of the Wust household. Her lack of any sense of financial responsibility to

Lilly left something to be desired. But her mischievous smile and slanting gray-blue eyes, her delightful Bohemian-Austrian accent and the way she cried *"Uj jegerl"* and clamped her hand over her mouth when caught unawares by something, made it hard for Lilly to summon up the severity to remind Lola that her rent was overdue. Instead, Lola bought a set of light-colored beechwood chairs and an end table as a Christmas gift for the balcony room.

With Lola's presence more men began to appear at the house again. One evening she brought home a student from Munich who was looking for a place to live, and Elenai, sensing a willing victim, played the wild woman to the shrieks of the others present.

"What's going on with all of you?" the young man asked, obviously distressed.

"Nothing at all, my dear young man," Elenai cooed, and Lola realized that this was one conquest that was lost.

Another time Lola was so late in returning home that Lilly and Felice gave up on her for the night. Erika Jung, Felice's hairdresser, and her friend Maria Kaufmann were guests for the evening. Inge had also frequented the chic salon on Friedenauer Strasse for a while, until things got a bit too colorful for her. Customers sat in small compartments divided by screens, and as they got their hair cut they would relate to each other the most intimate details of their love life. Anyone who was less than eager to join in promptly was pressured to do so. So Erika Jung was a guest for the evening with Maria, her blond girlfriend. Erika, her masculine haircut held in place with brilliantine, and Maria, an elegant and commanding presence, were dressed in men's trousers. Both women were in their mid-twenties. Maria lived alone in a huge apartment with carpets as high as grass; one's feet sank into them. Jaguar had taken Aimée there once, showing her off as if she were a trophy.

"If you go there with me now, you'll belong forever," she had said, preparing Aimée for the event.

Duly intimidated, Lilly arrived with Felice at the fifth-floor apartment in the imposing industrial-era building. And sure enough, the two women did their best to induct the novice into the joys of lesbian love. With one of their hostesses sitting on the other's lap, the air hummed with *"Küsschen,"* and *"Schätzchen"* and "Darling." When Erika began to fondle Maria's breasts, Aimée was so embarrassed she didn't know where to look.

On the evening of their visit to Lilly and Felice, it had gotten too late for Erika and Maria to go home. Lilly gave them one side of the marriage bed, but for a reason she later could not recall she didn't join Felice on the couch. As the other two soon pulled the covers off her, Lilly went into the children's room for Lola's eiderdown comforter. Lola showed up shortly thereafter. Tipsy and crashing around, she discovered the cover was missing from her cot and lay down in Albrecht's empty little bed.

Lola Sturmova:

> One fine day my boss, an Austrian from Enzesfeld, said: Let's go to the Chinese restaurant for lunch. And suddenly I looked up and thought, *My God, that man in uniform over there looks*

familiar. Didn't we go to school together? And then he handed
the headwaiter a note on which he had written: "Is that really
you or isn't it? Tom Lorek." Well, to make a long story short,
we met up and he said to me, I live not far from here and I've
got some good stuff over at my place. Send your boss packing
and we'll go over and fill each other in on what we've been
doing since we last saw each other. So I went, and I got a
little tipsy, my goodness, and to this day I have no idea how I
made it back to Lilly's! Every once in a while I would sit down
on the stairs and sing, until I finally reached the apartment.
When they heard someone fumbling around at the door they
came out, but by that time I was in bed. And they came into
the room—I didn't have a pillow, nothing, not a thing, only
Albrecht's little bed with its thin cover, where I lay down. I'd
get cold first here, then there, and I tossed and turned so much
that the whole bed collapsed. And Lilly and the other girls
came in and saw me lying on the floor, muttering, "Where's
my covers? I'm cold!"

In the bombing attacks that took place between the twenty-
second and the twenty-sixth of November, 3,758 people were
killed and almost a half million were left homeless. To keep up
the city's spirits Berliners were given special rations at the end
of November—a tin of fish, a can of condensed milk, a half-
kilo of fresh vegetables and fifty grams of coffee and tobacco.
On November 27 Goebbels visited the areas that had been
hardest hit, as well as several ration distribution centers. "One
gets the impression that the moral spirit of the Berlin popula-

tion borders on the religious," he wrote in his diary. "Women come up and make the sign of the cross over me and ask God to protect me. . . . The rations are extolled as excellent everywhere. . . . One can wrap these people around one's finger with the slightest display of kindness."

In mid-December Lilly urged Günther to pay her the money he had promised for herself and the children. The letters exchanged between Berlin and the front became increasingly angrier.

Christmas was celebrated with Lilly's parents under their large, decorated fir tree. And at the Böhler Works, Lola was given the responsibility of distributing presents to everyone, something that worked to the advantage of the Wust household. Aimée's gift to Jaguar was a white turtleneck sweater she had knitted for her. Jaguar wrote Aimée a poem:

That there was a time before you—I can't believe!
To me, we've forever been this way,
Together, side by side in life and in dreams,
Surrounded both by darkness and the light of day.

You belong to me! Since you arrived,
And slowly at first, then full of trust,
Placed your heart in my hands, I have strived
For the strength to build a life for us.

So I have hope for days yet to come,
As this year nods and slips into air,

Because before me, like some emblem,
I carry the copper gleam of your hair.

"I have such hopes for the coming year, above all, finally to have a quiet life," Aimée wrote to Jaguar on December 27:

A life lived for you, and, note this well, you have it in writing: a happy life with you only! Are you satisfied now? Jealous girl that you are, you think I'm writing to "my Hansel"! Silly, silly girl! You don't know how much I love you. Which is a good thing, actually, for if you knew how much, you would have me too securely in your claws, you old jaguar, you!

Only one thing matters! And that is that soon, very soon now, I will be lying in your arms, in your paws, that is. And then I will be the happiest person on God's green earth. Then all my worries and cares will be over and I will be safe from all the world's sorrows. My dearest one, in your white pullover, what do we care for others? We are enough to each other, we need no one but ourselves, but each other we need completely.

The year 1943 ended with a major bombing attack on the night of December 29, and 1944 began with major bombings on the nights of January 1 and 2. Everyone was kept busy sweeping debris, nailing cardboard over windows, searching for friends who had been bombed out and getting settled into basements. Everyone suffered from a permanent lack of sleep and irritability. At night an empty silence reigned in the dark streets, the wind whistling through bombed-out house fronts. Public transportation was infrequently in service. Radio London was amazed at the tenacity with which the German people set about rebuilding what had been destroyed.

As many women as possible were to be mobilized. Goebbels, as of July special commissioner in charge of total war mobilization, raised the age until which women were obligated to work from forty-five to fifty. Government agencies and administration offices were forced to devote thirty percent of their work force to the war effort. Theaters and restaurants closed. Women were accepted into the army.

Each month another transport left for Auschwitz, rarely with more than thirty people, most of them "illegals."

For Aimée and Jaguar, this was the quietest period of their life together. Their friends, many of whom had been bombed out, were busy with their own lives. Lola had fallen in love and was seldom to be seen. Aimée, who had always been devoted to crossword puzzles, created them for Jaguar. The answer to one puzzle, in which syllables were combined to form words, produced one of Lilly's favorite sayings: "You don't love me, I always knew it," to which was added the challenge, "Puzzle solvers and readers so inclined are invited to vindicate themselves."

Only once did they have a fight.

"What are you reading?" Jaguar asked. "Let me see," and took the thin volume out of Aimée's hands. "Honey!" Jaguar's indulgent tone held an element of contempt. "Waggerl!" She marched around the room as she read aloud: *The girl left the house, the thatch-roofed house on the pond. The house is old and gloomy, nothing more than a hut, but the fisherman's daughter is young and proud, a princess, as anyone in the village knew who had set eyes on her . . .*

"Can't you find anything better to read?"

"I like it, give it here!" Aimée flushed from her throat to her face, and she tried to grab the book away from Felice. Jaguar jumped out of her path and took refuge behind Günther's favorite armchair: *The girl's name is Veronica, a pretty name! The fisherman's daughter could easily have been somewhat less beautiful, it would scarcely have mattered. She is almost too pretty as it is, her forehead covered with lovely dark curls, her heavenly blue eyes . . .*

"Say, where did this yokel get to know Elenai?"

"You can spare me your disdain!" Aimée hissed. "I will not have you speak to me like this. You think you're the only ones who have accomplished anything in literature! That isn't so. We have good writers too!"

"All right, fine," Jaguar murmured, stunned.

Lilly had to put her acting talent to good use in overcoming unanticipated problems. When Felice infected Lilly with a boil it was no problem to get the medication they both needed. But when Jaguar came down with conjunctivitis, Lilly had to rub her eyes until they were bloodshot to simulate the condition believably. And with a toothache it was even more difficult. Inge finally located a dentist in Steglitz, whose name, incredibly enough, was Dr. Zahn ["Dr. Tooth"]. He agreed to see Felice without a health insurance certificate, and, more important, to treat her without registering her as a patient.

And there was a pharmacist on Bülowstrasse named Hagemann who filled Felice's prescriptions free of charge, and was
constantly supplying her with Dextropur for her baking needs.

Elenai Pollak:

I arranged a meeting one day with Herr Hagemann, through
my father, who needed certain medications. Hagemann was a
bachelor, and at thirty-five seemed an old man to me. But he was
interested in me and invited me to his place one day. It was then I
figured out that he only had one thing in mind, and I was put in
an awkward situation. I got the feeling he wasn't a Nazi, and so I
tried to establish a conversational relationship with him, in order to
avoid the obvious. But that didn't work, and I found myself in his
bed. I talked to Felice about it, and she immediately said, I want
to get to know him. What kind of person is he, perhaps he knows
something? That was always the important thing. And so all of a
sudden he has two Jewish girls standing in front of him. He was
highly flattered and right away started coming on to Felice. Both
of us smoked a lot—out of sheer nervousness about our perpetually
tense situation—and he had an infinite number of cigarettes. After
we all had drunk coffee together he left the room at some point
and Felice stuck his entire supply of cigarettes in her pocket.

"That'll keep us in smokes for the next few days," she said.

I was shocked. "We can't steal from this man, he's being
very nice to us." So when Hagemann returned I said to him,
"By the way, we just lifted all of your cigarettes." To which he
answered, "Yes, that's why I put them there."

Felice had an unbelievable gift for "organizing" things.
Whenever there was something to be gotten, she went for it.

By the end of January the quiet period was over. First, Jaguar presented a thousand Reichsmarks to a shocked Aimée: "In case anything happens to me." Then Inge's family was bombed out and moved to Lübben, her father's native village. After combing for jobs in the cultural sphere, Inge was forced to accept a position in a factory near Lübben that manufactured copper coil cable for submarines. Much to Aimée's displeasure, Jaguar often took off on the weekends to visit her. Then Lola called in tears from somewhere or other to reveal that she was pregnant. The father, Hans-Heinz Holste, known and detested by the Wust-Schragenheim household, was a revolting young man with thick, pouting lips.

"Ha, ha, ha," was Felice's wry comment [the German pronunciation of the man's initials, H.H.H.].

"Lola, calm down, we'll be there right away," Lilly said comfortingly, and the two of them set off for Zehlendorf to collect their unhappy friend. But Lola's tears merely occasioned sarcasm in their circle of women friends.

"This has to happen to you, of all people!"

"Be happy you're rid of the idiot! You can't really want someone from the Nordic race!"

Felice was the only one to take pity on her. "Lilly will take care of your baby, don't worry," she promised, giving Lola a tender hug.

Last of all, the doorbell rang one morning at 3 a.m. Felice sat up in bed with a start, her body tensed like an animal about to spring.

"For God's sake, what should I do?" It was the first time that Jaguar had shown fear.

Dressed in her silk pajamas, Felice rushed out to the balcony and crouched in a corner. Outside the door, a confused stranger was asking for someone who didn't even live in the building.

"Are you crazy, it's the middle of the night!" Lilly barked at him, and listened until his footsteps grew faint.

"It's nothing, dearest, come back to bed."

It was a long time before Felice fell asleep that night.

"It could have been them," she managed to say as she clung to Lilly, who tried in vain to warm a shivering Felice with her body.

"You are not to be afraid, I will never allow them to do anything to you. Never! They'll have to shoot me first!"

The next day Felice came down with a cold.

On March 1 the Pathology Building and gatehouse of the Jewish Hospital at Schulstrasse 78 in the Wedding district of Berlin were appropriated and put under the direction of Criminal Investigation Secretary Walter Dobberke as a "collection point for Jews."

Felice, who saw how hard Lilly was struggling to survive, fell into a depression now and then when she considered the future.

PESSIMISM

I know I cannot hold you,
If someone comes your way.
Quietly we will say adieu,
as when we first met, that April day.

Today it is enough to know
I love you, but that won't go far!
One day it will be essential, even so,
For you to have a maid and car.

I want to see you having fun,
You're not the most frugal woman around!
Even if my self-confidence abounds,
Even if I build castles on the moon's round
Surface, on earth I may not be the one.

The escalating war and increasingly bitter struggle for survival by illegal Jews put an end to group enterprises on Friedrichshaller Strasse. But Felice and Elenai maintained their friendship. They constantly rotated their meeting place, but often it was the small café on Winterfeldplatz where they first had met. When Lilly wasn't at home Felice would call Elenai. "You can come," she would say. The two women had agreed that what they had to say to each other could not be discussed in front of Lilly. They analyzed the military situation, reported to each other on which of their friends had been deported, and talked about their fear of being denounced. Was it wise to stay at one address for so long, or was there somewhere else Felice would be safer? But Felice dreaded making decisions, any kind of change frightened her. Elenai was never to know how emotionally entangled Felice was with Lilly.

At the same time, Elenai and Gregor tried to impress upon Lilly what a concentration camp was, and that Felice's life was in constant danger. A denunciation could destroy their idyllic life at any moment. Lilly often gave Elenai and Gregor the impression that she didn't really comprehend that Felice's situation fundamentally differed from hers, that for Felice there was no such thing as everyday life anymore.

"Shut up! I can't bear to hear any more of this!" Elenai would shout, when Lilly would go off on one of her raptures, stretching Elenai's nerves to the breaking point.

When Liesl Reichler capitulated to the difficulties she faced with her impending marriage to Günther Wust, father of four, and renounced the engagement, Lilly's mother had to travel to Silesia to bring Eberhard home. Several days later Lilly traveled with him to East Prussia, where the Rimkus family who had taken in Bernd would also now take in Eberhard. The trip lasted twenty hours. Inundated with the scent of lily of the valley, which covered the forest floor like hailstones after a storm, Lilly passed the night on a straw mattress.

And now it was Felice who expressed her desire through letters:

March 30, 1944

My Beloved,

What am I to do if you are sitting up all night in some horrible train and I cannot talk with you, cannot kiss you, write to you?

Exactly one year ago today I also was alone in your apartment. Surely we telephoned that evening, and surely

I was in your thoughts as much then as I am now. During this entire year I was, I think, alone just once with only the ticking of the clock, and that was on the evening you went to the theater with Gerd and the others. I spent that evening looking at all the little things that you hold in your hands every day, or even just look at.

A long time has passed since that evening, and you were always here. It is no wonder that, despite all the evenings I have spent alone in my furnished past, I find no peace on this evening, that I—just imagine, it's almost midnight!—cannot sleep. Perhaps because you are not asleep either? But you are so often awake long after I have fallen fast asleep. Which reminds me of something I've always wanted to ask: What do you think about on those long evenings? Sometimes I find it terrible that one person can love another so much, and share everything with that person, yet have that person's thinking remain so strange, and know it will always remain so. I'm just jealous.

April 1, 1944

It's time for you to return. I love you so much, and I'm so afraid that you've taken the wrong train, to arrive somewhere weeping. I'll never let you go off alone again!

During this period Lola took Reinhard to her mother's in Freiwaldau, and then went on to Enzesfeld, not far from Vienna. At her return, her mother opened the door and slapped her.

"You should be ashamed! Living with such perverse people!"

In his innocence Reinhard had revealed that his mother and Felice kissed each other and wrote letters to one another.

Early in 1944 Felice found a position as a stenotypist on Kochstrasse, in the newspaper district. She worked in the Berlin editorial office of the Essen *National-Zeitung*, "organ of the National Socialist Workers' Party."

Lilly:

Elenai had worked there first, and help was short. Felice had to be smuggled through about ninety-nine channels, but the worst was that she was hired as Frau Wust, mother of two. And I was demoted to the role of sister-in-law. But I had to be careful; once when I called I almost gave myself away. She never revealed to me what she did there; I know only that she typed lead articles for a man named Berns. There was some trouble at the paper once. Felice probably had something printed that was not what the boss wanted, but she was never discovered. She was terribly pleased about it at the time. I knew that she worked for the underground, but didn't know the what or how of it. I still have Felice's notebooks, in which she recorded her appointments, but what it all means is a mystery to me. I never found out. She often came home quite late at night; she would call from the Schmargendorf station, and I would get up and go to meet her. She always said, I'll tell you nothing, not the least little thing, it's too dangerous. She always said, If you're standing next to me and they grab me, then I want you to keep walking. Which I never would have done, never in my life! I would have found out thousands of things had we remained together longer. We just had too little time. We lived very intensely, but you must remember, there was a war on.

Lola Sturmova:

She worked, I think, at the *Völkischer Beobachter*, under the name of Schrader. Apparently she worked under my name as well, as a journalist, I believe. Whenever there was anything going on she would always bring home news of it—it was the *Völkischer Beobachter*, sorry, but I can't help it. She held jobs at several different places so that she could have access to the news. And she often came home with something. We kept up with the progress being made at the front, and there was the matter of the assassination [attempt on Hitler], she got the news of that from there too. I never asked her for details, because I thought what she told me was enough. I could figure out the rest.

She also brought home quite a few articles she had written under an abbreviated name, initials really. She had the articles smuggled to England through an officer I knew. He was "differently" inclined, was "Kaleu"—Captain Lieutenant— Henschel, that was his name. He said, Don't ask, I'll take care of it. Felice gave me a number of articles from the newspaper to give to him—she herself never met him. But she knew he would take care of it. He had a Saxon accent, and whenever I heard him talk I saw red, but he was a nice fellow. I tested him to be sure we were of the same mind despite the fact that he

was in the military. I got to know him at the OKH. And there
was this lieutenant colonel, a strange bird. I had just started
working at Böhler and he called there, and I kept lowering
his rank, addressing him as *Oberleutnant* [first lieutenant]
instead of *Oberstleutnant* [lieutenant colonel]. And one fine
day he arrived with a little book that listed the orders of rank.
Whenever I went over to the OKH or the Ministry of Aviation I always checked the little book first, so that I wouldn't
say something stupid. Well, so Kaleu Henschel got a big laugh
when I told him I had demoted the lieutenant colonel.

"So many people are being killed because of a schizo-
phrenic, a paralytic," he said.

Felice's employment at the *National-Zeitung* is described
by Georg Zivier in his book *Deutschland und seine Juden* (Germany and Its Jews), in the following words:

This pretty girl, who was a great help to the household
and particularly beloved in the air raid shelter, had lost
all sense of danger, and in her audacity even accepted
a position, under a false name, at the editorial offices
of a newspaper affiliated with the Nazi Party. If they
had found her out her landlady and all of her friends
and acquaintances from her building would have been
suspected of espionage and would have faced harsh
measures by the Gestapo.

In fact, the true situation was that Elenai had an aunt in
Buenos Aires who, as a member of the Association of Germans

Abroad (VDA), wished to emigrate to Germany. She found a position as executive secretary at the *National-Zeitung,* but then married an Austrian who wanted to return to his native city of Vienna. Before the couple departed, Elenai's aunt asked her if she wouldn't like to work for the newspaper. It was Elenai's job to take down in shorthand the verbal reports coming in over the phone, and to pass these on to the central editorial office in Essen, an activity she performed to the full satisfaction of her colleagues. Felice soon expressed her interest in working in the editorial office, and Elenai passed on the request to her boss.

"If she's as good as you, we'll accept her," he said.

"She's even better," Elenai responded, and Felice was hired. The only question remaining was which name she would work under, and it seemed just the thing to call herself Frau Wust, mother of two small children.

Then one day Felice had an idea.

"The foreign agencies transmit their reports each morning. I'm sure that we're not getting to see them all. If we show up at 8:30 they'll already have sorted through them and we'll miss the most crucial information. Let's arrive at 5:00 and take a look at what comes in in the mornings, before the assholes get there."

Elenai Pollak:
> So I had to go to the office with her at five in the morning—we had a key. And we looked through all the reports from the foreign agencies: Reuters and so forth. We made a

note of what was most important. I later became rather adept at memorizing things. It wasn't difficult for either of us to pass on entire lists of information. What we were doing wasn't conspiratorial, we didn't make use of the information in a political sense, passing it on to the underground, but only as it concerned our own illegal existence. The foreign press precisely registered what the Germans were doing, or were planning to do. It was so weird that they knew everything and yet never took any action. Information on the military situation was most important to us, for the closer the front moved, the closer came the day of liberation. We calculated it would come at the end of 1944. We had our maps, just like the general staff, and analyzed the situation each time another city was taken. We soon figured out the Russians' military strategy, it was relatively simple. We considered whether the time had come to leave Berlin and go to meet the Russians, in order possibly to escape having to endure the final catastrophes. But then we didn't dare, because the first reports started coming in on the rapes—which we didn't believe at first, of course. We were distressed by the fact that the Americans and the British obviously had a very cautious military strategy, and preferred to let the Russians do the fighting. Yet it was clear to us that it wouldn't last much longer.

Felice came up with another idea. "The *National-Zeitung* isn't a true party newspaper. Let's go over to the *Hakenkreuzbanner*, we'll find out more there."

"Felice, are you out of your mind?" Elenai said. "The

National-Zeitung is truly sufficient, please, not the *Haken-kreuzbanner* too! You just can't get enough!"

"Yes, but they run more articles on internal party affairs and I'd like to find out about that," Felice insisted.

This time Elenai won out, but Felice wouldn't let go of the idea. She would occasionally answer the phone with "Heil Hitler, *Hakenkreuzbanner*" when Inge called her from Lübben.

One day one of the editors gave Elenai a true shock. He made his hobby the study of races, and he had his eye on the exotic Elenai.

"I've been trying for some time now to figure out which race you belong to."

"Oh, why is that?" Elenai asked, her heart beginning to pound.

"You're a very distinctive type. You're tall and small-boned. You have a narrow face and a prominent nose. I've thought about it for a long time, and I've finally worked it out—you're the Indo-Germanic prototype."

In April 1944 Günther Wust had leave from the front. He stayed with Lilly and Felice during the day, and slept at his parents' at night. Lilly did everything to make his stay pleasant. Because Günther—having recovered from the shock of his divorce, and not under pressure to marry Liesl—met his financial obligations concerning the family from then on, Lilly saw no reason to resent him further. Their parents found all of this highly strange.

That same April, Greek and Hungarian Jews were deported to Auschwitz in the hundreds of thousands. Of four hundred thousand Hungarian Jews, two hundred and fifty thousand were gassed within eight weeks.

Günther, rested and feeling friendly toward Lilly and Felice, returned from his six-week leave to an idyllic village in Romania, where he found plenty of time to write letters. He described his new post in a letter dated May 12:

> My present position is the equivalent of chief clerk. My working quarters are in a separate office—not least because the captain, following several unpleasant incidents involving others, has placed great trust in me and discusses things with me he doesn't want the others to hear. . . . In addition to my office work I have roughly fifty men I am responsible for, and must see to it that orders are carried out punctually, such as arranging for cars, messengers, etc., and also that the men have proper quarters, that they keep their quarters in order, that accommodations are available for those passing through. Gradually now I am also holding roll call. I've scheduled an arms inspection for tomorrow, and now and then I call the whole group together and make announcements and so forth. So I'm slowly adapting to the responsibilities of staff sergeant—and in doing so have become more self-confident before a crowd.

This doesn't mean that I have to relinquish my calm, rather quiet manner. To the contrary, I get along quite well, am certainly not unpopular and am earning respect. And in the process, of course, I am becoming more ambitious. I'm just waiting for them to make me sergeant. Yesterday I ran across an order that indicated I would have to wait another year. . . . You will note from all of this that I am feeling quite content, not to mention healthy in body and spirit. My daily routine is nicely regulated: I rise at 6 a.m. and have until 7 to dress and eat breakfast. Then I work until noon and there follows a one-hour break, sometimes a bit longer. I always see to it that I lie down for an hour. Work stops between 7 and 8 p.m., followed by a horseback ride or a walk through the village until it gets dark. The rest of the evening is spent writing or reading or in pleasant conversation with one or another of my comrades, sharing red wine and cigarettes. Wine gradually has become a standard thing in the evening. I drink approximately a liter a day. I usually don't go to bed until 11. Seven hours sleep at night and one during the day—I feel alert and refreshed. I no longer get those attacks of fatigue I used to have.

Günther wrote his next letter on the twenty-first, and in it he made Lilly a surprising offer:

Listen, Lilly! In the course of my letter-writing, interrupted by an hour and a half of conversation with my office comrades, I have also finished off my wine and schnapps. This puts me in a lively mood, but not so much that I would go overboard. But now comes something you perhaps have expected, after receiving my recent letters. In consideration of the fact that, during my time as a soldier and even before, in the sphere of National Socialism and my work at the bank, I have succeeded in carrying through my ideas calmly and with a strong will, I now propose that we revive our marriage. We no longer possess the passion or the rebelliousness against our parents that brought us together in 1934, of course. Only a common awareness of our shared responsibilities toward the children could bring us back together again. I was thinking along these same lines when I made this offer last year around the second or third of May, with the condition that you observe my wishes in everything. You rejected that offer, saying I was merely speaking out of egotism. Nevertheless, I must now reiterate that condition. If your pride won't allow it, then it will be our sons who will suffer. One thing I learned on leave was that neither of us can do without any one of our children. So to avoid this we must live together. But I must reserve the right to fashion our life together according to the ancient Greek saying: Eis koiranos estō! ("Let there be one master only!").

In order not to upset Günther further during this difficult period, Lilly and Felice did not have the heart to reject his proposal outright, and continued to include him in the large and small issues of everyday life in Berlin. They told him, for example, that Bernd and Eberhard had been transferred from

East Prussia to Meuselwitz in Thuringia due to the advance of Soviet troops, that Lola was pregnant and that *Ha-Ha-Ha* had left her, and that Mother Sturm was unwilling to take her in.

Lola tried to free herself of her heavy burden up until the very last minute, which can be gathered from a letter that Felice wrote to her, perhaps in Freiwaldau, on June 16:

> Dear Lola,
>
> A quick note during my lunch break, so that I can give it to a colleague who will take it with him to Berlin, so that you will receive it that much sooner. We're wildly busy, as you can imagine under the circumstances. I never get home before midnight. Now to the issue at hand: I gave it my best effort, but nothing can be procured that quickly, as my pharmacist is away on a trip. I'm terribly sorry that I cannot give you more positive news at an important time like this. Nor do I wish to build up false hope, but didn't your doctor once give you a prescription for Argomensin? Do you still have any of it? It's the best thing, and that's probably all I could get anyway. But you have to do it soon, before your condition worsens, for then only a doctor can help, and that will cost money. We hope to see you healthy here again soon.
>
> Warm wishes from us both,
> Your Felice

At the beginning of June the Luftwaffe began for the first time to train women for antiaircraft service. "Women's Hands on the Searchlights," was the headline the *National-Zeitung* ran on June 18. It was Felice, perhaps, who typed the article, amused by the contortions the writer was forced to make in order to explain this sudden new role granted to German wives and mothers. The article stressed that women were not to be placed at antiaircraft guns or machine guns, as was the case in the United States, England and the Soviet Union, but rather would operate only measuring instruments, searchlights and electrical equipment. "For the German woman should never be militarized . . . that would be incompatible with her dignity and the position she holds in the national community." Any engagement in the armed forces was to be held to a minimum, "for under no circumstances should women become masculinized."

During this period Lilly increased the pressure on Felice to demand that Mutti finally return Felice's belongings.

Elenai Pollak:

> Felice told me that Lilly wanted to get her hands on her
> things. Felice found it was carrying things much too far that
> she constantly had to be in contact with Mutti because of this.
> She didn't feel it was the most important thing going on at
> the moment. And she was annoyed by Lilly's insistence that
> she absolutely had to have those things. Felice finally gave in
> because she didn't feel she was in any position to refuse Lilly.
> Her situation was too precarious for that. I'm sure that she
> was always reassuring Lilly that it would all work out at some
> point. She put off the problem, in her typical fashion. It's also

possible that Felice had not simply stored her things at Frau Selbach's, but that in her generosity she had said to her, just take what you want.

On June 8 Luise Selbach wrote Felice a letter in German script on a tiny sheet of paper, which today is barely legible in several places:

Dear Felice,

I am notifying you today that on Saturday the eighth, your grandmother's dress and jacket ensemble, as well as your summer dresses . . . will be sent to you there. You will receive a call about them. L. can arrange with the man a time for you to pick them up. Now about the fur coat: I assume you want to sell it. The story with Fräulein P., we talked about it before, is somewhat different now that she, as you yourself reported, has a good position, and so everything has been taken care of. She still has her parents, after all, and you are alone. Do you still want to carry out the original plan, is that still necessary? Whatever the outcome, it's not my affair in the end. But it is hard for me to imagine that you want to go away, that you can't even find it in your heart to come to us. Or does Frau W. love you so much that she intends to leave her four children for you? I can't imagine that. I can imagine, however, that you need money, that I can understand. So sell the fur to me—I assume that your dear grandmother would find it appropriate. So I'm asking that you name

a price, something along the lines of: You certify to me
that for a certain price . . . it can't be a fantastic price, of
course, but I could see something between eight and nine
thousand marks. Then, I hope, the thing would proceed
in such a way that both parties would be satisfied. I want
the coat and would never accept it from you as a gift. . . .
So, my girl, that's the way we'll do it tomorrow. You can
pick up the money here. Should you need an initial payment soon, let me know. I cannot imagine that you will
refuse me in this. If so, I wouldn't know what to think,
would no longer be able to believe anything you said. It
would be a great disappointment to me. Otherwise, you
must have more news to relate than I. Perhaps you soon
will be looking for a new apartment, it could be very nice
here. And then, of course, you would need furniture. And
in that case, too, a move here . . . with the "bomb ID" I
have, it would go well, I think. Don't forget the rugs. So
for today, my girl, I hope and believe that . . .

Greetings as well to Frau W.,

from Your Mother

Lilly had Felice respond to Günther's marriage proposal to
her. Jaguar accepted the role assigned to her by Lilly, that of
protectress of a delicate creature, though she—robbed of everything, even her own identity—certainly could have used
a caring mother herself. Although more than eight years
younger than Aimée, Felice's experience made her considerably older. "I am two thousand years older than you," she
would say.

Felice's letter to Günther has not survived, but Günther's response has:

June 20, 1944

Dear Felice!

. . . I know, too, that over the long run Lilly has accepted my authority, that she not only has bowed to it but in most arguments conceded that I was in the right. Perhaps it is an unfortunate characteristic of mine, perhaps I seem arrogant in this respect, but I cannot simply relinquish my personality. . . . My claim to dominance originated, without a doubt, from this basic feeling, both last year and this, as well. But I have found both then and now that the first response of the female psyche—yours as well as Lilly's—is to resist, and not to sufficiently evaluate the nature of the one making the demand. Besides which, the female psyche would rather accept countless small gifts than the burden of a great sacrifice. (Is male arrogance speaking here again?)

In his dream of a future life in peacetime, Günther has already accepted Felice and Lola and her "little worm" into the family. "It would be best for all of us to look for a seven-room apartment. Not such a bad idea at all."

Meanwhile, a totally different life continues at home:

My Dear Little, Big Aimée,

I am so happy with you and love you so much. You truly can count on the fact that I would never, never again go to Mutti. I love you so much because I know that you also love me, and that you always want the same thing, and think the same as I do. You know, don't you, that I am very happy to be able to work and earn money? I look forward all day to seeing you. But if I were always at home and couldn't work at all, I surely would not be as happy, but as dissatisfied as a man out of work.

I will always look out for you and take care of you, my little kitten.

Your Jaguar

July 16, 1944

My dear Jaguar,

I want to be as reliable to you as paper and pencil. I will always take care of you, iron your pants, wash your shirts and darn your socks. And I am happy, more than happy to be able to stay at home, and am immeasurably grateful to you for that. I am very glad that you are happy with your work. I have nothing against it, for basically I am terribly glad that you want to work for me and take care of me always. In return I will give you all of my love.

For eternity

Your Aimée

"SMALL CLIQUE OF TRAITORS WISHED TO ELIMINATE THE FUHRER ON BEHALF OF WORLD JUDAISM," screamed the July 21 headlines of special editions all over the city. That same day, the Majdanek concentration camp was liberated by the Soviet army.

On July 28 Günther Wust again wrote to Felice:

. . . The fact that Lilly has succeeded in convincing you, too, that she knows exactly what she wants shows me that you as well have too quickly confused the confident way in which she presents herself with inner confidence. I think you were a bit more skeptical a year ago. Perhaps it is true—and I would be happy were it so—that Lilly, seeking self-reliance in her present critical situation, has gained in inner strength. It would be all the better for the proposed agreement between Lilly and myself if it were made on a clear basis with clear boundaries. We then would be able to depend on each other that much more. Nonetheless, at this time I stand by my opinion that she is not inclined to stubbornness, is even rather easily influenced. And you, Felice, should know that, as you were more accomplished at leading her than I. . . . Look, Felice, despite your experience and self-reliance in life, you don't know what it's like to have children, and I defy anyone, no matter how clever and empathetic, who doesn't have children to fully comprehend what it is to be a happy parent. . . . In the last paragraph of your letter you spoke of seeing the future there differently than I. My remarks in this regard should not be taken too seriously. It may well be that my views differ from those of you there and yet—well, better to leave it at that! But believe me, my beliefs are strong, and have been so since I reached my political majority in 1926, on my twentieth birthday. Only my belief in people has been somewhat damaged. I am not a political person. And for that reason I do not inveigh against the fact that things slowly and consistently have moved further and further away from the ideals I held in my youth. And that is why I cling all the more to what is left of those ideals: the family.

That same day Felice recorded a kind of last will and testament:

I herewith again explicitly add to my letter of November 7, 1943, that the following possessions are to go to Frau Elisabeth Wust, née Kappler, Berlin-Schmargendorf, Friedrichshaller Str. 23:

1. The table and bed linens sent to L——without my permission by Frau Selbach, which are marked with the initials AS, AFS, ES, HB, EB, HK, P, and some of which are completely new.
2. The cabin trunk (red striped, marked FS) in which the above-named items are stored.
3. 600 (six hundred) Reichsmarks, which I gave to Frau Selbach in 1940 for safekeeping, minus the cost of alteration for the:
4. Persian lamb coat and muff, which Frau Selbach requested to purchase from me for RM 8,000 in her letter, attached, clearly attesting to my right of ownership.
5. Table silver, engraved AS, ES, HB, HK, P (also in L——).

All of the above-listed items are transferred to the possession of Frau Elisabeth Wust, née Kappler, as of today's date. My sister, Irene K., née Schragenheim, residing at present in England and who may be contacted through Madame Kummer, Geneva, Avenue de la Forêt 17, Switzerland, has been informed of my wishes and is in agreement with them.

As for obvious reasons I am unable to have a notary public certify this at this time, I must therefore request that it be recognized in its present form.

Berlin-Schmargendorf, July 28, 1944
Felice Schragenheim

August 1 was the first day of the Warsaw revolt of the Polish militia. Felice brought home five large sheets of "secret Reich documents" from the *National-Zeitung*, consisting of columns of numbers, underlined in red, that pertained to transports of Hungarian Jews. The secret papers were hidden in a small cupboard in the living room. In that same room, on the same spot on the wall where Hitler's likeness once had hung, was now a map of Europe that had been torn from a school atlas, on which Lilly and Felice, with growing satisfaction, used brightly colored pins to mark the action at the front. When the doorbell rang the map quickly was turned to the wall, revealing on its reverse side a picture of the *Schloss am Lustgarten*, the Berlin palace.

On August 7 Lilly traveled to Thuringia to visit Bernd, and to bring Eberhard home. She no longer wanted him to remain at the home of the high-ranking Nazi where he was

staying. On the way from the Meuselwitz station to Zipsendorf it began to storm, and Lilly removed her wooden-soled
sandals with the straps and walked the rest of the way barefoot. Eberhard's foster parents stared in astonishment at Lilly's
feet, covered in mud, the nails painted red.

August 8, 1944 (8:45 p.m.)

My Dear Kitten,

Have you arrived safely at last? Whenever you're away
I always reproach myself for allowing you to set off alone.
What if you didn't make your connection and there was no
one to pick you up? Hopefully you didn't weep. But you're
so good and brave.

I came home around five and there was no one standing on the balcony. . . . So I finally returned the book. The
doctor was at home alone and we had a nice talk about the
future and such. It will not be easy to switch back to being
a normal and responsible person, that's for sure. And he
said, perhaps correctly, that it wouldn't be the same if we
left, either, for we wouldn't like those on the outside. They
will have things and we won't, and they will be arrogant.
And whereas we would be saved some disappointment, we
also would miss our connections here. And were we even-
tually to return we would have to go through the same
thing all over again, for by that time those who stayed here
would have it all again, whereas we would have to start
over. But we both came to the conclusion that we will be
spared the need to worry about such things, for there is
no chance for us to leave, we shall remain here, and work

hard. And perhaps we will wish for the good old days, as crazy as that seems, when someone such as I had only to work occasionally and could lie on the Havel every day in the sun. I would like to take a bike trip with him next week and go swimming if possible. May I? You never let me do anything. But you'll let me do that, won't you?

Now I have a headache and am going to bed all alone. All alone.

The Friedrichs were not bombed out, they just received a little nudge. Christine sent me her monthly ration card. Inge got to work really late, and Elenai turned right around again once she saw the damage to Schöneweide. But she wasn't bombed out, fortunately. I may get together with Nora tomorrow. Your children are being very good. Lola is too. As is

> Your wild, noble and good-natured
> Jaguar who loves you

There was trouble at home the next evening when Lilly sent Eberhard down to the cellar bunker, for children were not permitted to remain in Berlin as long as the bombing continued.

On August 21 a blackout was in effect in Berlin from 9:12 p.m. to 5:24 a.m. Sunrise was at 5:53 a.m., sunset at 10:12 p.m. In its "Berlin Observer" column the *Völkischer Beobachter* ran an article on the harp, "instrument for a sensitive time." Haus Vaterland on Potsdamer Platz was featuring "The Big Bright

Cabaret Program," and at the Scala Theater on Ku'damm was a variety revue entitled *Utopia*.

The twenty-first of August, 1944, was a hot summer's day. Felice and Lola both had the day off from work, and Lola agreed to sacrifice her free time to take care of the children. Aimée and Jaguar set off on their bikes for a swim, crossing through Grunewald and then taking the road along the Havel down to the "big window," where woods and underbrush ran to sand, and they could look out over the wide stretch of river. They had a whole day to swim and lie in the sun, without Lola, without the children, perhaps even without bombs. Aimée could barely believe how happy she was. For weeks now she had been trying to talk Jaguar into taking some time off with her, for Felice had been working even on Sundays of late. The beach was empty of people on this Monday. "Hopefully Lola and the children will be all right," was the only thought that interrupted their murmurs of endearment. Jaguar had brought along her old camera, the Leica she guarded like a treasure. As always, Aimée made a fuss when Jaguar wanted to photograph her. Her prettiest feature, her chestnut-red hair, does not show up in black-and-white. She was wearing a navy blue beach outfit of thick linen, with breast and hip pockets stitched and riveted in white. Aimée had more fun playing photographer herself, trailing down Jaguar's long legs with the camera, legs usually concealed by long pants. On this Monday on the Havel, a self-timer was used to take the only photographs of Aimée and Jaguar in which they are alone together. Lilly, with her short legs, appears awkward before the lens, her arms demurely and impassively at her sides, while Felice looks willfully into the camera, serious and fearless. Before they started out on the long journey home that afternoon Jaguar posed once more, barefoot and dressed in shorts of white linen with her father's bow tie boldly fastened to the collar of her blouse. The shadows at the "big window" were beginning to lengthen.

Out of breath from the long bicycle ride in the hot afternoon sun they locked the bicycles in the cellar and ran up to the apartment two steps at a time, eager finally to relieve Lola of the burden of the children.

"Were they good?" Lilly trilled happily as soon as the door opened. But Lola's gray-blue eyes were wide with fright. At the same moment that her lips silently formed the word "Gestapo," two men stepped out of the darkness behind her.

"Who are you? Come in here."

Aimée and Jaguar were pushed into the living room, and Lola was ordered to join Albrecht, Eberhard, and Reinhard in the children's room.

"You needn't bother to deny it," the menacing SS man with the black hair barked at Felice. "You are the Jewess Schragenheim." He held a photo of Felice under her nose that had been taken on Luise Selbach's balcony. Felice said nothing.

To Lilly he said, "You knew that Schragenheim is a Jew." Lilly said nothing.

Then they were separated. Lilly was ordered to follow the squat, stocky man in the brown uniform into the bedroom while Felice remained behind with his superior. How long had Lilly known Felice, the short one wanted to know, and when did she move in with her. Lilly answered the questions truth-fully.

Then she was taken back into the living room where the two were cross-examined further for the names of friends and acquaintances, for addresses . . .

At the moment that both men turned their attention to Lilly, Felice dashed out of the room. It was the peak of summer and all the doors and windows in the apartment were open, cre-ating a draft when Felice opened the apartment door. A door slammed shut. The short man set off after Felice. "Stop her!" he shouted. Felice bounded down the stairs as if possessed, her footsteps echoing through the stairwell. She ran through the yard, into the back building, and up to Frau Beimling's. It took only seconds for old Frau Beimling to grasp the situation, and shove Felice behind the couch.

"There, she went up there," fat Herr Rauche screamed in excitement, running out of his ground-floor flat in his under-shirt.

The squat man, having found Felice, kicked at her, forcing her out from behind the couch. He then dragged her down the steps of the back building and back up to Lilly's apartment.

The investigation continued. Where did Felice get her food ration cards, they asked and, again and again, did Lilly know that Schragenheim was a Jew? Lilly feigned ignorance.

"You know that you can be sent to a concentration camp for sheltering illegal Jews," the squat one shouted. Lilly said nothing.

After roughly two hours more SS men arrived. They had been waiting in a truck a few buildings away.

"Now give each other a kiss," the black-haired commander said with a malicious grin. Then he yelled, "And you, young woman, we should take you with us. But we'll let you go this time because of your poor innocent children."

Without a word, Felice removed the ring with the green stone from her middle finger, handed it to Lilly, and kissed her on the forehead.

Then she was led away.

Lola Sturmova:

I was at home with Albrecht, Eberhard, and Reinhard when someone started ringing the doorbell wildly. I opened the door and he grabbed me—I was already pregnant at the time—and said: "Schragenheim!"

"Who might that be?"

"Don't try to deny it, Schragenheim!"

"I don't know any Schragenheim."

"Let's see your identification papers." So I showed him my ID. "We'll wait here until she arrives," he said.

Jesus, it was awful. I couldn't even get word to the other lady, the one who lived below us. I had to go to the bathroom, but he followed me and I had to leave the door open! I wanted quickly to write something down and give it to Albrecht or Reinhard to lower from the balcony. I already had some string, but then I dropped the idea because he was standing right there behind me. At first there were two of them, and then more . . . the whole house was surrounded, and then they hunted down Felice. One of them had a photo of Felice that he showed me. And I said, I know her, but. . . . Then they asked since when did I know her, since when did I live here, where was I employed. They also talked to my boss, the Austrian, and he said, *no, no Jew.* But the best thing was, he had shown me a photo of his company and said, That's me. It was in Czernowitz, he'd said. And my father had been a commanding officer in Czernowitz, in the old republic. They were all Jews! So I said to him, So, you're Jewish? It was a Jewish regiment. He wasn't a Jew, but he had been assigned to that company. He told them that Felice worked at the *Völkischer Beobachter*, and that she passed on information. Apparently there was some sort of station down in the cellar where she was sending the reports to England, that's what the "catchers" said when they arrived. I said, nope, don't know anything, we only have a radio down there so that when the bombs fall we can find out where they are, the British. They went down to the cellar, took the keys and went down, but they didn't find anything.

Once the men had left, Lola cautiously opened the door to the children's room. Lilly was beside herself, screaming and crying. Albrecht and Reinhard were pressed against the wall, terrified. That night Lilly didn't allow the children to go to the bunker. Lola and Lilly stayed up all night.

"We have to do something," Lola urged. "The papers! Burn them. Yes, burn them," she murmured, more to herself than to Lilly, who sat staring into space. Lola pulled the "secret Reich documents" from the dark brown cabinet, then went to her room to gather up other material that Felice had given her for "Kaleu" Henschel in the last few weeks. She then stuffed all of it into the green tile stove in the balcony room.

"Jesus, they were standing right in front of it!"

"No, not that," Lilly ordered, her voice breaking, as Lola prepared to add to the fire books by Lion Feuchtwanger, Felice's "uncle."

Lilly knew nothing of most of the things that Felice had brought home from the newspaper office. Lola and Felice had always tried to keep as much from her as possible, because of the children.

The next morning, when Lilly went into the kitchen to prepare the children's breakfast, exhausted, her eyes swollen, she found a poem in a coffee cup:

Much of what I think about
Is like a poem to my ear,
I give to you. I cannot shout,
And it seems you cannot hear.

Words exist, which when they're spoken,
Cannot bear the light of day,
Said aloud, something gets broken,
And can't be made right in any way.

Nor are they words that I can say.
So you must now bend down to me,
That I might seek in some small way,
To communicate them silently.

Words there are that can't be spoken,
Not without something broken

Last things will not tolerate
Even a whisper.

So you must now bend down to me,
And softly close your eyes
I want to tell you silently,
My dearly beloved You.

"She didn't even say good-bye to me," Eberhard wailed.
And Lilly could not find her gold watch, which had been in
the bedroom during the interrogation.

No one has ever found out how Felice's photograph came into
the hands of the Gestapo.

SIX

On August 21, 1944, Elisabeth Wust began a diary. She was never to be without it, always finding new hiding places for it, sometimes under the bathtub, or in the linen closet, or behind a loose brick in the cellar.

Lilly's diary, August 21, 1944:

Today it happened, the horrible thing I had blocked even the slightest thought of: They took my beloved away from me.

Dear God, protect the girl I love above all else. Give her back to me safe and sound. I screamed and cried, and the children with me, all except Albrecht. He just stood there and smiled, the chubby thing. He doesn't understand. I came to my senses for the children's sake. I didn't look out the window, I simply didn't have the strength to, and I didn't want you to see my tears. Lola was so sweet.

*She saw you wave as they put you in that heavily guarded
car and took you away. She was comforting, but what
good is comfort.*

*I picked up Christine from the station that evening.
She cried a lot. I think she loves you a little. And who
wouldn't love you? Before that, when I went to the cellar
with Lola to get some clothes from the suitcase for the
children, a light flashed on at the Rauches' when we shut
the cellar door. He probably wanted to spy on me to see
what I was taking from the cellar in secret. Maybe he had
been instructed by the Gestapo, or maybe it's just his own
zealotry. My God, six fearless men to trap one single girl.
Six men! And Rauche, full of his own self-importance. I
will never forget the vile thing he did. Never.*

When Christine Friedrichs heard the unhappy news she
called Inge in Lübben. Inge immediately removed from her
room all her forbidden books. When Felice was picked up she
was carrying a postal ID made out to Inge Wolf, which Inge
had had made for her some time earlier.

And then Inge had a thought. A woman who was apprenticing at Collignon's, and with whom she got along well, had
a father who was a Nazi big shot at the Reich Security Main
Office. Perhaps he could tell them where Felice had been taken.

On Tuesday morning Frau Blei, the editorial secretary at
the *National-Zeitung*, called and asked to speak to Frau Wust,
the name under which Felice was working at the newspaper.

A short time later Inge and Lilly marched into the gloomy building on Prinz-Albrecht-Strasse that housed Gestapo headquarters. As her summer things were in the wash, Lilly wore her house dirndl with the bright trim at the neck, hem and on the puffy sleeves, and little white socks, which she discovered a hole in at the last minute. With their hearts pounding, Inge and Lilly asked to speak to Herr Doktor Emil Berndorff, *SS-Sturmbannführer,* senior government officer, and detective superintendent of the Section IV Office for Investigating and Combating the Enemy, and in charge of protective custody cases. They mentioned the name of his daughter Ilse. Too intimidated to utter so much as a word to one another, they sat rigidly on a bench until the detective superintendent, in a not unfriendly fashion, bade them to come in.

"I have heard that Schragenheim was using an identification with my name on it," Inge said. "I have no idea how it came into her possession, I just wanted to tell you."

"My dear woman, she could have been one of those from the twentieth of July [attempt to assassinate Hitler]!"

"But Herr Detective Superintendent, she's only a young woman."

"Yes, well, one cannot be too careful."

Lilly:

> As we went in, I remembered that they had almost beaten my brother to death in the basement of that same building. We waited for a long time, and Inge sat on the bench, intimidated. Then I'd had enough of that, and I went up to this burly guy

in the reception area and let him have it: "How much longer do we have to wait?" I didn't care about anything, they could have locked me up for that. I really surprised him. "You must wait a bit longer. Hopefully he'll be here soon." Inge was terribly afraid, but I had no fear at all, and was as cocky as could be. But it was the same later: If you were spirited enough and didn't put up with anything, they didn't know what to do with you. It isn't that I am a courageous person. So then I let Berndorff have it too: "Unbelievable, you can't just misplace someone like that. I want to know where she is." He threw us out fairly quickly, but before he did he said to me, "What are you thinking of, young lady? I can't tell you that. We pull the strings for the entire Reich." The cur knew exactly where Felice was!

That evening the telephone rang. Lola picked up the receiver and a male voice said, "Schulstrasse," and hung up.

"My God!" Lilly whispered, "that's the Jewish Hospital. That's where the transports to the East leave from!"

The next morning—Frau Blei from the *National-Zeitung* had called once again—Lilly took the S-Bahn to the Gesundbrunnen station. Loaded down with fruit and the tomatoes that Felice loved so, she hurried along the long wall of the Jewish Hospital to the side entrance at Schulstrasse 78, where the Pathology Building, separated from the other buildings by barbed wire, was being used as a collection camp for Jews. Through a large iron archway a smaller door led to the two-story gatekeeper's lodge to the right, where the administration was housed, and to Pathology to the left, where the prisoners were kept. The guardroom for the police was located on the ground floor. Lilly identified herself and asked for permission to visit Felice Schragenheim.

Three steps led to a door which opened into a large room. Four or five people sat to the back of the room at the right. Busy with correspondence, they nevertheless kept a close eye on everything that was going on in the room. Behind them, several more steps led to the prisoners' quarters. It was from there that Felice was summoned, a yellow star on her chest.

What a difference from the smiling Felice of two days before!

"Good heavens, who was it that blabbed?" Lilly whispered. "Potty Peyser."

Charlotte Peyser, a friend of Felice from school, had been picked up with her girlfriend by the Gestapo in Vienna and brought to Berlin, where she and Felice ran into each other again in the collection camp on Schulstrasse.

Backes, one of the Jewish police (*Ordner*) at Schulstrasse, who had pulled Felice out from behind the couch two days before and dragged her back to Lilly's, walked into the room at that point. He had nothing better to do than to report Lilly's presence to the head of the camp, who immediately summoned both women for questioning. Walter Dobberke, the bullnecked *SS-Hauptscharführer*, with his short military haircut and poker face, was concerned above all with the bicycles. Detective Secretary Herbert Titze, the commander of the team of six men who arrested Felice, had reported that the two women returned home on bicycles. Jews were not permitted to own bicycles: Whom did they belong to? Dobberke and Titze wanted to know.

"To me, who else?" Lilly answered curtly.

Dobberke, addressed as "Kommissar" at the camp, treated Lilly with utmost politeness. It was well known that the man was cantankerous, kept a whip ready at hand in an office cabinet and had a weakness for pretty women.

Right after Felice was brought to Schulstrasse, she was forced to sign a declaration of property. According to it, her property included an inheritance in the amount of twenty thousand Reichsmarks, and diverse furniture, linens, and items of women's clothing. At her new "address" at Schulstrasse 78, Felice received a communication from the Gestapo, dated May 1, 1944, informing her that all of her property had been "conscripted for the benefit of the German Reich."

Lilly's diary, August 23, 1944:

> I was a mountain of courage. Even when that disgusting Backes saw me standing there, and of course had to report it to the camp commander, Dobberke, right away, that vulgar man. This Dobberke, and Titze as well, treated me in an odd way. Dobberke was almost kind. They harassed us, it's true, but precisely because of that we got to see each other much longer than we had expected. No one can take that from us,

*no one. From now on I'll go there every day, and you'll have
many, many tomatoes, among other things.*

Lilly sent off telegrams that said, "Felice seriously ill," to
London, New York and Geneva, as well as to Luise Selbach.

Each day Lilly hurried to Schulstrasse with the best food
she could find in Berlin at the end of the fifth year of war. One
of the younger policemen—pacified by the French cigarettes
Inge had bought from French laborers where she worked in
Lübben—even began a flirtation with Lilly. Lilly went along
willingly, enveloping him in her charm, for he could open the
door to Felice for her. After he went so far as to show her his
work schedule, Lilly always appeared when he was on duty,
and promised him a photo of herself.

Lilly discussed with Elenai how they could get money to
Felice. With money she could buy a lot of things, maybe even
her life.

Elenai's situation was also becoming increasingly precarious. When she could no longer come up with an excuse for
Felice's absence from work at the *National-Zeitung*, she too
stopped going to work. She went underground, and went to
Lübben to stay with Inge Wolf. And it was high time, for her
Aryan stepfather, under whose protection she had been living,
had died early that summer. And Elenai had been denounced
by someone in her hometown of Erfurt, where a *Gauleiter*
named Fritz Sauckel was wreaking havoc, and this resulted in
her being summoned by the Gestapo.

"Leave. Now," was the advice the Gestapo gave her.

Felice at first was locked up in the "bunker," with mostly young people, all of whom were suspected of trying to escape. Twice a day prisoners were taken to the bathroom and to a small court-yard where they were able to walk around. There were eight to a cell, and they all shared one table, a few stools, and slept on the floor. Felice later was taken to one of the hospital's larger rooms, where the prisoners—"U-boats" for the most part—could walk about the empty rooms freely. As always, Felice won everyone's heart, particularly that of Ludwig Neustadt, an *Ordner* (Jewish police). It was he who had called Lilly on the twenty-second of August to tell her where Felice was being held. Soon after Felice's imprisonment, the small, unassum-ing blond—he didn't wear the Jewish star—arrived at Frie-drichshaller Strasse to pick up clothes for Felice. Lilly packed Felice's favorite gray pants, her rust-red checkered jacket, the white sweater, a pair of shoes and, most essential, underwear and socks. As Neustadt and Lilly were sitting at the kitchen table talking about Felice, the air raid alarm went off and they rushed to the cellar.

"Every day there's something new with her!" one of the women living in the building remarked caustically. Ever since the Gestapo turned out in force on their street, most of the building's residents avoided Lilly. Even "Aunt" Grasenick, widowed in World War I, who often celebrated the children's birthdays with them and loved Albrecht as if he were her own grandchild, looked the other way when they met on the stairs. Lilly had run down to her apartment in a panic after Felice was taken away. "Is being Jewish a person's own fault?" she'd sobbed. Even then she had noticed that Frau Grasenick had moved away from her.

Lilly's diary, August 26, 1944:

> You shall read this diary when you are no longer the "Jewess Schragenheim," but a person among other persons. Dear God, let us live together or die. Do not allow for only one of us to survive. I will never get over not seeing my Felice again. Never in a lifetime.

On Sunday Lilly took Albrecht, Reinhard and Eberhard with her to Schulstrasse. This time they waited for Felice in the guardroom. Even the policemen enjoyed having the children there. They were wearing their knitted summer shorts, their brown legs ending in worn-out sandals. One of them eyed Eberhard curiously. "Who is this child's father?" he demanded to know.

Albrecht had gotten his first "man's" haircut for the occasion. "Hice! Hice!" he called as Felice was led in, rushing over to throw his chubby arms around her. Jaguar picked up Albrecht with tears streaming down her face.

"You have a star pocket," he said, playing dreamily with the yellow patch at Felice's breast.

Lilly had instructed the children not to tell anyone about their visit. Without comprehending why, they nevertheless knew quite well that this time their mother was serious.

On Monday Lilly was discovered by Titze. "Get out!" he roared, forbidding her to come back for a whole week. But Lilly marched straight to the Gestapo office on Französische Strasse and requested an official visitor's pass, which she obtained. She was back in the guardroom again by Tuesday. Without a word, Lilly's favorite guard brought Felice into the large room.

Suddenly a very attractive, slender young woman with reddish blond hair and cold blue eyes walked through the room, talking and laughing shrilly with the policemen, only to dance out again, with her long legs and high heels.

"That's her," Felice whispered, almost in awe. It was the Jewish "catcher," Stella, into whose hands Felice had almost fallen when she went to meet Gerd Ehrlich on Savignyplatz.

On Wednesday there was more trouble in store for Lilly at the Schulstrasse camp, this time from the boss himself.

"What do you think you're doing?" Dobberke bellowed at Lilly, barely able to contain himself. "Unbelievable! I forbid you to come here. Don't show your face at this camp again, or I'll lock you up. Now get out of here!"

Outside the front gate stood a Jewish gatekeeper.

"What could they do to me?" Lilly asked him.

"Oh, it wouldn't be so bad, a bit of concentration camp."

That evening Ludwig Neustadt called to tell Lilly that it soon would be decided where Felice was to be taken. Lilly should not appear at Schulstrasse again, he said. He would keep her informed.

Lilly sent Lola and Nora, a friend of Felice, to see her. The policeman in the guardroom promised to deliver their packages to her. Felice didn't want to see Inge Wolf; the two of them must have had a major altercation.

In the midst of Lilly's fear for Felice, she received a further bad sign. The letters and a package of cookies that Lilly had sent to the front came back marked "recipient unknown." Günther Wust's last letter was dated August 18.

Lilly's diary, September 2, 1944:

> *Our day, my beloved. If only I could see you. Ludwig called right on time, and I will see him this afternoon. I don't know if you're really receiving all of the things I sent. I went with Lola to Schulstrasse. Today of all days, you should not be without something nice from me. I stood on the corner very secretively because I was afraid someone from the camp would see me. Lola said she even got to speak to you. Oh, my beloved, I cried all the way back to Schmargendorf. It is so unspeakably difficult to be reasonable. Did you bite the apple I had bitten? Did it taste good? Did you think of the first day we met, and how, at the end of it, you gave me an apple, and how I, freezing, held it so tightly at the streetcar stop at the Ufa-Palast? I was and I remain Eve. If only I could lie safely in your arms. Tomorrow you will have been gone two weeks already. Two eternally long weeks. Who knows how many weeks will follow.*

September 4 was Lilly's father's birthday, and the two of them quarreled. Lilly should stop worrying about Jews, he thundered, and endangering herself and others in the process. "They made a remark to Lola that I cannot forgive them for," Lilly wrote in her diary. "I wholly and confidently belong to you and your life. I am finished with everything that lies behind me. You are my future. And note this well, Felice Schragen-heim, even if you are no longer here, so shall it remain."

On September 5 Lilly tried once again to reach Günther: "I got the feeling that all the letters I have written lately were for nothing," she wrote to him. "I particularly regret this be-cause of a truly endlessly detailed 19-page (that's nineteen!) letter I wrote you." Lilly again related how the children were doing, but did not mention Felice's arrest.

On September 6 Ludwig Neustadt called to report happily that Felice was being transferred to Theresienstadt. That after-noon Lilly met with him at the Wedding district train station, where he gave her a letter from Felice:

My Dear Aimée,

I cannot write much here, only many thanks for your letter and for everything else. And be brave. I'll write to you soon. Then you'll send me some things, won't you? As things went so well for me here—"It is impossible not to love me," etc.—and as everyone, particularly "this one," was so nice to me, it shall certainly continue to be so. Cross your fingers and say hello to everyone who is taking care of you. All my love to the children and to "Sweetie-Pie," my kitten!

Auf Wiedersehen!!
Your Caged Jaguar

Felice and Lilly saw each other for the last time on September 7, and Felice signed a declaration of property of a different sort:

I herewith authorize Frau Elisabeth Wust, of Friedrichshaller
Strasse 23, Berlin-Schmargendorf, to request from Frau Luise
Selbach at any time the delivery of my Persian lamb coat and
muff, which she is holding, as well as my house and bed linens
and my table silver, and to take them into safekeeping for me.

Felice Schragenheim
Collection Camp of the Jewish Community
Berlin, September 7, 1944

They were allowed a half-hour together, more time than
ever before, but it was in the small guardroom, where even
whispered conversation could be overheard. Lilly presented
Felice with a lock of her red hair, and Felice, touched by the
gesture, wrapped it around her comb. Felice returned Lilly's
gloves, which she had gotten from her the day before. There
was a little note stuck in one of them, and a round orange box
with two pills:

My Adorable Pussycat,

Be good and brave and think of me! The nurse I recently introduced you to gave me these Pervitin pills. She is
so nice to me, as is everyone else. And that shall remain so
in Th[eresienstadt]! Cross your fingers for me. I love you so
much, and will be back soon!!

My Aimée
Your Jaguar

Lilly never figured out exactly why it was a stimulant that Nurse
Tatjana gave her, when at that point it was a sedative she needed.

When Lilly got to the corner she suddenly turned around and ran back to the camp. The policeman in the guardroom raised his head in surprise.

"Go back and get Felice Schragenheim again, I beg of you," she said breathlessly. He stood up without a word and returned with Felice.

"Felice," Lilly whispered, "is it true that you love Christine?"

"Who planted that idea in your head?"

"Christine. She told me."

"Ach, Sweetie-Pie, you needn't believe everything that's floating around in the air."

"Felice, I'll kill myself, I'll throw myself out the window if it's true!"

"Sweetheart, you must believe me. It is very important for you to believe me: I love only you."

"Ladies, we have to put an end to this at some point," the policeman warned, and Lilly was pushed gently out the door.

Early in the morning of September 8, 1944, the Jewess Felice Sara Schragenheim, transport number 14890-I/116, was taken to Theresienstadt, "ghetto for the aged," 350 kilometers from Berlin. It was the next to the last transport to leave Berlin for that destination. The trip on the slowly moving train lasted until late that evening.

Lilly's diary, September 10, 1944:

Thursday, the seventh of September, arrived. Oh, Felice, my heart wants to stop with the pain. You were so calm and cheerful, my darling. It was certainly for my sake.

My God, I felt like my heart was being torn out of my body, and had to smile instead—smile and stroke your hands in secret. I made my way to the streetcar trembling, almost staggering.

I had a terrible experience the day before. Waiting at the stop for the number 41 streetcar, I saw a procession coming toward me. A procession of women prisoners was coming along Osloer Strasse. They were from a branch of the Oranienburg prison and were dressed in striped clothing, with shaved heads, and barefoot. Felice, I wanted to scream, I wanted to rush into their midst. But I didn't move, I couldn't utter a sound. It was as if I had turned to stone. It was like a vision. Tears streamed from my eyes. Dear God, help, don't let my girl go through something so inhuman. Dear God, help. It was so horrible, because this miserable gray procession marched by not five hundred steps away from you. How am I to bear this? But God saw to it that you were taken to Theresienstadt.

Ludwig called on Sunday evening. We want to meet on Tuesday. I'm truly looking forward to it. He can't tell me enough about you. We both have already sent several packages to Theresienstadt. You see how much you are loved. No wonder you're such a vain rascal. Everyone loves you. But I insist that you love only me, do you hear? I'm going to bed soon. Are you already asleep? How are you doing? If only you will be as fortunate as you were here. I miss you so terribly, and have cried so much I look awful. I'm so worried. Do you think of me? I'll find a star in the sky that maybe you can see, too, and it will bind our two souls together. I will pray and pray and pray. Tomorrow we'll finally receive clothing ration cards again, and I'll go right away to buy the children winter coats. And then I have something else planned. Perhaps I will succeed in it. Good night, my girl. I want to kiss you.

On September 12 Ludwig Neustadt handed Lilly a long letter from Jaguar:

September 7, 1944

My Dear Aimée,

When I came here fourteen days ago I never would have believed you would make a scene on my behalf, despite the police and the barred windows. It was wonderful, it was totally you! By the way, you were wrong. And I, by the way, could see you much longer than you saw me, for I stood at the window by the toilet, but you couldn't know that and didn't turn around.

I can't give you an account of the last seventeen days. It would be longer than one of Berns's lead articles. My roommates are "at work" until three, but despite my ability to turn a deaf ear to any kind of interruption—I seem to be the only person in this madhouse who truly enjoys reading—I can't concentrate today. Also, I'm without—among other things—my typewriter.

If things continue as they have up until now, none of you need worry about me. So wish me luck. Everyone has been so wonderful to me that I simply have to believe in my own irresistibility. Too bad it's not possible for me to meet myself. It must be a pleasure. No, seriously, if I'm not eaten up by bugs or killed in some similarly tragic manner, you'll be ironing my pants again soon! Anyway, when I was still living in the "bunker" under lock and key, I shared a room with a woman who finally sewed up my pants as you had planned to do four weeks ago. This woman is so bored that she's always pleading with everyone to give her their sewing. So she's busy with my pink underthings and my socks.

You needn't be afraid that I've fallen into bad company: in addition to the unsurpassable Ludwig, high society, in the form of the (almost aristocratic) nurse-lady you met briefly and the officer-chemist (even more aristocratic and a truly fantastic fellow) she is pursuing, has embraced me. In this way I can often get away from "Jewish suffering" (nauseating!) during the day. And I have nerves of steel. I particularly noticed that yesterday, when the transport left for the East. And I can sleep. In our room there is a woman who snores like a—well, there is no comparison actually. Others snore along in harmony. And I sleep. I was asleep ten minutes after we arrived at this building, that was my reaction. And if I wasn't asleep I was beaming at everyone. There is scarcely any sign of sympathy here. People are either totally occupied with themselves or are numb. At most, one can be liked, and that is best earned with "keep smiling."

At any rate, everyone envies me my good friends, who

are taking such good care of me from the outside. Which is no more than I deserve, right? After having not been able to eat anything for the first two days after I arrived here, I now have an enormous appetite. Tonight I have been invited to *"Herr Ordner's"* for supper. Unfortunately I can't dress for the occasion. He will forgive me. As I assume that he is a tactful young man and won't read this letter, I can go ahead and write what you already know, that he is simply fantastic, sweet and nice and caring and—successful, as this letter attests.

I was just interrupted: The "boss" himself just came into the room to tell a woman that she has been reclaimed by her employer and can remain in Berlin. He managed to overlook three burning cigarettes and two missing stars. The sun of his mercy reached its zenith.

My hands are stained with ink, I have a cramp in my arm and in addition it's time to "be served" coffee and bread with marmalade. The coffee tastes like bicarbonate of soda, so we brew our own and eat cookies with it in the physician's room, and talk about things that happened seventeen days ago—and, in this case, that's a great deal.

So, everyone stay healthy. I'll write as soon as possible. Greetings to those who filled our apartment and bothered us to a greater or lesser degree: our good friends.

Kiss the children and keep your chin up, all right?

Auf Wiedersehen

Felice

P.S. "Potty" was sent East yesterday, but her bride remained behind weeping, and with a case of tuberculosis to boot.

Nevertheless I'm sorry for her. She's going to Th– [Theresienstadt] on my transport. The dogcatcher is also gone. Other than that there is hardly a Berliner here—whether *Ordner,* official, or "inmate"—in whose mouth my parents hadn't poked around.

SEVEN

With Felice's deed of donation in hand, Lilly tried to collect Felice's belongings with a zeal that startled and disconcerted Gregor and Felice's friends. Lilly's mother and Lola, who was in the last term of her pregnancy, set out to ascertain Luise Selbach's whereabouts, and to collect Felice's things from her friends. They were told that, except for the youngest daughter, Olga, who had been drafted into labor service in the East, the family had been picked up and taken away, and that six crates had been removed from the house at the same time. Felice's grandmother's coat reportedly was not included. "You'll never see the Selbachs again!" said Mutti's acquaintance, the market woman Roese, triumphantly, reporting that Mutti and her husband had slit their wrists and been taken to the hospital in Hirschberg. Lola, for her part, heard that Mutti had had nothing good to say about Lilly. Felice was a nice girl, Mutti had said, and had sunk so low only because of "that Wust"; Felice had ignored Frau Selbach's many requests to come to the "Forst," but had she accepted the invitation she also would have had to change her behavior.

" 'That Wust' is obviously unaware of the fact that deeds of donation from Jews are null and void," Roese said, rejecting Lola's demand that she return the Persian lamb coat, which Lola guessed she had in her possession.

"I'll make a note of that statement for later," Lilly noted in her diary.

The truth behind Lilly's diary entry was this: On September 14, 1944, the Gestapo arrived at the "Forst" and arrested Olga's sisters.

"Get yourselves ready, we're coming back," they said to Herr and Frau Selbach as they led off the two daughters, still wearing their summer dresses. Mutti and her husband locked the dog in the house and went up to the forest preserve, where the forest was most dense. Once there they took sleeping pills and cut open their wrists. Despite the considerable distance to the nearest farm, the neighbors must nevertheless have heard the dog howling. When they broke down the door the dog shot out like an arrow and led them to the Selbachs. They were carried to the sitting room, where the doctor said they would have died from the strong sleeping pills before they would have bled to death. Then they were taken to the hospital in Hirschberg. After they had partially recovered, the Aryan husband was put in jail and his Jewish wife incarcerated with penal servitude. Herr Selbach was released shortly after Christmas 1944. Mutti and one of their daughters were supposed to be deported to Bergen-Belsen, but by then it was too late. The machinery of destruction was already being dismantled.

On February 1, 1945, Lilly tried equally unsuccessfully to collect Felice's linens from Christine Friedrichs's mother. "That doesn't concern you," she was brusquely informed over the telephone. "What makes you think these are your linens? Felice Schragenheim entrusted them to me. They belong to Fräulein Schragenheim and not to you." And Lilly noted in her diary: "She told me to my face that I only wanted to enrich myself with your belongings. Dearest, she said that to me! I could just have smashed everything. I was even angry at you, at your judgment of human nature. Otherwise I wouldn't have found myself at these people's mercy. Must I endure that?"

Elenai Pollak:

Felice's belongings were incredible treasures to Lilly, which was due to some degree to the trend during that period of appropriating Jewish property. They stole it; they denounced people to get at their possessions. Almost everyone participated in this theft, from the little people on up. This country was one single land of thieves. And this of course was passed on to the Nazi women, this greed: Let's get our hands on it before someone else does. Lilly merely projected her own wishes onto Frau Selbach, accusing her of practically everything Lilly herself wanted. I can still remember precisely this disgusting situation, Felice hinted at it again and again. She was always on the go because of these things, which they didn't even need. They had enough linens. But they didn't have a fur coat. And anyway, Lilly already had a whole pile of things from Felice. She was always wearing Felice's clothes and took over everything Felice owned. She had already seen to it earlier that she got several things. Right at the beginning she put pressure on Felice to come over and pick up the bookcase and books that she had stored at my place.

"I have come up with a plan. Dear God, help me!" Lilly mysteriously confided to her diary for the second time, on September 25. That was the day the "German *Volkssturm*" was proclaimed, conscripting all men between the ages of sixteen and sixty who were able to bear arms.

Lola had an idea.

On the twenty-sixth of September Lilly and Lola made the rounds of agencies, with Lola pretending that she had to go to her mother's in the Sudetenland, to give birth to her child. Their efforts resulted in a pale green travel permit, which stated that Eleonora Sturm was allowed to travel to the protectorate of Bohemia and Moravia.

Lilly wanted to go to Theresienstadt.

Elenai Pollak:

I was fairly horrified, first of all because I had heard reports from others that you couldn't get into this ghetto. So I was greatly worried, also by the fact that she wouldn't wait and think about it first. Why at that point, when, in terms of the potential for horror, things were going more or less better than expected in Theresienstadt—why did she have to go there? It was understandable that she wanted to get food to Felice. But what I didn't understand was that she had to deliver it herself. I talked to Gregor about it, and he was just as horrified as I: "What does she think she's doing, is she not all there?" We were also surprised that she would do something like this in a situation where we assumed she was endangering herself as well. After all, it was known that she had harbored a Jew. We couldn't understand that, matter-of-factly and without reflecting on the danger involved, she would just go there as if she were visiting a health resort. We told her that right off, and when that didn't work, we pointed out that it could do Felice harm. That under the circumstances, she could be the cause of something totally unforeseeable. But she didn't care. It was as if she were possessed. She wanted to go and wouldn't listen to anything we had to say. We could say what we wanted, nothing got through to her. So there was nothing left to do but withdraw and say, whatever happens, happens, and hopefully it won't be the worst.

Shortly after 8 p.m. on September 27 Lilly arrived at the Anhalter Station to board an empty compartment of the Prague-Brünn-Vienna train. She carried with her a suitcase full of food and warm clothing, and Lola's pass was in her suit pocket. At the Lovosice border, when she was asked for her pale green travel permit, the Sudeten guard did not notice that Lilly was not Lola. In Lovosice Lilly waited for the second train to Bauschowitz-Theresienstadt [Terezín], so that she would not arrive too early. She nevertheless got off the train at the Bohusovice station at 5 a.m. The two-hour wait there was anything but pleasant, for the non-German-speaking native population reacted toward her with hatred. At 7 a.m. Lilly picked up her heavy bag and bulging briefcase and set off in the direction of Theresienstadt, the Czechs giving her directions only begrudgingly. On leaving the village of Bauschowitz she encountered a troop of "volunteer workers" who were wearing the yellow star and were guarded by soldiers.

When she reached the outskirts of Terezín she asked a man on a bicycle the way to the ghetto.

"What do you think you do?" he replied excitedly in broken German. "Yes, you know an official, then can do something. You know no one, then has no use. What do you think you do? They won't let you through. What do you think you do?"

Lilly decided it would be better to leave the suitcase at an inn close to the SS military hospital. There she met the first person on her journey who was friendly to her, a peasant woman who advised her to ask for the German headquarters. As she talked to Lilly the woman continually looked around her in fear. Her husband was Czech, she told Lilly, she herself was Yugoslavian, and their seventeen-year-old son was doing forced labor. Her husband delivered the mail to Theresienstadt, and that is how she knew that packages usually reached their addressees. Anyone who wasn't receiving packages would starve. The woman begged Lilly not to tell anyone of their conversation.

Suddenly there was a barrier blocking the road. Lilly showed her Maternal Cross certificate and in a firm voice asked to be directed to German headquarters. She soon came to a guardhouse, and a second barrier blocking the cross street that actually led to the camp. It was a lovely road lined with chestnut trees, and Lilly bent down and tucked three chestnuts into her pocket as a memento. In front of her was the first line of fortifications: three or four embankments of warm red brick, crowned and surrounded by soft green grass—gently rolling hills in which people were housed. She passed a guard every fifty meters, repeating each time that she wished to go to headquarters. After one final turn she saw before her the buildings of Terezín, one- and two-story houses painted in the imperial yellow of Austria, each with a high red roof. From that point on she was accompanied by a Czech gendarme, a brightly uniformed Četník. The clean but dusty street led to a large square with shops. There were many people on the streets, too many people, dragging themselves along, yellow stars the only touch of color in a sea of dismal gray. Lilly glanced at a man in nickel-plated glasses who was sweeping the street with a birch broom, his face deathly pale. When she sought out his eyes they were empty, as if he were no longer among the living. She looked through the ground-floor windows of the overflowing *Ubikationen* (barracks): beds, mattresses, rags, pots, plates, clothing—there was scarcely any room left for people. The streets ran in perfectly straight lines that crossed at right angles. The buildings were identified by black letters and numbers painted on their corners.

At the junction of Lange Strasse and Neue Gasse, Lilly and her Četník escort arrived at the commandant's office. Lilly mounted the few steps to find herself standing before the omnipotent *SS-Oberscharführer* Rudolf Heindl seated at his desk and talking with a young married couple who was visiting him.

"What do you want?" he barked at her, his guttural pronunciation betraying a Viennese struggling with High German. Lilly handed him her Maternal Cross certificate.

"I'm passing through on my way to Brünn, and wanted to ask you if I may deliver something to my friend, Felice Schragenheim. I know she is here."

"You want *what?*" Heindl repeated in disbelief, turning a bright purple.

"I brought my friend food every day when she was still at the Jewish collection camp on Schulstrasse. I had no difficulties in doing so, and as I happened to be passing through here, I took the opportunity to bring her something again. Please, I beg of you!"

Heindl was shocked into silence for a moment at Lilly's audacity. Then he screamed at her: "What can you be thinking of? I've never seen anything like this! Travels right into the protectorate, where no one is supposed to be traveling at all, pushes in here and demands permission to give food to Jews. I'll be looking into this! Tell me, how is it that you came to be friends with a Jew? Do you have other such girlfriends? And where did you get that food? Give it to your children instead."

"I came to know—and to love—my friend as a person," Lilly replied calmly. "I found out only later that she is Jewish. There is no one who can convince me that I should just strike her from my memory. My children love her dearly."

"Your friend the Jew," Heindl screamed, glancing at his visitors in a play for approval. "I forbid it. And you, a German woman? Aren't you at all ashamed of yourself? Have you no racial pride?"

Lilly silently congratulated herself on having decided to leave the suitcase at the inn.

"But don't you worry—I'll report you to Berlin. There must be some strange things going on there. Now get out, and don't show your face here again!"

He gave one final imperious gesture, and Lilly found herself outside at the guard station. She then retraced her path: Czech headquarters, line of fortification, chestnut trees, road barrier. When she picked up her suitcase it seemed heavier. There were Jews at the train station loading mail and packages for Terezín. Lilly sat down on her suitcase to wait for the train to Berlin. A freight train being shunted to one side slowly rolled past Lilly as it switched to another track. She watched in horror as a cattle car passed by, the people inside it staring out at her through the tiny, barred windows. Lilly lowered her eyes in shame and then began to sob loudly at the inconceivable thought that her dark-haired, sweet-scented girl might be among them. People stared at her in astonishment and the thought ran through her head that perhaps she was being observed. But nothing mattered to Aimée anymore. She had been to Theresienstadt and could not see Jaguar.

For hours until it reached Leuna the train to Berlin crossed through a fiery hell.

Arriving at home Lilly found three faded brown postal confirmations, signed by Felice and stating that she had received the five packages Lilly had sent to her at Theresienstadt. She also discovered Jaguar's address: Bahnhofstrasse 6. "Had I only known it beforehand," she wrote in her diary. "But I was happy, in spite of the torment: your handwriting, my beloved. I carry the cards with me always."

Elenai Pollak:

I can still remember how triumphant she was when she returned. "I did it, I got in! I spoke with the head Nazi! I was thrown out, it's true, but I showed them!" She gave not a thought to what might happen to Felice, she was thinking of herself again. I was constantly troubled and confused by all of these many contradictions.

Several days later Ludwig Neustadt delivered to Lilly a postcard that Felice had sent to his address.

September 14, 1944

My Dears,

Many, many thanks for the bread, rice and sandwich spread! Postal regulations here are such that I can write only once every eight weeks, and each addressee may write to me only once every four weeks, and only in care of the Reich Agency. But there is no limit on the number of packages I may receive, and they can be addressed to me directly, as before. They cannot include any written messages and are distributed daily. I'll confirm the arrival of each with a preprinted card!

Today is the second anniversary of Grandmother's death. I am healthy and hope that all of you are doing fine as well. My warmest wishes and kisses from your

Felice Schragenheim

It was in this way that Lilly found out that Felice's grandmother, Hulda Karewski, had died at Theresienstadt on September 14, 1942.

Lilly sent Felice two small packages almost daily, with sugar, sausages, noodles, bread, meal, butter, cookies, fruit, potatoes, saccharine, dried vegetables and onions, as well as gauze, kneesocks, darning yarn, rubber bands, toothpaste and cellulose cotton.

On October 9 Lilly took a highly pregnant Lola to the train station. Lola had gotten it into her head that she wanted to go to a maternity home in Sommerfeld to deliver her baby. Lola hadn't felt well all day, and Lilly had tried without success to convince her not to go. A major air raid alarm went off as Lola's train was departing, and she went into labor shortly after passing through Frankfurt/Oder. YOUNG MOTHER SURPRISED BY STORK ON TRAIN, a newspaper later reported.

Lola Sturmova:

> It started on the train. It was a hospital train that was also carrying soldiers on leave from the front. And I had only a blanket and a cushion, and then they made a kind of carrier for me. My doctor said: You have time yet, and then suddenly my water broke. They had to go around collecting water so that he could wash the baby a little. They heated the water by putting it in a helmet and holding it over a candle. What is it? I asked. A boy, he said. So, I said, you'll have to remove something, I wanted a girl. Give him to me then, he said. His name was Captain Rockowski, he was from Radibor, and his wife couldn't have children. No, I said, you can't have him. I wanted a child, I was just disappointed that it was a boy. And the Russians kept flying over outside. . . . The last car had to be uncoupled, the Russians were firing on it so heavily. And that's how I got to Sommerfeld.

On the same day that Lola Sturm from Sudetenland brought her son Thomas into the world on a train, Jewess Felice Schragenheim was underway as well—in a cattle car, transport number Ep–342, destination Auschwitz.

On October 11, 1944, a woman unknown to Lilly and her friends sent a postcard from Theresienstadt addressed to "M. Zivier":

Dear M—,

    I am fine, thanks. Hope you are too. Have heard nothing from Felice. Hope she's healthy and happy. My best, and greetings to everyone.

                                          Beate Mohr

It was four weeks before news of this card reached Lilly.

Lilly's diary, October 16, 1944:

Dearest, it is eight weeks today since they took you away, an eternity. I am so terribly unhappy. I'm alive, but the way I live! The children are here. I go into the city. I shop. I get together with Gregor. I do this and that every day. But the pain eats away at me constantly. It is my constant companion. Tell me that you love me. I love you. You probably will never know just how much.

On October 30 Ludwig Neustadt called and Lilly met him at a restaurant near the collection camp. With him he brought a postcard from Felice, which he let Lilly read.

Lilly's diary, October 30, 1944:

> *My beloved. Ten weeks without you. I cry and cry, and stare blankly into space for hours, worn out by the pain, love, happy memories, darkened hopes for the future. I groan in the face of my powerlessness. Before, I loved you because you loved me. Today I love you regardless, and more than I ever expected. My diary is one long love letter to you. Do you know where I am writing this? At the Mecklenburger Restaurant. I came back here again after the air raid alarm because I hadn't paid my check. I've met three women here. They're all between the ages of forty and fifty, and my assumption about them turned out to be correct. Actually I was interested in only one of them. But Aimée, I can almost hear you say. The little dark-haired reticent one is very interesting. But Aimée!*
>
> *They are total intellectuals and enormously clever. Conversing with them is a joy. They know all about foreign literature. I had the* Well of Loneliness *with me, and they knew the book well. We had a very nice evening last Wednesday, but today, unfortunately, they aren't here. Are you jealous now, my sweet?*
>
> *Ludwig called this morning. Finally. And then he called again. I met him in a restaurant on Schulstrasse, across from the camp, and read your postcard. What am I to write now? I want to die. Oh, I no longer want to live.*

On November 1 *Reichsführer-SS* Heinrich Himmler ordered all gassings at Auschwitz to cease and all traces of them to be destroyed.

On November 8 Ludwig Neustadt called to tell Lilly that Felice was no longer at Theresienstadt, but had been taken to a camp near Breslau.

On November 14 Lilly's parents received a letter from Felice postmarked Trachenberg, known today as Zmigród, located on the road between Wrocław and Rawicz:

November 3, 1944

Dear Parents,

I have not written for a long time, but I think I have a sufficient excuse. I also secretly suspect that you have long since forgotten me and are busy trying to get your daughter, my Aimée, married off to some gentleman—for four hundred Reichsmarks. Yes, well, I almost found myself in the position of never again being able to worry about it. But only almost, for the gods were otherwise disposed and put me in a proper hospital bed with a light case of scarlet fever, where I hope to remain until December 9. In addition, they sent me a good person, a man who is the janitor here and who is determined to help me whenever he can. I have requested that our former middleman send a package from Lilly to me in care of him. I didn't write to her myself, nor shall I, for I am afraid I will infect the children. (Though my skin is not peeling and I don't have a fever.) And secondly, I'm not sure where Lilly is. On October 9 an *Obersturmführer* in Theresienstadt asked me if I knew why she . . . etc., etc. They showed a great interest in her, and she may not know this. I'm asking you, dear parents, to give her the enclosed letter if possible, or to write to me (with no return address and indeterminate salutation) and tell me what is going on. I am understandably greatly concerned about wife and child—don't grin, Papa! I hope you both are well. Don't mention this letter to anyone but Lilly.

With Best Wishes and a Thousand Greetings! F—

November 3, 1944

My adorable kitten,

Barely does the Jaguar turn his back before you're up to such wild things that the evil hunter has already been asking Jaguar about you, and poor Jaguar can no longer sleep at night. He's had a very hard time of it, the noble Jaguar, and lost much of his beauty. You must have a new bracelet made for him from Grandmother's watch chain, and keep it for him until he returns! How good that pants, jackets, and curls have been recorded in photographs. Now sit down and write Jaguar a long and loving kitty letter. Without return address and in such a way that should someone else read it, he wouldn't be able to figure out who you and I are. Josef doesn't read the letters, the good man, so write a very, very sweet letter, do you hear? And tell no one that you have heard from me. Do you still love me now that my ears stick out and I have lung troubles? I'm so worried about you. That's the worst thing about all of this. Write a long letter! Kiss the children. A hug for you and "199,000" kisses from

Your Jaguar

Return add.: Josef Golombek, Municipal Hospital, Trachenberg, Silesia.

P.S. Even if you can't write more often, I hope to be able to.
Please include a few stamps.

Lilly had to smile. Felice with her ears sticking out! Felice
was always trying to hide her large and very pale ears behind
her hair, which was not exactly thick. It did not take long for
Lilly to discover this sensitive point. She had only to tuck Felice's hair behind her ears and say, "Grandmother?" and she
could be sure that the "little stick" would follow. Around New
Year's, when the needles had begun to drop off the Christmas
tree, Lilly had cut off the branches in order to burn them, with
Albrecht's enthusiastic assistance. But the trunk had been too
large to break into smaller pieces, so it had remained behind
the stove as a memento of Christmas.

"Albrecht, go get 'little stick,'" Felice would call when she
and Lilly had a fight. Lilly would take off screaming and bar-
ricade herself in the bedroom.

Several days after this first letter arrived from Silesia, Lilly
received another long letter, which had been written in several
installments in pencil on the lined squares of notepad paper.

November 7, 1944

Dear Aimée,

Surely your long letter will arrive today—it seems that
Josef delivers the mail around noon—and then I will send
this off later this evening. Yesterday the packages arrived
and I was so happy—about the letter, the one postmark,
and of course about the contents. The baked goods are so
wonderful! And your knitting as well! And you packed it

all so beautifully. And on the blue jacket—for which, if I am correct, I must thank Lola, and for a pair of socks as well—I found a red hair! I'll wrap it around my brown comb right away. Besides my toothbrush it is the only thing I have managed to save. The lock of hair I had wrapped around it before got lost when I was carrying the comb in the lining of my sleeve. When one is as poor as we, without even pockets on our coats, we stick our few possessions in our sleeves! My kitten, surely you sat up for many nights preparing all of this for me. And now I am sitting here wrapped in my checkered blanket, wearing my blue jacket, which smells wonderful, looking like "high up on the pasture where there is no sin," and I'm overjoyed at each new item! But I already have written all of this in the letter Ludwig will bring you, which certainly you will receive before this one. And now I am waiting for mail from you. Afterward, if something comes, I will continue this letter.

November 8, 1944

Nothing arrived yesterday. And today? Today for certain: There's so much I want to write you, my Eve Dolorosa. Are you indeed that, without me? But I don't know where to begin. My temperature has stayed above 101 for a few days now and I feel a bit funny in the head. I think about you constantly and worry about you. Are you doing all right with money? And nothing happens to you when the sirens go off? Are you eating properly? Are the children healthy? Have there—most importantly—been any unpleasant incidents, as it seems they aren't letting you out of their sight? I had no idea that one could think the same thoughts over and over again, day and night, month after month, recalling each little detail, isn't that so? Do you remember how nice it was in Caputh the first time, and how wonderfully silly we were, and how happy! And that evening in the hospital when your roommate was fast asleep and we didn't know it. And, and, and. Do you still say "mein liebes Herzchen?" How I would love to have some of those horrible, horrible herbs to eat that you put in the potato soup! Sometimes I think I never shall again. The chances are so slim. And I spend my sleepless nights reproaching myself for having gotten you mixed up with such an uncertain existence as mine. When I return I'll be arriving with a considerably advanced case of tuberculosis. Please, my kitten, please, should someone come along who is nice and wants to marry you, accept him. It has nothing to do with our love, which shall remain no matter what. After all, you have four small human beings depending on you, and your husband would surely allow you to take a trip with me now and then. My Aimée, don't be angry that I am writing this, but I can't sleep, I'm so busy thinking. You needn't be sad for me right now. I am doing excellently here. Everyone is nice, something we no longer were accustomed to, and we'll stay here until the ninth of December for sure. If I continue to have a temperature, perhaps it will be for even longer. I watch my temperature chart with dread every day now, hoping time will rush by and nothing will happen. Josef brings the mail in the evening, and then he always takes our letters away with him. Have I remembered to tell you that I love you? Yes, and I want you so. I wish you could take me in your arms and hold me tight and comfort me, and then everything would be all right. I want to be able to say "Sweetie-Pie" to you again. And Albrecht is three now. Has he finally been housebroken? You once listed Bernd as the sender of a package to me. I took that to mean that you have him at home again, and Lola's child as well. My poor dear. But you'll write me all about it, won't you? Is Gregor taking care of you? Not too well, hopefully! And what is Elenai up to? I want to know everything, but most of all how you are, and be honest, don't gloss over anything because you're afraid that I'll worry. For I worry anyway, my dear. Say hello to Madame Kummer for me! But don't mention me to anyone else, everyone should continue to think that I'm just not around anymore. I've decided to send this letter this evening no matter what, and to write another tomorrow in answer to yours. I embrace you and give you a thousand kisses.

Your True, Noble, Wounded Jaguar

When you get my next letter, answer it too, all right? Enclose photos of all of you. Have you developed the film from August 21? Hopefully your letter will arrive today.

November 9

No letter arrived! Today perhaps? I don't want to send this one until I've received yours. I'm not doing too well today. Perhaps I'll get my period one of these days; I haven't had it since Berlin. But it's the same with everyone; it's a symptom of detention. The bra fits wonderfully, it's only a bit large. A.S. [Aimée Schragenheim], my beloved. I don't feel like writing much today, I'd rather be answering your letter! You understand, don't you, that I am sharing the things you send with my friend? I understood that to be the reason you marked some things and not others. She's nice and has had a much harder time of it than I, for in B–, or A– [Birkenau or Auschwitz], it's the same thing. She was separated from her husband and doesn't even know if he's still alive. And she has no home anymore—she's from Amsterdam—and no one else in the world. It took great effort to convince Josef to accept three cookies and two pieces of cake, because he's always bringing us something. He says it's his duty to help us, he says he must and that he simply cannot accept anything for it. And now we eat all the time, and I'm terribly proud when the Dutchwoman, who is quite fussy, praises your creations. And they taste so-o-o good.

November 10

Yesterday nothing arrived from you in the mail. And today is almost over. We just got the results of our second swab test: negative. We'll have one more taken and if it too is negative then they'll send us away. So I was wrong about the six weeks, and I'm truly afraid that I'll be sent back to the camp. I feel like someone who has just managed to get his head above icy water only to be pushed back down into it again. But I'll only say that to you, for only my kitten may know that the brave Jaguar is afraid. Pray for him, all right?

November 11

No mail yesterday either! I no longer know what that means. Did your parents not receive my letter? If not—I'll mail this one today—write me a long, long letter right away, with pictures (and list the sender again as A. Karsten).

1069389056 kisses

from Jaguar

Your letter just arrived!!!

Lilly's answer to this letter never reached Felice. It was written in Felice's green ink on Felice's brown stationery, with the initials "F.S." printed at a slant at the top of the sheet. Lilly made a copy of it before taking it to the post office:

My Jaguar—do you recognize the stationery?

Well, I'm completely and totally Eve-Dolorosa without you; Eve has almost disappeared, only Dolorosa remains. Oh, my dearest, without you, every day without you! How many weeks is it now! I cannot live without love, of course, it is the essence of my life. There is room for nothing else in my thoughts. From morning to evening I live only with the hope of seeing you again. God cannot punish us in this way, we haven't even truly been given the chance to have a life yet, and we must be given that chance. Dear God, protect my love! It is unbearable; I tell you I won't survive it! I cannot live without you, I cannot G. probably will not return either. Am I—I know it shows a lack of character to say so—to go through life suffering? That is why I am pleading with you: Do not lose courage. I beg of you a million times: Keep alive the hope that we will see each other again. It's the only thing that makes life bearable for us. I know only too well that I am asking the near-impossible of you—I could scream, scream for hours and blame mankind—what it is doing to you drives me to despair. But please, please, you who are so passionately loved, you must hope, hope, hope. . . . I am praying for you, for us all, with each breath I take! My heart has been reduced to a trembling mass. How I wept at your letter, dearest, I cannot read it without tears. If only I could hold you in my arms, stroke you, kiss you! Things are so terribly hard without having you near to keep me calm.

L. is at home, what do you say to that? Her mother fetched her from the maternity home—she wasn't doing well there, so now she's home—with her baby. It was so sudden! . . . I have decided to give up another room. I won't make hardly anything from it, but I won't have to starve, and I can't go to work. Nor do I welcome the idea, for I'm not well. Yes, my dear, physically I'm doing very, very poorly, and would collapse for sure before two weeks went by. You needn't worry about me, I'm not nearly as ill as you, not nearly. And if the two of us survive we'll have to nurse each other back to health, isn't that so? We'll have so much to make up for. Dearest, we must have hope, my sweet! You should not have me on your conscience, you silly thing you. Without you I would never have known what love is, what love is capable of. How happy we were, how happy! Do you remember how I rushed to meet you each time! Do you remember how your arm never went numb? Do you remember how, when we were first together, I always traced your mouth with my finger? Do you remember when and where I wore the yellow scarf on my head for the first time? That I always walked to meet you at the train station at night, and happily fell into your arms? Dear God, all of that cannot have ended, it cannot have! Remember how we lay around on Sunday mornings? Oh, I must love you, and only you, for eternity. It is my fate, a fate I gladly accept. And you—only me? You will love only me? I felt it that time at the hospital, when you came through the door and I said to you, "I'm so sick."

The jacket and socks are from E., not from L. Did you really not receive any of my cards? L. had a boy! N. could be healthier, why didn't she just stay there! E. is now a great comfort to me, I've gotten closer to her, you'd be surprised. But she is truly the only one who cares about me. She is a great comrade and more dependable to me in my sorrow than I ever could have imagined. I. is almost always in L., at a factory, and still terribly cheeky. E. always has a clear head, and I need that more than ever. . . . My parents say hello, and to keep your chin up. God, what do they know, they have no concept of what your life is like, or that of your friends. My God, how will I face Irene? But I won't do it without you. K. sends delightful cards, but unfortunately she misunderstood me, and wrote concerning some "Christmas family portrait" she wanted. I thought my heart would jump out of my chest when I read that yesterday. Our good Lu. didn't give me your letter, on top of which he maintained that you asked him to tear it up immediately. He calls faithfully, but I don't think he's completely honest with me. He truly wants the best for you. Am I really to blame for your present situation? I cannot believe that, even though my conscience troubles me constantly. If I didn't believe that you still need me I would have put an end to it all long ago. You can ask anyone who knows me, I was tired to death. But you still need me and I will be there for you to the end. We must have hope, for God's sake, we must hope and—pray. Don't lose courage; I will lose it with you if you do. Look, we've always said we belong among those people who somehow survive even the most horrible things. And we want to hold on to that belief, my beloved. At Lu.'s suggestion I'm sending you another package today. He shall too. J. should not be mad, but understand. Please do me the favor of eating everything right away. You don't know if you will still be there tomorrow, and then you will at least have something in your stomach. Divide it with your friend and give the unfortunate woman my best wishes. I could put my arms around J., even though he is a man. I agree with him completely, it is his duty! This time the torte I baked doesn't have a filling, but a lot of butter instead. I hope it tastes good! Please eat the sausage and the butter as quickly as possible, don't save anything, and ask J. if I can send something again. Hopefully! Nothing tastes good to me here if I think you are doing without. There's also a body-warmer in the package. You'll recognize what it's made of. I cut up the green pullover, it's so wonderfully warm; from the lower part I made the body-warmer, and from the sleeves I made the gloves. Aren't I clever? I did a lot of darning on them so no one could see how nice they are. You can undo it and then you'll have something to darn with. Anyone who takes a close look at them (and the colorful jacket!) will know that they're perfectly all right. But I was afraid they would take things away from you that didn't look mended. So wear them as they are, they'll be even warmer if you do. And write if there's anything you need. Oh, I do hope you'll be there for a long, long time. If only I could help, my darling! I'm so powerless! Please, please, write as much as you can. Am I permitted to write again? I want to just hide away on my birthday; it could have been so different. Oh, I can't think about it, thinking is so terribly painful. Are you allowed to keep the pictures? And which should I send? I carry the film and the briefcase (with everything of value to me in it—it's as full as it was in your best of times) with me always. I haven't developed the film yet, I'm afraid we'll be bombed out and they're so precious to me; will it hurt the film if it just lies around? Gregor is sweet, and Dörthe as well. Sometimes he's too sweet and then he gets mad because I'm so indisputably loyal to you. It's true, isn't it my love, that loyal people are necessary, too, to body and soul!

I live from one mail delivery to the next. If it's at all possible, write again very, very soon and tell me that you love me. Put your arms around me, and I will do the same, and remain

Your Beloved
and Eternal Kitten

Trachenberg Hospital, November 12, 1944

Dear Parents,

Many thanks for your nice letter. I hope that my request met with success and that I will now get news of everything, also of you. I'm doing very well. I no longer have a fever, only the skin on my fingers is peeling, and food tastes good again. It's just that everything moves so slowly. But I mustn't be impatient. Nevertheless, I was so sure I'd be returning by the twenty-fourth of November. And it doesn't look as if that will happen. That's terribly sad, don't you think? Be well and accept my best wishes and kisses!

F.

November 12, 1944

My Aimée,

Your letter arrived yesterday, it had been opened by the censor! But the censor probably thought: That is a truly fortunate man, to be so loved! *Du*, your letter is so wonderful. But please, please answer all of my questions. It's all right to be cautious, but not that cautious! No, I want to know whom you have rented which room to, what you do all day, whether Gregor comes by often, whom else you talk to, what Madame Kummer has to say in her letters, what the children and our parents are doing, whether Lola had a girl, what you did about Mutti and the coat, and everything, everything else. I want to know everything, do you hear! And while we're at it, why the big bad wolf attacked Little Red Riding

Hood, and then wanted to ask me so many questions.

If you aren't using it for something, please send Inge's blue wool dress, all right? It could be sent as a sixty-pfennig letter, surely. And from now on always give a return address, as you did on your recent package. And then please, please, a few photos, and answer all my questions.

By the way, Josef spoke with the head nurse, and she says we will stay here for six weeks, we've been granted a temporary reprieve, that is, until December 9. So I'll be writing often. As my skin is peeling I prefer not to send the letters directly to you. That worked before. Be brave, my sweet. Then you'll get a long kiss, and can give the children some of it,

from Jaguar

If it's not too much trouble, and if you have any, could you send a little sausage or cheese? I'm shameless, aren't I?

On November 14 or 15, 1944, Felice found just enough time to write a few words on a scrap of paper in a shaky hand before she was taken away:

My Beloved,
The nurse just came in and said we're being taken away. Pray for me and keep your fingers crossed!

Always, Your
F—

Lilly's diary, November 17, 1944:

> *It wasn't supposed to happen: You're back in the camp.*
> *My poor, poor dear. You can't have recuperated fully.*
> *When I received your second long letter of November 14*
> *I cried all day long. I am terribly, profoundly afraid. You*
> *must not lose courage, my beloved. You must have hope,*
> *I'm praying for you day and night. . . . If only this were*
> *a dream. Where are you now? What are they doing to*
> *you again? And when will I have news from you? How*
> *awful that you didn't receive my second package. I was so*
> *looking forward to knowing that you finally had enough*
> *to eat. Is there a God?*

Two letters that Lilly wrote to Josef Golombek on November 14 and 18 came back to Berlin covered with stamps.
"Acceptance Refused" was written in thick blue letters on one
of the two envelopes. As Lilly listed neither her real name nor
address on the envelope, the letters were sent back and forth
across Berlin for a while until, in mid-December, they finally
landed *poste restante* in Berlin-Wilmersdorf, with the notice:
Forwarding address unknown.

EIGHT

Felice was taken to the Gross-Rosen concentration camp. Gross-Rosen was a huge complex of work camps that stretched across Lower Silesia, Sudentenland, and the eastern part of what was to become the GDR. The Lower Silesian village of Rogoźnica itself was located sixty kilometers from Wrocław (Breslau). The camp, which was owned by DEST, the German Excavation and Stone Works, Inc., had been established in May 1939 near the granite quarry of Gross-Rosen. Opened on August 2, 1940, as headquarters of the Sachsenhausen concentration camp, it became a separate camp on May 1 of the following year, with a series of "external camp detachments," or subcamps, engaged in labor for major German industrial firms.

Either factories were established close to the camps or the external detachments were located in proximity to the armament factories. Each of these subcamps maintained a "prisoner force" of several hundred slave laborers, but in most cases a thousand or many more prisoners were involved. In the final two years of the war more and more of these subcamps were established, so that there were about a hundred such units on record.

They produced goods for the German industrial firms of Rheinmetall-Borsig, IG-Farben, Siemens-Halske, the FAMO (Vehicle and Motor) Works, Dynamit Nobel, Vereinigte Deutsche Metallwerke, Krupp, Vereinigte Textilwerke, the aircraft works of Aerobau, the Concordia Spinning Mill and many others. Unskilled laborers were paid four Reichsmarks a day, skilled laborers six Reichsmarks. In December 1944 a net surplus of roughly thirty million Reichsmarks was transferred to Berlin.

A total of roughly 130,000 prisoners passed through Gross-Rosen, forty to fifty thousand of whom died at the camp or during evacuation. The concentration camp of Gross-Rosen was also used by the Breslau Gestapo for executions. All files on prisoners who died there were burned in early 1945.

After the SS reorganized its method for exploiting Jewish labor, and due to the evacuations of the Płaszów and Auschwitz-Birkenau camps, more and more Jews were brought to Gross-Rosen starting in late 1943. When the work camps of "Organization Schmelt" were integrated into the Gross-Rosen camp complex, the "supply" of women continued without interruption until January 1945: Jewish women especially from Poland and Hungary, but also from Romania, Austria, Yugoslavia, Belgium, and France, as well as from Czechoslovakia, the Netherlands, and—like Felice—from the German

Reich. They were assigned especially to the external camp detachments, forty-six in all, of which four were mixed sex. On January 1, 1945, there were roughly eighty thousand prisoners in the entire Gross-Rosen system, 26,000 of whom were Jewish women. Like Buchenwald and Stutthof, Gross-Rosen was among the camps with a large share of female prisoners in their subcamps. Many of the women's camps served the textile industry, others were created for Jewish women who—like Felice—were put to work building fortifications at the eastern border of the province of Lower Silesia. In January and February 1945 about half of the prisoners in the women's subcamps were marched into the interior of the German Reich to Bergen-Belsen, Buchenwald, Flossenbürg, Mauthausen, and Dora-Mittelbau. An unknown number of women unable to continue on the death march were shot along the way or froze to death. A larger group of prisoners on the death march managed to escape one night. Those who were left behind because they were sick, and who were not shot—as in Kurzbach—were liberated by the Red Army on May 8 and 9, 1945.

Little has been written on Gross-Rosen, and nothing at all on the women's camps. "The fate of the women of Gross-Rosen, now there's a topic! There's not one book on it, not one study," Mieczysław Mołdawa, former inmate and author of a work on Gross-Rosen, wrote to me from Warsaw.

At the end of February 1944 Stella Leibler, a Polish stenographer, was brought to the women's branch camp of Peterswaldau bei Wałbrzych (Waldenburg). Today Wałbrzych houses the small archive of the Gross-Rosen camp.

Stella Leibler:

Peterswaldau was not yet a concentration camp when we arrived there. It was housed in the servants' quarters of a castle belonging to a Count von Frick. We slept in two-tiered bunk beds and there were lockers in the corridors, half a locker to each person.

On the day after our arrival we were taken to an arms factory. I had just gotten over a case of typhus a short time before and was very weak and afraid that I would be given work where I would have to stand all day. I was assigned to a machine that stamped out directional pointers. To stamp the aluminum pointers I had to use all the strength in both my hands to press a lever. But that wasn't the heaviest work. The room also contained machines operated by girls who had to stand as they worked, and these machines manufactured bomb parts. Even heavier was the work in the section where so-called "bomb bodies" were bathed in acid. This labor was so hazardous to your health that the girls who worked there were even given milk to drink. Sometimes we had to carry the crates with the finished parts to the castle's chapel, where they were stored. The crates were so heavy that we sometimes almost fainted before we got there.

The rations they gave us were just enough to starve on: one-third of a loaf of black bread each day, a little piece of margarine, a little piece of sausage, cheese or marmalade, or a heavy black syrup made of beets. At noon we got half a bowl of vegetable soup.

One day a doctor arrived. We had to strip naked so that he could determine whether or not we would be allowed

to remain at the camp. Several days later an officer of the
Wehrmacht arrived in the company of female guards who
collected all of our valuables. Even our suitcases were taken
from us. We were issued one change of underwear and outer
garment and assigned numbers. My number was 26,764.
That's when hell began. When we needed to relieve ourselves
we had to stand at attention and say, "Frau Guard, may I be
excused?" Whether or not we were allowed to go depended
entirely on her mood; several times the foreman had to inter-
vene. The guards beat us.

One day we returned from work in a pouring rain. We
reported for roll call on entering the camp and waited for the
guard who had the authority to dismiss us. It's hard to say how
long we stood there, perhaps an hour or so, maybe an hour
and a half. When finally we were dismissed we had to help
each other pull our feet out of the mud. It was as if we had
taken root there. We had to hold each other up, we were so
weak from standing in the pouring rain.

A *Scharführer* from Auschwitz once came to the camp for
two weeks, and that is how we found out about the extent of
the suffering there. On Sundays, the only day we could spend
the whole day in camp, they held drills. It is a sign of how bad
things were that during this period two girls ran away and
two others had their heads shaved. One of them had become
friends with a German woman who sat next to her at the factory, and the other girl, a heavy smoker, had given a note to a
worker who wasn't an inmate, asking for a pack of cigarettes.

After some time went by—it was August of 1944—we
were transferred from the castle to a building that formerly

had been a spinning or weaving mill. Our place in the count's castle was taken by men and women who had been brought to Peterswaldau from Warsaw, following the Warsaw uprising. The mill had once belonged to a Jew named Zwanziger. It was a bleak building with a courtyard. For lack of space we were put in bunk beds three high, and there were no lockers at all. We kept our change of underclothes and outer garment, along with our ration of bread, under the straw sacks we slept on. The toilets were located in the courtyard. We were locked in at night and couldn't get to the toilets, so they gave us one single bucket to share, which of course was insufficient for a roomful of twenty women. It is difficult for me to describe what we had to go through in order to hold out until morning.

Activity at the factory was frenzied, and a night shift was introduced. One day as we were leaving the factory to report for roll call, a colleague stumbled and sprained her foot. I ran over to help her when one of the women guards rushed up to me and began beating me on the back with her fists. Everything went black, and I was half-unconscious from the pain when I took my place in line.

In the fourteen months I spent at the camp, three or four transports left from there to go to Gross-Rosen. One of them never arrived. They had ordered all those too weak to walk to report for transport, to take them to a "sanatorium," they said. Those who reported were old women and girls who were totally exhausted, and they took these women out to a field and shot them.

Each day before we entered the munitions factory we went down a steep stone stairway to the cloakroom where we hung up our coats. On frosty days these steps were covered in ice. The female guards made a game of pushing the girls down the steps.

Due to a shortage of materials less and less work was being done in the munitions factories. The heavy machines were oiled and ready for transport. There was a rumor that we would be sent to work underground, where the work conditions were inhuman. The rumor was that after two months we would go blind, and then we would be shot.

Meanwhile, my health was getting worse. I once suffered a weak spell while I was working and my Kapo led me out to the corridor, and allowed me to sit on a windowsill. The guard came down the steps and said, "Well, what are you two doing here?" My Kapo said, "If you felt like she does, you'd sit down too." The guard jumped on her at this and began hitting her with her fists. My Kapo—Jetka Ringer, from Auschwitz—was a good person, she never yelled. She did what she could to help us, within the realm of the possible. The head Kapo was a beast. She screamed and beat us and kicked us.

Later I became seriously ill. I could hardly drag myself back to the camp. After a doctor examined me she complained, "You wait to come to me until you're almost dead, how am I supposed to help you then?" She sent me to an infirmary where I stayed for a few days until I felt better.

In the meantime the front was moving ever closer. They began digging trenches as a defense against the tanks, and the women inmates were supposed to help with this. They lined us up in rows of four. Two women—the Jewish elder and the doctor—walked down the rows and weeded out those who were too weak. I was among them. When they counted us it turned out that one of us had to go back and join the others; they had dismissed one too many of us. Despite my weakened condition I volunteered, and off we marched. We passed through some city or other, maybe it was Reichenbach, which is called Dzierżoniów today. You could see the fighting from there. We saw one building that had been cut in two by a bomb, you could see inside the rooms. This foot march was my final feat. We were not taken back to work in the factory, but they made us do one more thing. We had to throw crates of bombs—bombs we had made—into a pond so that they wouldn't fall into enemy hands. That was a happy day for us.

Unfortunately, I was not only unable to lift the crates, I couldn't even walk. How many of the girls died? One died during inspection call, and she immediately was carried away. Now that liberation was near more than one of us was on her way to the grave. And then something happened that was a first in the history of the concentration camps. An utterly exhausted woman by the name of Freda Lieberman, who held a master's degree in German, was transferred to a convent a few weeks before liberation. Who had authorized this? It could only have been the camp commandant.

So wrote Stella Leibler in a letter to me dated June 10, 1992. However, things were actually very different. Freda Lieberman, a Germanist, was born in 1914 in Trzebinia. Her name is now Friederike Cohensius and she lives in Nahariya, Israel. She wrote to me the following description of her stay in Peterswaldau:

We had to do heavy work in a factory. Working and starving. One day I fainted and was brought to the infirmary. When I opened my eyes it was dark and then I heard a voice: "Don't be afraid, we just want to do some experiments." I was laid naked on a table and then the pain started. Injections, taking blood. . . . I am not able to describe what I went through. The man was wearing a white smock and his assistant called him Dr. Wagner. It is important for science, he said. The Germans were notorious liars and invented the story about the convent in order to explain my disappearance to the other slave laborers.

When the remaining prisoners in the camp were liberated, Freda Lieberman was found on a cot, unable to move, and brought to the hospital in Wałbrzych. After recovering she stayed in Wałbrzych and spent two years working there as the director of the Department for Education and Culture. In this position she was responsible for the city's first Polish schools, libraries, cinemas, theaters, and newspapers. She became an honorary citizen of the city in 1997.

Felice arrived at Auschwitz from Theresienstadt on October 9, 1944. It was a time when Jewish workers were in great demand by the war industry, so policies dictating their extermination were coming to an end. On October 7 a desperate *Sonderkommando* armed with explosives, three hand grenades, and insulated flat-nose pliers to cut through the barbed wire dared to stage an uprising at Auschwitz. Crematorium III was set on

290 · Erica Fischer

fire and 450 camp inmates and three SS men were killed. Four women who worked in the Union factory and had supplied the commando with the explosives were publicly hanged.

In Auschwitz the women had to undress and were given new clothes. Beate Mohr, who Felice knew from Theresienstadt—and who now lives in San Francisco—received an evening gown. It got shorter and shorter every day, since she tore strips off bit by bit to use the fabric as toilet paper. The women's heads were shaved and they were given a prisoner number, which was used from then on instead of their name.

After one week, Felice and Beate, as young women classified as fit for work, were forced to take a two-week-long foot march to Gross-Rosen, and from there, together with a thousand others, to the women's subcamp at Kurzbach (Buckolowe), about fifty kilometers north of Wrocław. Most of the women were Hungarian, Slovakian, and Romanian Jews who had been in Auschwitz since early summer 1944. There was also a group of women made up of Polish Jews from the Lodz ghetto, as well as Dutch, Czech, Austrian, and German Jews, most of whom had been deported from Theresienstadt to Auschwitz in October 1944. They were housed in two former stables of the Hatzfeld Palace. The buildings were surrounded by barbed wire and provided the most primitive lodgings. The infirmary was located in a smaller building, the former pigsty. There were quite a few mothers and daughters in the camp together. The prisoners did not wear prisoners' uniforms, but light civilian clothing. In order to make it difficult to escape, the clothes were marked with oil paint on the back. To protect themselves from the severe cold the women draped themselves in blankets during the day; at night they were damp and didn't keep them warm. Many women were given only paper sacks to use as blankets at night. They wore wooden clogs. Each day the prisoners received a bit of soup, bread, and coffee. Two Hungarian farmers taught Felice and Beate how to ration the meager portions of bread. One of them even had a knife. She cut the bread into thin slices and chewed very slowly. Those who gobbled down their bread quickly had worse chances of survival. Sometimes they also received raw meat, from which it was easy to get sick. And now and then they got a bit of jam.

The Todt Organization gave them their instructions and oversaw their work. The prisoners were assigned to groups of one hundred women each. After a long march of several kilometers to get to work, the women had to cut down trees and dig tank ditches using primitive tools. The frozen ground in winter made this a murderous ordeal without any prospects of success. Malnourishment, cold, abuse, and the exhausting work caused many women to become unable to work, and the infirmary was overflowing. An unknown number of women died in the camp. Their bodies were carried in a cart to a forest near Książęca Wieś, where they were buried.

Ruth Klüger, a Viennese Jew living in California and Göttingen today, has written in her 1992 book, *weiter leben* [English: Ruth Kluger, *Still Alive: A Holocaust Girlhood Remembered* (New York: Feminist Press at the City University of New York, 2001)], about the time she spent at Christianstadt, a subcamp of Gross-Rosen. The camp lay in the vicinity of the eastern German city of Guben, and supplied female slave laborers to the Dynamit Nobel firm. Nevertheless, for twelve-year-old Ruth, who was sent there only because she claimed during a "selection" at Auschwitz that she was fifteen, the labor camp gave her a chance to escape the sure death that had been awaiting her. At Christianstadt she slept with her mother in a green barracks that had been divided into rooms, each room housing six to twelve women. Occasionally a prisoner was punished by having her hair shorn, but generally, she wrote, the female personnel at the camp were not as brutal as the men of the SS.

The winter of 1944–45 was a particularly cold one. Mornings, Ruth and the other women were wakened by sirens and had to report for roll call in the dark. They were given a black brew that only resembled coffee and a piece of bread to take with them, and then were marched off in rows of three. A guard walked beside them, attempting to keep the women in step with her whistle. All of the women were so undernourished that none of them menstruated, a fact Felice had mentioned in one of her letters.

The women of Christianstadt worked clearing forests. They dug up the stumps of felled trees and carried them away, split wood and hauled rails. Occasionally they were loaned out to the civilian population to sit in attics and arrange rows of onions to be braided with string. The villagers stared at them as if they were wild animals. Ruth sometimes had to work in the quarry at Gross-Rosen, where her thin clothing offered little protection against the terribly bitter cold. She wrapped her feet in newspaper, which helped somewhat, but the sores on her feet became infected. Later the women were given warmer clothing for the winter, chosen from a pile of bright things that probably had come from Auschwitz. They had to cut a piece out of the upper back of each item of clothing and sew a yellow patch in its place.

With the approach of the Soviet army in January, the women hoped that the Germans would simply surrender the camp to the Russians. Instead, the Germans evacuated the prisoners on foot. These deportations from one camp to another at the end of the war, writes Ruth Klüger in retrospect, often were not intended as death marches—it was just that the German organizational capacity had collapsed. Ruth and her mother were among those evacuated. Following an exhausting day's march, the SS, which was in charge, confiscated a barn, and the women passed the night there, crowded unbearably close together. On the second evening Ruth and her mother managed to escape.

Lilly hoped that Felice would be able to save herself in a similar fashion.

NINE

On December 8, 1944, Lilly received a summons bearing the round, terror-inspiring stamp of the Gestapo, ordering her to report to Jewish Section IV D1 at Französische Strasse 47 at noon on Wednesday, December 13. She decided to bring Bernd home from Thuringia, so that the children would not be separated in case she was detained after questioning. That Saturday evening Lilly set off for Meuselwitz, where she arrived at five in the morning. From there it was a forty-five minute walk to Zipsendorf.

Bernd Wust:

> When she picked me up she told me the others were already at home, and that the Russians were approaching and that was why we all needed to be together. But right after that she started with the story of Felice. That's all she talked about for the half-hour or hour it took us to walk through the village and back to the train station in Meuselwitz. There weren't many people on the street there either, three or four maybe.

It was a small village with one main road, the way villages are in Thuringia and Saxony. I remember Mutti talking about Felice in a loud voice, and suddenly I said, "Oh God, someone's coming!" And Mutti answered, "Oh, nonsense!" Then she told me about the Jews and why Felice was taken away. Then when we got home to Schmargendorf she spent the next few days telling me everything there was to tell. Christians were no good, just look at the Nazis, that sort of thing. She suddenly had decided that we all should be Jews, if not from birth then somehow. To me, everything was happening very quickly, I was shocked, actually. We had teachers in Thuringia who were 150 percent Nazi. We—the whole class—marched to sports class to the accompaniment of Wehrmacht songs; we thought that was great, and we played army sometimes, too. But I had begun to notice certain discrepancies: The Führer was winning, yet we were being bombed. The fact that the Russians were approaching was for me, as a ten-year-old, a fluke; the Führer in his wisdom was giving them a little rope, he would be victorious in the end. Then they told us about the V-weapons. We thought that was great. But then the bombs started falling, and we were in a lignite mining area, Leuna wasn't far. So, well, there we were, standing in the fields saying, what happened to the German defense? What happened to our secret weapon? The sky was filled with American planes, the entire horizon, with a few flak planes in between, and once in a while an American plane would crash. Well fine, we were glad about that of course, but somehow. . . . And when as a ten-year-old I would carry on about the Führer to the shopkeepers and the neighbors, well, even a child could tell they weren't sincere in what they were saying, they had their reservations. And I felt that perhaps. So when Mutti told me the whole story I was . . . naturally I was horrified at first, but God, it was also very exciting because I knew it was dangerous. It was a game to me.

When Lilly's friends found out about her Gestapo summons it affirmed their opinion that her trip to Theresienstadt had been sheer madness, and perhaps had even played a role in Felice's being deported to the East. Lilly's parents prepared to take the four children into their home. Everyone was in a state of upset except Lilly. "I don't know how it is that at the moment of greatest danger I can keep my wits about me," she wrote in her diary. "It is not only Felice who has nerves of steel."

That Wednesday Lilly wore the blue ensemble that Felice had commissioned Käthe Herrmann's father in Königs Wusterhausen to make for her. She put on Felice's blue cloth coat with the faux pockets and proceeded to the Gestapo office on Französische Strasse, around the corner from the Deutsche Bank on Behrenstrasse where her father worked. But before she went she gave the folder with Felice's papers and her own diary to Elenai, who, to Lilly's surprise, had stood by her in this period as no one else had. They agreed that Elenai would wait for Lilly in the bar opposite the Gestapo building. If Lilly did not return from the interrogation Elenai was to take the documents to Inge in Lübben. But the air raid sirens went off and Elenai could not stay there any longer, so she went to her apartment near Nollendorfplatz and waited impatiently until

Lilly's call finally came. Bernd, well aware of his responsibility, stayed at home with his three younger brothers, all of whom were down with chicken pox. When Lilly returned home he was standing in the doorway, white as a sheet and armed with a child's rake, exhausted but proud.

Lilly's diary, December 18, 1944:

> *They grilled me for four long hours, tormenting me with their questions. An air raid warning sounded for a half-hour in the middle of it all, but the beasts wouldn't let me out of their clutches, though they knew that my children were sick and at home alone. I was so afraid! Several times they said to me, "Well, that's what you get." Oh, my sweet thing, what is any of that compared with you. First they took down my whole life story and then went over our entire history from beginning to end. Questions, nothing but questions. Insidious, nasty, spiteful, friendly, calculatedly well-meaning and base questions, questions, questions, threats, threats and promises. I think you would have been proud of your Aimée. She stood the test well.*

As Lilly was climbing the narrow marble steps of the rust-red building in Berlin's banking quarter, her summons clutched in her hand, she encountered a Jewish *Ordner* she knew from Schulstrasse as he was dragging a wooden bench out of an office on the second floor. He didn't say a word, but turned pale and gave her a frightened look. Since March 1943 the Gestapo's Jewish Section IV D1 had been housed behind barred doors on the third floor of the elegant, four-story, turn-of-the-century buildings, its eaves embellished with grape-bearing cherubs. The Jewish Section handled the cases of Jews who had gone underground, or of Aryans who had "aided and abetted" Jews. The brown-paneled interrogation room measured roughly thirty square meters in size. To the right of the door sat a police officer whose job it was to arrest her, she was later told with pleasure. Through the half-open sliding door leading to the next room Lilly could make out a large group of men in uniforms. Five men took part in the interrogation, and a crude blond woman with red cheeks recorded the proceedings on a typewriter. The cardigan she was wearing was fastened appropriately with iron crosses.

Now and then she stood up from the table as if so indignant that she could no longer contain herself. "God, your poor unfortunate children!" she would sigh, her eyes upcast for effect.

Lilly was forced to talk about her friendship with Felice. She had met Felice at the beginning of December 1942, at the Café Berlin, she said truthfully, leaving Inge out of the story. They had met several times after that to go out together. Felice later had visited Lilly at home; Lilly had never been to Felice's home. She lived with acquaintances; Lilly did not know the address. No, they weren't Jews, as far as she knew. Felice had told her that she worked in Babelsberg. What kind of work did she do? Lilly had no idea. Then Felice moved in with her, first for a few days and then on April 2 for good. Lilly had neglected to register this officially, believing it wasn't necessary to do so with friends. Felice was not a subtenant, after all, but her friend. The Gestapo cross-examined Lilly on the registration issue for half an hour.

"You knew Schragenheim was a Jew. You did know. Talk!" they shouted at her. Lilly hadn't known, she said.

Lilly was astounded to discover that, rather than being afraid, she was totally alert. She needed to remain vigilant to perceive the traps they were setting for her; she could not afford to be inattentive. One careless answer and she, and Felice and their friends, would be done for.

"I got to know and love my friend as a person, and only found out who she really was on August 21," Lilly stated, repeating what she had said at Theresienstadt.

Felice worked sporadically, Lilly told them, but was seldom at home. She gave Lilly coupons for butter now and then, but not regularly. Where did Felice get the coupons, they wanted to know. "She didn't get them from the block warden," Lilly answered, thinking, *"nebbish."* Felice also had travel coupons and money. From where? No idea. She didn't pay rent, but when she went shopping with Lilly's ration cards she often brought back toys for the children. Did she have friends? Jewish friends? "Listen, there's a war on. With four children I have more than enough to do without prying into other people's affairs."

And then the woman with the iron crosses on her cardigan got up from her typewriter and went over to the table where the chief interrogator, who was named Burchard or something similar, was seated, and whispered to him. Then she bent down to Lilly while Burchard pretended to organize his papers.

"You didn't have sexual relations with the Jewess, did

you?" she asked in a soft, confidential voice. "No," Lilly replied incredulously, with an uncomprehending smile.

"There was no question of lesbian love between us," was the answer recorded in the protocol.

Then Lilly had to recount the events of August 21.

"How did you know that Schragenheim—don't always refer to her as your friend, I will not tolerate it—was at the Schulstrasse camp?"

"From acquaintances."

"Jews, in all probability."

"How would I be able to tell?"

They then made threats against those acquaintances who had revealed that Felice was on Schulstrasse. Lilly told them about Titze and that she was at the Schulstrasse address five times in order to take Felice a few items of food and clothing. Her interrogators seemed to know exactly how many times Lilly had visited Felice.

"What were you thinking? By then you knew that she was a Jew. You knew it by then."

"Who told you that Schragenheim was being sent to Theresienstadt?"

One of the police officers on duty mentioned in passing that she might have been sent there, Lilly answered.

Did she know where Felice was at the present time?

No.

So then what happened?

So then on September 28 she went to Theresienstadt.

There was a great deal of murmuring at this among Lilly's interrogators.

"Something like this is totally outside our experience—
you just up and follow a Jew, of all people, to Theresienstadt,
and with a general travel ban in effect. What did you do there?
Tell us!"

The Czech military guards probably assumed that she
wanted to speak with the *Hauptsturmführer* personally, Lilly
said, and that's why they allowed her through the blockades.

"And then?"

"After five minutes of conversation with him I was back
outside."

"We're happy to hear that."

In the middle of the interrogation the sirens went off and
everyone rushed to the cellar except Lilly, who was told to
leave the room and wait on a bench outside.

Once the interrogation resumed, she was asked about the
acquaintance she had traveled with. Lilly didn't know whether
or not they had been to Brünn asking questions about Lola.

She had just wanted to take a few items of clothing and
some food to her friend in Theresienstadt, Lilly answered.

"Where did you actually get all this food?"

They knew all about the packages she had sent to Felice
daily. She answered that she had written to Felice approximately five times. Then Lilly spied several of her own postcards
to Jaguar in the thick file on the desk, Jaguar's green ink was
unmistakable. So Felice had never gotten her cards.

"So by then you knew precisely that . . ." [" . . . namely,
that you are a totally enchanting Jewish girl," Lilly added in
her diary.]

Lilly then told them that after that, she had heard nothing

further from Felice. What excuse did Lilly have to offer for herself, she was asked.

"It was terrible for me that my best friend—"

"I will not tolerate that!"

"—was taken from me like that. My children loved her very much as well."

Then the topic of Lilly's divorce came up, divorce from a poor unfortunate soldier fighting at the front.

"Don't think for a minute that we believe you. Schragenheim told us something else entirely. There's no reason for her to protect you anymore."

Lilly stuck to her story. In the end Burchard left the room to consult with the group of men. Following a good deal of loud chatter, they all coursed into the room, and Lilly had to sign a paper stating that because she had befriended a Jew she actually belonged in a concentration camp, but that due to her four children who were dependent on her . . . and that if there were even the slightest impropriety in the future, a concentration camp was exactly where she would be sent, etc., etc. Lilly could feel that the Nazi henchmen were furious at her composure, even as they threatened to send her to a concentration camp. And then—after a great deal of being sent back and forth from one room to another—she was actually allowed to go home.

"—only out of consideration for your poor, innocent children."

"And you've probably never heard of the words 'National Socialism' either!" one of them bellowed at her as she left.

Lilly's parents, too, accused their daughter of lacking a sense of responsibility toward her children. This led to a huge family altercation, as a result of which the Kapplers forbade her any further contact with her friends.

Lilly was placed under police surveillance. "Fine, I consider it an honor," she wrote in her diary. She had to report to her local police station at the Schmargendorf town hall on Berkaer Platz every other day.

"Why do you have to report here?" she was asked by the officer on duty at her first visit on December 14.

"Don't you know?" Lilly answered, undaunted, and refused to say. Let him find out for himself if he was so interested. She wasn't afraid of this man with the fat stomach; he lived in the building next door to her and was a painter by profession.

On her fifth visit it occurred to her to have the date and exact time of her appearances documented. Who knew what it might be good for in the future?

"It's not customary," the fat man said.

"The Gestapo told me to do so," Lilly lied.

Lilly was accompanied to the police station by her eldest son, who was already grown up enough to offer her his protection.

"Heil Hitler!" Bernd would say, standing rigidly at attention as he had learned in school.

"You can say 'Good day.' That's what you say at home, isn't it?" the man behind the desk growled irritably.

When Lilly answered the phone at home the line would crackle. She advised her friends not to visit for a while.

On January 5, 1945, seven men and seven women were deported from Berlin to Auschwitz. It was on that day that Lilly finally received mail from Felice. The pale envelope with the round postmark dated January 3, 1945, bore the text: "Rawitsch— Old German City in the East—Gate to the Warthegau." It was addressed to her parents, in a child's neat, slanting script that Lilly was unfamiliar with, and contained two letters:

December 18, 1944

My Dearest,

A thousand Christmas greetings to you, your parents, and the children. I am well again, even despite the cold attic, and am still quite weak but "verra beesy." Unfortunately I never received your long letter, it wasn't in the cards. But tomorrow I'm going to T[rachenberg] for a delousing (but I don't have any!), and I hope to be able to mail this then. Please think of me always, and pray for the brave and yearning

Jaguar

December 26, 1944

My Dear Ones,

I'm going for a delousing—without lice—a second time so that I might tell you that a Christmas package arrived on the eighteenth, which unfortunately had been sent back and forth so much that all the food had spoiled. But the green gloves and the socks are wonderful, as are the chest protector and the shawl. And everything with "AS" [Aimée Schragenheim]! So I received something for Christmas after all, otherwise there was no sign of it here. I thank you a thousand times for everything, think of me always. I can put all of it to good use because I'm always outside and it has already dropped to fifty-nine degrees here. It's amazing what one is capable of, even without a Teddy coat and long pants. I love you very much. All my love to you, your parents, and the boys.

Kisses, kisses, kisses from

Jaguar

and Happy New Year.

On reading the passage about the delousing, Lilly sadly remembered a touching scene in the midst of her tears.

"I don't know why I itch so much," Felice had once complained. And in fact, to everyone's horror, she had lice! Someone from her circle of friends had loaned Felice a pair of pants, according to Felice, and now she was paying the price. Lilly had shaved Felice with Lola's help, and it was sweet how it embarrassed Felice.

Lilly's diary, January 5, 1945:

Your letter, you poor caged one, you. Now I can live again until your next letter. You shall return. I must be-

*lieve that, otherwise I'll lose my mind. My longing for
you makes my blood race through my veins all the faster.
I can almost touch you. Felice, I love you. And you? My
beautiful, clever girl. Unfortunately, the war is making
our situation wretched once again. It just won't come to
an end, and on top of that I'm in financial straits. I don't
want to touch the thousand marks, you might suddenly
need the money. Let's wait and see. I want to finish this
volume of my diary and take it to Inge in Lübben; I want
to be sure it's somewhere safe. Inge will pick me up at the
train station. She works there at a factory, and has to
stand at a machine all day. She was terribly unhappy at
first. Hopefully Elenai won't come with me. She recently
behaved quite badly to Frau Wolf.*

Reports were circulating that the camps in the East were
being closed down. Her head pounding, Lilly stuck pins in her
map of Europe denoting that the front was drawing ever nearer.

On January 25 at 2:45 p.m. she reported to the police for
the last time.

Lilly's diary, January 25, 1945:

*To think that you might already be safe. My God, what
hope. When will I hear from you again? Last week I sent
you a package, which you'll probably never get. Warm
stockings, warm underwear and woolen gloves. Never
mind. We're used to it, after all. I don't dare imagine*

how the snow is heaped up where you are, and the cold. They must not have had much time to think things over, their own people barely had time to make their getaway. Every day we hear the most horrible stories. Only yesterday they unloaded thirty-two people in Lübben who had frozen to death, and there were so many children among them. The children of the Führer. Unloading bodies has become part of the daily routine of every town of any size at all. Every single road to Frankfurt/Oder is blocked with people who are fleeing, with horses and wagons. Do you know what they say when they see the transports? "The Jews are coming." They come in freight cars, in open lorries. The Russian breakthrough has been going on for a week now, and everyone in Berlin is in a panic. The gas has been shut off completely. We're all supposed to share the stove for cooking, but what are we to cook with when there's so little coal to be had? I haven't received my ration for a long time now. And the lights are turned off with no warning beforehand. For hours. We can no longer write letters, only cards are permitted. Travel is out of the question, they won't let you go farther than seventy-five kilometers. Thank God I can get to Lübben. But express and local trains don't exist anymore, so I'll have to figure out how to get the things from Lübben. Better that the Russians pick me up with my things than pick up my things without me. Travel time on the S-Bahn, subway and streetcars is held to a minimum, so now the wait at the Schmargendorf station is truly enjoyable, my dearest!

*Between ten in the morning and two in the afternoon
practically nothing at all is moving. Each day the papers
bring new joys. My God, if only you were somewhere safe
and allowed to be a human being again.*

Lilly's diary, February 4, 1945:

*I was going to continue writing yesterday, but there was
a major bombing. The inner city got the rest of it. The
Potsdamer and Anhalter train stations, Alexanderplatz,
the Jannowitz Bridge, Witzleben, the Tempelhof airport.
There's nothing moving at all between Tempelhof and
Hermannplatz, and barricades have been set up everywhere. Nothing but piles of rubble. Nothing in our immediate vicinity was destroyed, thank God. My parents
and Nora and Elenai are fine, but I've heard not a peep
from the others. The telephone is out so we can't keep
in touch with each other. I haven't heard from Gregor
for a week; he's been bothered by a bad tooth. I've survived for you, my beloved. Today the wireless informed
us that due to the repatriation of* Volksgenossen *from
the Eastern territories, and the loss of these territories, it
will be necessary to introduce restrictions for the upcom-
ing ration periods 72 and 73. We are supposed to stretch
eight weeks' rations over nine weeks. As of tomorrow we'll
have only dried potatoes. When they start talking on the
radio about economizing . . .*

*Berlin resembles a frantic ant colony. Newspapers
and the radio report on the people's unshakable deter-*

mination to defend themselves, and say that the Volk *is standing behind its Führer. Yesterday Goebbels delivered a speech to Berliners, saying that it is the citizenry's first duty to stay calm, that there was absolutely no danger, and so forth. We get a new* Gauleiter *every day. Everything is quaking and creaking, our situation truly is serious. I want to save the canned goods I've put aside—you're not back yet—for an emergency. They're in the basement, where it's still cold. And finally, finally, peace seems nigh.*

"I'm deeply shaken," Lilly wrote in her diary on February 9. Since the end of October she had been going to the Mecklenburger Restaurant on evenings when she couldn't bear to stay at home, and there she had met the three mysterious and educated women who fascinated her in the same way Felice had at the Café Berlin. Only the eldest of them wore dresses, the other two were always attired in discreetly elegant outfits of English wool, their hair combed straight back from the face in the masculine style. Lilly particularly was drawn to the youngest of the three, who despite her severe features radiated softness.

"I'd like to get to know her," Lilly said to Gregor sometime during October 1944 over a bowl of soup at the Mecklenburger. Under the pretense of having left a glove behind, Lilly returned to the restaurant with Gregor and spoke to Petel.

Evening after evening they met there to discuss world literature, proceeding to the restaurant's air raid shelter when the sirens went off. On February 7, as they were all sitting in the shelter, Lilly invited the three ladies to visit her at home. Their reaction was more than subdued, which Lilly attributed to the fact that the youngest and eldest of the women didn't seem to get along. But the next day Katja, the small, third member of the group, who wore a pair of thick-lensed glasses, invited Lilly to a café on Heydenstrasse. The two women chatted about this and that until Katja put a direct question to Lilly.

"Tell me, little Pythia, you wouldn't be a spy by any chance, would you?"

This came as a total surprise to Lilly. Only a few days before she had talked more openly with the three women than was prudent. She had related an argument she had on the telephone with Christine Friedrichs's mother, who had accused Lilly of wanting to get rich on Jewish possessions when it was forbidden to own property belonging to Jews. And this because Lilly had wanted to pick up her own and Felice's clothing from the Friedrichs's house in Brandenburg. At which point in the story Lilly blurted out, "You will have figured out by now that my friend is Jewish."

The three women had exchanged knowing glances, and Lucie, the eldest, had said softly, "Either you don't know people very well, or you're still too young to comprehend such viciousness."

Lilly succeeded in allaying the suspicion her red hair had aroused: The three women had taken her for Stella Goldschlag—the Jewish "catcher" whose path Lilly had crossed on Schulstrasse. And Lilly finally discovered who Katja, Lucie and Petel were: Dr. Katja Laserstein, forty-five; Dr. Rose Ollendorf, known as Petel von Petrus, forty; and Lucie Friedlaender, fifty-one.

Lilly's diary, February 9, 1945:

The poor things. They're in the same situation as you, my sweet, only they've been in it longer. My God, there's someone I can help again. So you can see that I'm in the best of company. Something like this could only happen to me, to me of all people! With Berlin such a big city and so full of people. But I must get to know them! My God, the way these women survive. You were in heaven compared to them, despite everything. They live in a summerhouse and can only go in and out after dark. They wash in restaurants and discreetly dry their things on the chairs they're sitting on. All that is over now. They shall sleep in real beds again, and no longer have to wander from train station to café to restaurant and back again just in order to have some place to rest. Nor shall they have to sit on some cold park bench to pass the time somehow. I'll figure it out. Luckily, the war is almost over. The murderers are being forced to think of their own safety now. It will work out. I don't think they'll credit me with being that bold. I've been talking to everyone in the building about my cousins from Frankfurt who were bombed out and whom I now, unfortunately, have to take in. It must work.

The neighbors took no particular notice of Lilly's new guests. They had become accustomed to unusual behavior from her and, on top of this, they had other things to worry about. Preparations were being made for the final battle. All men who were still at home had to have a doctor attest to their fitness for the *Volkssturm*, a territorial militia of older men and young boys unsuited for regular military service. The city was teeming with refugees, Berliners were not mincing words about their true situation, and the police had ceased to interfere. Nevertheless, Katja, Petel, and Lucie avoided the air raid shelter in Lilly's building, returning now and then to their summerhouse on Wiesbadener Strasse to spend the night.

Lilly's diary, February 24, 1945:

> *The air raid alarm goes off twice a night, and there's always a lot going on. There's a considerable amount of shooting. I love you so much, Felice. I'm so lonely, though now I have people around me who are worthy of my love and care. I love you all the more through them. I'm so busy with them and never at home, as my friends justifiably complain. And yet I'm lonely. I yearn for you terribly. They understand my suffering best of all, for they are like us. You understand. They love one another and it makes me long for you more and more. You, my only beloved.*

Lilly's diary, February 28, 1945:

> *Gregor calls them "the witches." Though God knows, they're dear witches. Our life gets more and more difficult, there's no such thing as comfort anymore. The lights go off three times a day, and even in the evenings. Some-*

times the alarms sound when the lights are off and we then have to rush down to the basement in total darkness. Everyone is secretly grumbling. Even Frau Mory, Frau Eichmann's daughter, said, "Oh, it's not courage we lack, but the urge." Funny, isn't it?

My provisions are running out, see witches above. I have plenty of dried potatoes, but bread is in short supply. There are now eight of us living on five ration cards. I don't know what the next weeks will bring or what we will have to eat by then. I cook with gas despite the ban on it. Bernd and our guests need to eat, after all. I use the coal I have for the oven, and not for the communal stove as ordered. I have no intention of sitting around with the children in the cold of April.

Lilly's diary, March 9, 1945:

The alarm sounded at eight forty-five tonight. My three ladies had to disappear quickly. They really have to hurry because we don't want anyone in the building to run into them and subject them to any particular scrutiny. So at the first warning they duck into the nearest public basement. In a bunker they can ask you for papers. Usually I go with them, but sometimes I have to keep up pretenses and stay here and complain about my burdensome relatives. Everyone believes they truly are my relatives. The alarm goes off every evening, and sometimes at night. This is the seventeenth one today, just as we were preparing to drink our coffee. I baked a pudding cake in your honor [for Felice's birthday], and a nice potato salad, secretly at night, because the gas is on then. My witches are worthy stand-ins for my noble and oh so wild Jaguar. They're so nice to me, and all of their best wishes are with us.

Good Lord, they just laid down a bomb carpet some-where nearby. What a racket! Boy, oh boy. Everyone turned pale at that one. Say, was that a greeting from you? A little loud. And the ground wobbled and shook. The day before yesterday a card arrived from Emmi-Luise Kummer, as charming as ever. She wrote: God lives and will help. Will he, my sweet? The outlook for Berlin is less than rosy. If Berlin becomes a battlefield—and that it will be for certain, in the truest sense of the word—then we'll be in for something frightful.

On March 15, 1945, Irene Cahn believed her sister still to be in Theresienstadt. "I don't know if I mentioned that my parents-in-law, Paul and Eva Cahn, are in the same place as 'Lice, they even live at Bahnhofstrasse 25," she wrote to Emmi-Luise Kummer in Switzerland. "Is it possible that 'Lice knows them, and that my grandmother, who was also there, was able to see 'Lice?"

Lilly's diary, March 18, 1945:

Where? In the basement, of course. It's shortly after eight-thirty at night. Today we had a terrible attack, three thousand bombers over Berlin. It truly was the worst day of bombing yet. But thank God there was little sign of it where we are. We stood on the stone square that belongs to our building and saw the whole mess of them fly over. Almost like being at the theater. Flying silverfish. When they looked like they were get- ting too close we hurried back down to the basement. The distance is always deceptive, but unfortunately I saw two planes shot down. Herr and Frau Rauche and Herr Wendt wanted to kill the parachutists with their bare hands. Nice people, they are. God spare those poor men. Will Germans be received the same way in En- gland? Perhaps no one here will think of that. Hopefully there are good people there.

I'm in bed with a light flu. I look like I've been crying, and now and then when no one's looking I do cry. I feel so miserable, and there's no Felice to fight over pills with. Thirty weeks ago today we were forced apart. It will be March 29 soon, the day two years ago on which I wrote to you, blushing. "When shall be our wedding day?" And then April 2 will arrive. I so had hoped that Berlin would be showing another face by now. God knows why the Russians suddenly are taking their time in conquering Berlin. The war continues. The signs are mounting that the Thousand Year Reich is coming to an end, it's true. Rations have been curtailed greatly. We're often given lard instead of butter, and there have been no special rations despite the constant bombings. Every evening on the radio there's yet some-

one new championing Berlin. Every bridge in the city is barricaded and thousands of streets as well, to hamper an enemy breakthrough. Since the offensive began in the East, and particularly in the West, the Allies systematically have destroyed all of Germany's transportation routes, all the industrial storage and warehouses. A constant stream of bombs of every caliber falls continually on cities that are already terribly damaged. And now the war is coming so damned near. But it is lasting too long, much too long for those of us waiting for it to stop. All the men in Berlin have been called up for the so-called Volkssturm. *Last Sunday they were armed with antitank rocket launchers and had to swear an oath to the Führer. Bread supplies often run out by five in the afternoon, and an astounding number of people line up for rolls. Pastries are few and far between.*

Lilly's diary, April 4, 1945:

My God, it can't last much longer. It could be over any day now. One night recently the radio suddenly went off the air and we thought peace finally had arrived. We can barely rein in our impatience.

Dearest, for the last few days I can't get—you know— out of my head. Two years ago I was in urgent need of rest. And what did you do, you beast? Poor, ailing and weak Aimée hardly got any rest at all. How little sleep we got then; my heart races at the memory. Oh, Felice, you don't

*have any idea how you changed. A very self-confident,
yet inwardly lonely girl turned into a person who finally
knew where she belonged, who had a home and a family.
We grew, both of us together, drawn to each other like
magnets. On April 2, 1943, when we decided that we
wanted to stay together forever, neither of us knew we
couldn't escape our fate. We were in love, I shy and afraid
of the unknown, and you passionately resolute, but secretly
afraid that I would be shocked by my own behavior. At
that point you didn't want to trust how happy you were.
Oh, my beloved black-haired girl with your big ears.*

On April 10 Irene Cahn wrote a letter thanking Madame
Kummer for her efforts to get Felice to Switzerland, so that
Käte Schragenheim could then book her passage to Palestine.
Lilly, in one of her letters to Irene sent through Emmi-Luise
Kummer, apparently had told Irene about the difficulty she
was having getting Mutti to return Hulda Karewski's fur coat.
"The affair with the fur coat is a mystery to me," Irene wrote,
"but it's not really important. The person who has it should
just keep it."

Lilly's diary, April 10, 1945:

*Since April 9 we've had a new ration card system. Butter
has practically disappeared, now it's lard. We get 2,000
grams of bread a week, 250 grams of meat, 225 grams
of grain, 65.2 grams of cheese, 800 grams of marmalade
or 335 grams of sugar—but there is no sugar in period*

74—100 grams of ersatz coffee, 375 grams of lard. It has been stated explicitly that distributors are to weigh foodstuffs fairly, so that sometimes the rations we are due are not available. They're making marmalade out of all kinds of things now. My mother told me how to make it from beets, so we would have something to spread on bread. The bread ration of 500 grams per week for children under six is hardest. What can I do? I also have to consider my three ladies. I get queasy just thinking about it. My store of potatoes has been greatly reduced, and there's no more cereal at all. I've still got two pounds of flour and three cans of milk. I used up too much when my witches first arrived, and now I'm feeling it. I don't regret a minute of it, of course. Nevertheless, I get discouraged thinking about the immediate future. How am I to steer my little multitude into the promised peacetime if there's not enough to eat? The children say "Mutti, I'm hungry," often enough as it is. This wretched war, in addition to everything else we've got it to deal with. Who knows if we'll make it out of the war. And if we do, who knows if they will be able to tell the difference between us and the Volksgenossen. *My God, we've had it up to here with all of it, nor do we believe that people here will change. Heroic battles and anti-Semitism. Revolting. I no longer want to have anything to do with this Germany, thank you very much. Not with this one.*

On April 9 all public transportation ceased operation. On April 11 the Buchenwald concentration camp was turned over to U.S. troops. On April 13 the Red Army marched into Vienna.

Lilly's diary, April 13, 1945:

The Western Powers have reached Magdeburg. Hurrah. Who knows when they will get to Berlin. We have been told that Berlin, like all other cities, is to be defended down to the last stone, the last person. The Russians stopped at Küstrin and Frankfurt on the Oder. The Americans are right outside Leipzig, and according to reports yesterday, sixty kilometers from the Czech border. My God, what a snail's pace! Now I must abandon any hope of mail getting through. We truly are cut off from the outside world, surrounded by the enemy. I'm so anxious. If only it would go faster, come to an end. Perhaps you'll find us half-starved amid the ashes and ruins. Oh, my dearest, come for me. I'm so impatient, as are my witches. When Albrecht sees my crying he always says, "Mutti, Aunt Felice is coming back." He's learned how to say "Felice." You live in the hearts of my/our children. My dearest girl, I have your picture before me. I'm waiting for you. I cannot be without you.

Lilly's diary, April 15, 1945:

Will you ever read this diary? Who knows what will become of us. We have reached the decisive moment. The Russians are approaching from the East, the Anglo-

Americans are at the Elbe. Both are roughly the same distance from Berlin. Will Berlin become a battlefield? The Americans have already marched through Thuringia; it's fortunate that I got Bernd out of there. Now they're marching on Dresden. Germany has been divided into two parts. Hamburg and Bremen will be taken in the next few days. The Americans are also approaching Berlin from the direction of Celle. We're caught in a trap, it can't last much longer now. Even the worst Nazis are afraid. Let them be, I grant them that happily. Not one of those bigwigs should believe that he is safe from punishment. If there is any justice.

Today we were without electricity for a total of twelve hours, we were just now in the basement. We'll live in the basement like rats for the next few days until freedom comes. I've made a place for Bernd's cot down there, and that is where he and I sleep. The three little ones sleep together on one small children's bed, and my three ladies sleep in armchairs—Lucie, unfortunately, right in front of the cellar door. There simply was nowhere else to put her. Our suitcases and boxes are all piled up on top of each other. The air raid sirens go off almost constantly, and we are happy not to have to run out of the house schlepping suitcases back and forth. We're protected here only from bomb splinters, of course. But what does it matter, at least we're among ourselves, and don't have to listen to our neighbors' asinine talk. And thank God no one is interested in the eight of us, eagerly awaiting freedom as we are. But you must hurry if you wish to still find us.

Yesterday, in three waves of bombings, they totally destroyed beautiful Potsdam, which miraculously had been spared until then. I just heard Frau Mory and Frau Eichmann whispering: "I never would have believed it. That it has come to this. How awful." They were talking with worried expressions about the approach of the Russians and the anticipated major offensive against Berlin. My God, how these people deserve it! At every convenient, and inconvenient, opportunity they were always yapping, "It's all the fault of the Jews!" They think they know everything, and believe steadfastly in the Führer. And a fine Führer it is who allows all of Germany to go up in smoke because of his crackbrained schemes. His top party officials are bolting as far and as fast as they can. The German Volk *can die, for all they care, and it is dying.*

On April 16 the Red Army launched its major offensive against Berlin. In the Jewish collection camp on Schulstrasse, Walter Dobberke came to blows with two particularly fanatic members of the Gestapo, who were trying to carry out an order from the Reich Security Main Office calling for the execution of all patients remaining in the Jewish Hospital, some eight hundred in all. Dobberke managed to prevent this.

Lilly's diary, April 20, 1945:

My dear, is the hour of our reunion near? Since this morning all hell has broken loose. The Volkssturm *and all sol-*

*diers are to report to the Spandau district. As of tomorrow
all traffic will come to a total standstill. For two weeks
now as it is, commuter traffic was allowed only between
5:30 and 9 a.m., and between 4 and 6 p.m. All bicycles
have been expropriated, but not ours. I simply pretended
I wasn't home. I stood right inside the door for fifteen
minutes, shaking something awful. I have no intention
of surrendering your beloved bicycle, the one we battled
so fiercely for on August 23, 1944, the day of the interrogation at Schulstrasse. I'll throw my own bicycle in their
faces first. But not before I've smashed it half to bits.*

Lilly's diary, April 25, 1945:

*We're in a fine mess now, my sweet. So much has hap-
pened in the last few days I couldn't fit it all into this
diary for you. Last Friday I wrote that things were finally coming to a head. But it was only the Russians who
stormed Berlin. Where are the Americans? They had to
distribute emergency rations on Sunday. I stood in line
at each shop for roughly six hours. Everything was available but bread and lard. And the things you could hear
standing on line! The wildest slogans, and a great deal
of panic that it was the Russians who are overrunning
Berlin. Where are the Western Powers? All of the children
have been with me since Monday. The children's bunker
is closed, the nurses have fled. I forced my way into the
deserted bunker with Bernd and Eberhard and stomped
on the lovely portrait of Hitler.*

As I'm writing this, umpteen enemy planes are buzzing overhead, throwing grenades, and our own antiaircraft are firing from Dahlem, and endless bombs are falling. Our nerves are completely shot. Out on the street everyone presses himself against a wall or ducks into a corridor at the whistle of the artillery guns. How quickly it has become routine to take cover. It makes it seem like we were living in peaceful times just eight days ago, in comparison.

I'm sitting in the kitchen, where I've moved the table over to the balcony door and am cooking on the stove. There's no gas and almost no electricity. And anyway, turning on the electricity is punishable by death. We're only permitted to listen to the radio, to the rousing speeches of higher-up criminals. I can see nothing but clouds of smoke on the horizon, and can hear only the constant rat-a-tat of machine guns. There is heavy fighting in Dahlem-Dorf, from there they're firing multiple rocket launchers right into the middle of the city. Soldiers and members of the Volkssturm, armed with rocket launchers, are marching through Schmargendorf. We are not happy to see them. What do they intend to do, defend us until there's not a stone left standing? Every hour we reckon with: Bang, a bomb, Hurrah, we're still alive. Our conquest! The streets are barricaded, a machine gun nest has been set up on the balcony of every corner building. Who knows what will be in store for us should our protectors decide to defend us to the bitter end.

I've had no word from my parents. They're far behind the Russian line of fighting, safe from Hitler's insanity. Hopefully, dear God, they survived without being harmed. I now wear our rings on a string around my neck to keep them safe, my beloved you. I couldn't bear to lose them. Everyone is suddenly burying his valuables, now that there's a rumor going around that the conquerors are confiscating everything of value. My lord, the explosions and the shooting! The front moves closer and closer. Bernd, pale as his other basement-brothers, just ran up, all excited. "Mutti, they're advancing from Schumacherplatz." That's very close, and we're all sitting here cool as cucumbers! From here we watch our proud soldiers of the Wehrmacht, who have dug themselves in next to the streetcar shelter. We feel sorry for the poor fellows after all. Did you know that the words "Jews are prohibited from sitting on the benches" were painted on a wall of the shelter? I never noticed it when we were sitting there. All places of work are shut down, the streetcars and subways aren't running, all streets are closed off. Almost all the shops are closed. Just splendid, this war. Heaven help us. And in two weeks there will be nothing at all left to eat, unless some fantastic miracle should occur. Will we survive conquest and hunger? Pray for us, my one and only. Perhaps this diary will be all that is left of my great love for you. Dear God, let us find one another again. Let us forget, together, what we have suffered. Dear God. I will love you, Felice Schragenheim, until I die.

TEN

On May 2 the Red Army reached Berlin. Because of the large paved square next to Friedrichshaller Strasse 23, the Soviets requisitioned the building and designated it a military command headquarters. They set up multiple rocket launchers on the square and commenced firing on the inner city. The noise was indescribable.

Lilly went on the offensive. "What am I supposed to do with my small children?" she barked at the Russian officers and turned up her coat collar to reveal Felice's yellow star, which she had sewn there. "We nix Nazis, we Jews. War over, you our liberators."

Finally, the third officer she spoke to understood her, and Lilly was in fact assigned beds for all eight members of her household, in the basement of the post office on Kolberger Platz. They spent two days and two nights in the camp with roughly one hundred other women and children. Every fifteen minutes the Russians came for more women, who were taken upstairs to the post office where the officers had set up quarters, and were raped. But many of the soldiers simply carried out their "conquests" on the spot.

Lilly was sitting on a chair next to her sleeping children.

"You, Frau, come!" A rifle butt bored into Lilly's side as a soldier pulled her to her feet.

"*Matka*," another soldier cried, and used his weapon to push Lilly back down into her chair so hard that even days later a contusion was still evident. But children did not always offer protection. Many mothers were raped before their children's eyes. Some women hid behind coarse jokes, or feigned indifference. "Ow, you're ripping my panties," a voice would say in the darkness. "He didn't do anything to me at all," another added, "probably didn't know how."

Many of the women were so paralyzed with fear that they prepared themselves to become victims even before it was demanded of them. When one weeping young woman gave Albrecht a piece of chocolate a Soviet soldier had given her, Lilly refused it saying, "Keep it, you paid a high price for it." One soldier pulled the blanket off the bed in which Petel was snuggled close to Katja, and then huffed indignantly, having taken Petel for a man.

"Do you understand what's going on?" Lilly asked Bernd.

"No," he lied, and spared Lilly the explanation.

"They should be happy," was Gregor's callous comment. "They haven't gotten any for a long time."

Bernd Wust:

The officer took us along with him from the front of the post office on Kolberger Platz to the courtyard. It was a typical military existence, very interesting to me as a young boy. Three days later I could identify all of the epaulettes. Then they put us in the basement, and that's where the rapes occurred. I didn't know what was going on physically, I just heard them shouting. When I asked Mutti what rape meant—everybody was always talking about it—there was an outburst of laughter all around, I still remember that.

The Russians came down one set of stairs and twice it happened that one of the older men in the basement was brave enough to go up another set of stairs to complain to an officer. And then I saw the Russian officer beat one of his soldiers so black and blue that he barely survived. Another time someone else went up and came flying right back down the stairs again, because someone was lying in wait for him at the top.

Whereas most of the women found a dark corner to hide in, not daring even to step outside, Lilly was determined to leave the basement. A fearful Lucie tried in vain to restrain her.

"Don't you understand, these are our liberators," Lilly said.

On one of her outings, Lilly made the acquaintance of the area commandant, a Jewish lieutenant by the name of Kuczynski, whose sole dream was finally to be able to return to his work as a mathematician at the Kiev Observatory. When Lilly pretended to be an "*Ivrej*," a Jew, he found a room for her in nearby Reichenhaller Strasse, in the home of a native Russian woman.

"But be careful, they don't like us there either," Kuczynski warned her.

The eight of them had one bed, in which Lilly and the children slept. Katja slept in an armchair, Petel in a chair, and Lucie, the physically weak "senior citizen," got the deck chair. When Katja tried to claim the deck chair for herself, Lilly snapped at her.

"You're supposed to be friends, how could you! You should be ashamed of yourself, acting this way!"

"It's all right, Lilly," Lucie placated her, reaching for Lilly's hand in the darkness. In the difficult period of their shared "U-boat" existence, Katja had left Lucie for Petel. Now that their lives were no longer in danger, their unstable love triangle was beginning to crumble.

Kuczynski assured the women that they were under his protection and didn't need to lock their door. One of the Soviet officers who went in and out of the building often played with the children. He drew a picture of four fir trees for Lilly, asking, "Do you understand?"

"Yes," Lilly answered.

Then he drew another fir next to them. "You understand?"

"No," Lilly said.

He repeated his offer, this time with apples. When Lilly again pretended not to understand he began to get angry, but then laughed and trotted off. For security's sake Lilly decided to lock the door after all. Shortly thereafter they all were startled when someone pounded at it. They waited with bated breath until they heard the sound of boots fading away in the corridor. When they opened the door, they almost tripped over three open tins of meat sitting on the floor outside.

Reichenhaller Strasse resembled a tent camp from the Thirty Years War, so crowded with horses that one could barely pass through them. Across the street was the ice cream shop they all knew so well, and home was quite near, yet the distance seemed insurmountable. It took five days for Lilly to gather the courage to go back to Friedrichshaller Strasse to get clothes for the children, taking Eberhard with her and holding his hand for protection. Barely had she started up the stairs when a Soviet officer was right behind them.

"Nooo, what you're thinking is *nix*," Lilly said, wagging her finger at him.

It was a standoff, the soldier speaking Russian to her and Lilly answering in German. Each time Lilly started up the stairs he was on her heels. Finally Lilly relented, but Eberhard got a piece of bread and a can of sardines in exchange.

Eberhard Wust:

> There was a water tank on Kolberger Platz, and after the
> war people filled it up with all kinds of rubble that had been
> cleared away. We played there as children and were always
> finding something interesting. When the Russians came we
> had bread again for the first time. I can remember going
> somewhere with Mutti and bread was being handed out. I was
> given a piece that I was supposed to eat right away, which I
> didn't want to do because the bread was too dry. It had been
> sliced with a knife, and cut into squares rather than slices.
> Hunger? You had to eat whatever was put on the table. I can
> remember that Mutti cooked gruel once, she seared some flour
> and mixed it with water, there wasn't much more to it than
> that. But she put a lot of salt in it, and then made us eat it.

After one week they were allowed to return to their apartment, which was much the worse for wear. Both gramophones, the bicycles and all of their records had been stolen. Lilly later found some of their clothes and the silver in the basement. When Kuczynski was transferred out of Berlin he asked Lilly for Felice's yellow star as a souvenir. Lilly made herself a new one, and every night in the hallway in front of her door she drew a huge Star of David in chalk, a magic token that she erased every morning, out of fear of her neighbors.

Ten days after the war ended Katja and Petel moved back into Katja's apartment in the Steglitz district of Berlin. They found it exactly as Katja had left it in 1939, even the pictures were still hanging on the walls. Lucie Friedlaender, who had gone to school with Felice's mother, moved in with Lilly. The corpulent woman talked incessantly of food.

Lilly's diary, June 12, 1945:

> *Unfortunately, the food rations we were promised are not materializing. Sometimes I can offer the children only a watery soup with a few kernels of barley and maybe a few greens. Bread is scarce and bad, and I spend all day preparing the most impossible ersatz things to spread on it. I cook the soup on an inverted iron. We have electricity but no gas, nor do I have wood or coal for the stove. I've already chopped up some of the furniture I don't need, for kindling. People comb the ruins for anything that will burn, fences are carried away by night. Everyone has an eye out for wood, for their warm meal.*
>
> *And now, my beloved, I wait for you, anxious and afraid. All my dear ones wait with me. I tremble at every*

sound, every step I hear. My ears deceive me at every turn. I have run out of patience. My nerves are so strained waiting for you that I imagine I hear your voice everywhere, at home and on the street, saying, "Aimée." Felice, for God's sake, come. I can't take it any longer. When am I finally to hold you in my arms again? Your Aimée, our children and our home are waiting and waiting. Come, this waiting is terrible.

Lilly began searching for Felice. Frau Kappler or Lucie watched the children while she wandered the bombed-out streets, where lilacs bloomed despite the pervasive aura of doom. She made inquiries, added to the postings for missing persons, had Felice's name announced over the radio, wrote letters to people she heard had been in Gross-Rosen, searched for Felice through the UNRRA, the United Nations Relief and Rehabilitation Administration. On the way to the "Red City Hall" the horrible stink of corpses rose from the ruins of the bombed-out suburban train station at Potsdamer Platz. On Französische Strasse she discovered a lone hobbyhorse in a shop, and took it home for the children. As she was making her way home through the deserted streets, her trophy in her hand, a man came toward her.

"Good lord, girl, why are you walking when you can ride?" he said in a heavy Berlin dialect.

As Lilly was walking on Iranische Strasse once, she encountered a group of people dressed in striped prisoner uniforms. They were dancing and laughing, blocking the entire street.

Lilly asked them where they were coming from and if they knew anything about Gross-Rosen. Across from the Jewish Hospital was a stately building with large French windows. It was here that those returning from the concentration camps were housed, in the light and spacious rooms of a sanatorium. Lilly posted a missing persons notice there and knocked at every door to ask about Felice. She also searched for the Dutch Jewish woman who had been assigned a bed next to Felice's at the Trachenberg Hospital.

NEVER!

The hours pass so quickly by,
The clock hands turn indifferently—
It makes no sense, I don't know why:
This waiting . . . have you left me?

With hope my days I justify,
I hate my night dreams fervently—
It doesn't make sense, I don't know why:
This waiting . . . have you left me?

I abandon myself to doubt, I cry,
I walk the alleys in jealousy—
It doesn't make sense, I don't know why:
This waiting . . . have you left me?

But deep within I know the reply,
And that is why I take it calmly—

It does make sense, I do know why:
While alive you would never leave me!

[LILLY, AUGUST 3, 1945]

On August 12 Lilly succeeded in reaching Irene in London by mail. The letter was delivered personally by Irene's brother-in-law, Richard Cahn, who had changed his name to Collins and was stationed as a British soldier in Germany.

Dear Irene,

How happy I am that we finally can communicate directly with one another. It will pain you to know that I cannot report anything concrete about 'Lice. What I would give were that not so. . . . During the period following August 21 when I was alone so much of the time, I kept taking out the picture of the two of you to look at, so that you were in my presence at least visually. All of your pictures, as well as a number of papers (family record, wills, etc.), are in my possession, I always carried them with me everywhere—due to the many bombings—and constantly guarded them. I am fortunate—I don't understand why, exactly—in having been spared house searches. Did your brother-in-law tell you that I have both of you "on the wall"? That might seem a bit strange to you, but please remember that I know you as 'Lice's sister, and I ask you in all sincerity to accord me a bit of the affection you feel for your sister. You do not know me as well as I know you, of course, but I so hope that will change when—and I hope to God it is soon—we all see each other again, or get to know each other, as the case may be. . . . Dear Irene, your sister was so unbelievably brave, more brave than I have ever seen anyone be; I am absolutely certain that she was an angel to all of her fellow sufferers. The Russians reached their area at the end of January or the beginning of February, so we may assume with certainty that she is alive. Where could she be? Up until now only a fraction of those who survived have returned. She knows exactly how anxiously I am waiting for her, she wishes nothing more, after all, than to return home. I expect her any day, any hour—the waiting is terrible. I've already issued a message to her three times on the radio, and posted her picture in the camp on Iranische Strasse. I've done everything I could; each week I go to the Jewish community to see what I can find out. Perhaps one day I'll be lucky.

Lilly's diary, August 15, 1945:

I'm so afraid of August 21 approaching. If only I could give Irene more positive news than I communicated in the letter her brother-in-law, Richard Kahn, took with him to England. He is a soldier stationed with the occupation forces in Spandau, which, like Wilmersdorf, belongs to the British sector. I wrote to her about 'Lice, whom she knows so much better than I. I want the chance—oh God, help us—to call her 'Lice someday too. It sounds so sweet: my brave 'Lice.

Since we have been under British occupation the situation with rations has gotten much better. But there are still shortages, and because we aren't working (everyone wants to) we get the least—card 5. Lucie as well.

Lately, I've had nothing but worry with her. She can't sleep at night, and then she doesn't get up until the afternoon. Once overly fastidious, she now neglects her appearance in every way; it's hard to watch. And she complains constantly. Everything, but everything, is too much for her. She wasn't in good health when she came to live with me. She said to me once that she feels her old nervous disorder returning. I've spoken volumes trying to get this idea out of her head. Sometimes I get quite rude. My heavens, I've got troubles enough. The children look pitiful, they're always hungry. They don't get enough vitamins or enough fat. They have nothing more than their little bit of rations, after all.

On August 17 Lilly received a postcard from Ilse Ploog in Berlin-Heiligensee that gave her hope:

Lilly,

Our "Stift" is alive! Arthur met a man on the train to Eberswalde who was with Stift in Gross-Rosen. He—the man—says he also met Stift later, in "freedom." He recalls it quite well. Stift was intending to go somewhere—he's forgotten where—for four or five weeks to recuperate. As I don't know if I can make it up to your place tomorrow or the day after, when I come to town (which I absolutely must do because of the bread coupons), I at least wanted to send you this card as a preliminary report. It's important, after all, and at one time I would have reached for the phone and called you in the middle of the night. But my time in Berlin is limited, for Arthur is sick in bed. I hope this card will prove to be superfluous, and that Stift has already arrived, and is in good shape. That would be the best news of all!

On August 17, Lucie took an overdose of Veronal.

Lilly's diary, August 17, 1945, 1 a.m.:

At eleven at night I took her to the Martin Luther Hospital on a handcart. I spent an hour and a half just looking for something to carry her on. Then the fire department came to my aid with this two-wheeled cart. They almost didn't want to admit Lucie, the hospital was so full, but I made a big fuss.

She must have taken the Veronal the night before. I knew that she always took something to be able to sleep, so I let her sleep late, it was my big wash day. I was in her room that morning because I received a card from Ilse, who wrote that Arthur had met a man in Eberswalde who said he knew you. I rushed into Lucie's room with the card, in tears, but she was sleeping and I didn't want to wake her.

That afternoon a woman arrived to deliver a half-pound of barley to her from Petel. Lucie was still asleep. The blackout shade was down, so I just opened the window a little. The room was hot and dark.

That evening around six I wanted to go out to visit friends, and when I went to her room again Lucie was still asleep in the same position. She had a blanket pulled up to her chin. There were drops of sweat on her forehead, so I uncovered her a bit and saw that she was fully dressed. It was then that I suspected she might have taken poison. I knew from Petel that she hoarded pills, and I knew that she was tired of living.

Had I not been so inexperienced about how people who have taken poison look in their sleep, I would have taken her to the hospital that afternoon. And now that I suspected something, I still couldn't believe it. So I went over to Rosel's and it got later, of course. When I came home at eight-thirty and Lucie still hadn't changed position, I ran all over the building, but no one knew how to help me. Finally Bernd went to get the children's doctor, Dr. Kain. He gave Lucie a shot and me little hope.

Subconsciously, Lucie must have been trying to get up. The whole time I was running around trying to find something to carry her in, which took over an hour, poor Bernd continually was trying to get the unfortunate woman to lie back down. She didn't react to me when I spoke to her in a loud voice.

It was after curfew and the cart was hard to manage. We ran more than walked to the hospital, and were stopped three times by British soldiers. The night doctor gave Lucie another shot and told me to talk to her in a loud voice. I shook her and called her by name over and over again. She reacted with a vague "Ja." *I tried to bring her further out of her unconscious state, but she didn't want to, she only became more fitful. The doctor gave up and sent me home after taking care of the formalities. Poor Lucinde.*

Lilly:

Lucie didn't survive our sudden freedom. I talked and talked to her about it. She would be the first to leave Germany, I said, and she really would have been. Her sister applied right away for Lucie to be able to go to her in Australia. Lucie's other sister had been taken to Auschwitz right after she had been operated on at the sanatorium on Joachimstaler Strasse. I searched for information about her, too. She died during transport.

It was devastating to Lucie that Petel had left her, and that certainly played a role. Petel should have shown more concern for her. I was totally distraught at the time. I was crazy for a while there at the beginning. Every time the bell rang, every time I heard a step I thought it was Felice returning. And Lucie knew that. No one could have understood that better than she. I talked about dying; I didn't want to live. And she said to me, "You know, Lilly, one doesn't die so quickly." She had made her decision then already.

Once I walked in and she was sobbing. I stroked her hair and put my arms around her. And she embraced me so hungrily that I'll never forget it. I've regretted ever since not doing so more often. But I was always busy with the children and with preparations for some indeterminate meal or other, with food. And Lucie got more and more apathetic and couldn't even eat anything anymore.

On August 18 Lilly received the first response to an announcement she had posted at the Jewish Hospital. The German script was shaky, as if that of an old man:

August 15, 1945

Fräulein Schragenheim took the same path as my daughter, and therefore probably was in Bergen-Belsen.

Further details in person. 12–1 p.m., 6–7 p.m.

Respectfully,

Dr. Grünberger

Iranische Strasse, Room 70

Lilly hurried to Iranische Strasse the next day. Dr. Grünberger, roughly forty years old, had recently returned from Auschwitz. He spoke in a kind, soft voice. "Puppe" ("Doll"), his daughter Hanne-Lore, had been at Gross-Rosen. The camp was shut down at the end of January 1945, and the women were sent to Bergen-Belsen. He promised to ask his daughter about Felice and to visit Lilly as soon as he could.

Lilly then rushed to the Neukölln district to see a Frau Linke, who also had responded to her notice. She had been with Felice in Theresienstadt. "They killed the young ones and left us old ones behind," she said, weeping, adding that Felice had been an angel at Theresienstadt, simply incredible.

She radiated great calm and confidence. And she was always together with a woman who wore pants, Frau Linke said.

Lilly's diary, August 21, 1945:

> *6:30 a.m. One year without Felice. My heart feels heavy as lead. I'll straighten the apartment now, and then make myself pretty. For you, Felice. Perhaps this terrible day of remembrance will bring us something better. Oh my beloved, I'm trembling, it pains me so. Lilo was here yesterday. Everyone, everyone consoles me and gives me hope.*
>
> *Even Frau Linke, whom I saw on Sunday. Felice, who was the woman in the pants you were always together with at Theresienstadt? Was it that Sternberg woman? I'm bursting with jealousy, and Frau Linke smiled when she noticed, unfortunately. It's ridiculous, I'm in the grip of paranoia. Have you, in the course of one year, so quickly forgotten your Aimée, who waits for you, trembling? I love you so much. I cannot give up even a tiny piece of you.*
>
> *Around midnight:*
>
> *I so would have liked to be alone today. I wanted only to wait for you. But Gregor arrived right after Rosel left. I walked with him for a bit and then went to see Lucie at the hospital. They had strapped her down tightly. The day before yesterday, in her struggle with death, or with life, she fell out of the bed and split her head open. I stood at her bedside, terribly sad, and stroked her hair. What else could I do for her? Perhaps it is best if she dies.*

When I came home again, Käthe Herrmann surprised me with a visit. Today of all days! The good woman looked quite disheveled. I could barely contain myself talking to her: Hadn't she ever noticed that you were Jewish, and Gregor, Ilse, Lilo and so forth and so on. Now, of course, she doesn't want to have been anything back then. An hour later Dr. Grünberger appeared unexpectedly. Käthe shook his hand nicely. Just imagine, a Jew! I was so filled with spite I could have screamed. I felt that hysterical. But she wasn't so comfortable when she had to sit there without batting an eyelash and listen to what they had done to all of you. It didn't do her any harm to hear it. Basically I like her, as I know you do. She's a nice person in spite of it all.

Just imagine, Dr. Grünberger, the good man, brought a loaf of bread, a tin of liverwurst, a half-pound of powdered milk, a quarter-pound of margarine and ten sugar cubes for us. What a joy, and such a sacrifice. I'm almost a total stranger to him, after all. He was a lawyer in Breslau, and is optimistic enough to believe that those dear "custodaryans" of his beautiful things will be returning them to him soon.

While I was walking him to the station, Petel arrived. She had just come from the Martin Luther Hospital, where the doctor had told her that Lucie probably would not survive the night. It was very strange for us to think that we might never see Lucie again alive. Petel was depressed and sad. What could I say to her? No one should accuse anyone of anything, but I couldn't help thinking of the little piece of paper I found in Lucie's

*handbag as I was looking for the papers I needed for the
hospital. Though I've forgotten almost all the French I
learned at school, I could understand enough to know
that her words in French were a cry for help from Petel.
If only Petel had looked after Lucie a little more.*

*And I'm sad. Though I had my problems with Lucie,
she was here at least, and now I'm even more alone. Lucie
is better off as it is. She was finished, and more than just
psychologically. Hunger ration card number 5 did its part
as well. It is scandalous that the Jews who survived get the
same number 5 card as the worst Nazis. They're only now
in the process of remedying that. In the meantime Lucie
starved to death. For as long as I live I'll hold the Allies
responsible for that.*

*I am terribly afraid that you've left the country. I heard
this might be true. Is that what you've done? And I wait here,
thinking the dumbest things. Do you know that it's my life
I'm waiting for? Come back, no matter where you are, and
take me in your arms. Let us forget the world and its insanity. Dear and only God, give me my girl back again. One
year alone, one whole year I have lived with my memories,
one whole year, trembling with the hope of seeing you again.
Good God, I almost can no longer pray.*

Lucie Friedlaender died at the Martin Luther Hospital on
Auguste-Victoria-Strasse during the night of August 21, 1945.
She was buried in the Weissensee Jewish Cemetery on August
26, the second burial to be held there since the end of the war.
Petel and Lilly were the only mourners. "As we walked along

behind her I had the feeling that millions were following along behind us," Lilly wrote in her diary.

In September Lilly received an answer to the long letter she had written to Irene on August 12:

> I wrote to Frau Kummer last week, right after Richard's first report of your meeting. She had not been able to do anything further for 'Lice, of course, but I so hope that she will arrive at your place soon. Nothing could have happened to her, don't you agree? I spoke today with a friend of my mother, and she said that 'Lice could learn any language in five minutes and could get by in any country. I think so too, but I'd like to know where she is. . . . Did 'Lice really have something with her lung from the scarlet fever? Mrs. Kummer wrote something to that effect. The dear woman did everything she could for 'Lice. And it is certainly not her fault that 'Lice isn't in Switzerland.

MEMORY

With each breath that I take,
I see you here before me.
Plunge into memory's wake—
And end up weeping bitterly.

So I live in a time that no longer is there,
And today is immersed in yesterday.
I burrow into your sweet-smelling hair
And bear you joking and chatting away.

I wrap myself up, tuck into your arms,
I cannot resist your laughter—
Beguiled, enchanted by your charms,
It is sad to awaken thereafter.

[LILLY, OCTOBER 26, 1945]

Lilly's diary, December 9, 1945:

I must believe that you are alive and that someday, per-
haps quite soon, great and merciful God, you will stand
at my door and say, "Aimée." Then I will fall into your
arms and cry the last tears I have left in me. I will make
you forget everything that has happened in the past and
give you the best that I have in me—my life for you until
I die. Felice, my dear, come into my arms, I want to kiss
you and feel your soft mouth upon mine. The memory of
your mouth—I felt the whole earth move, and my blood
as it coursed through my body. My willpower dissolved
when I drank in your kisses, do you remember? I was no
longer in control of my senses, consumed by my passion for
you. I was lost in you, lost in the tumult of feeling, your
mouth on mine, forever. I savored those wild kisses and
became one with you. Our bodies pressed against each
other, kindled by mutual desire. Your hands slid hungrily
over me, stroking my breasts, my body, and then, then
you took me. And I you. For the first time in my life I
gave, I didn't just take, I demanded. How passionately I
loved your body, I loved it so much. I felt my way with my

hands over the body I love so, and you strained against me, gave yourself to me, taut and hard at first, and then openly, freely you surrendered, moaning in excitement. Then I covered you in kisses, beside myself with desire. Everything coursed through and around us in the heat of the moment. I could have murdered you in an instant. I screamed, I was nearly mad, as were you, as were you, not content until we were numb with exhaustion. We were one, it was the fulfillment of our love.

Murder in the literal sense of the word. How we loved one another. My God, I'm already saying "loved."

Shortly thereafter, at the end of 1945 or beginning of 1946, Lilly wrote a letter to Irene, which she copied before sending off, as she did with all of her important correspondence:

My Dear Irene,

I send to you and Derek my greetings and best wishes for the New Year, which hopefully will find you well. It is so nice that you found Derek, it is so good to have someone you love for yourself alone. If I wish anyone the best from the bottom of my heart, then it is you, sister of my beloved Felice! One day you will read the letters Felice and I wrote to each other and know what we meant to each other— one day. Since 'Lice was taken from me on August 21, '44, I have dreaded the day when I must write to you, stand before you alone—I have given up hope since I found out that in January/February roughly seven hundred women from Gross-Rosen were transported to Bergen-Belsen and there—in Belsen—almost all of them died of typhus. Even today it is not one hundred percent certain that she was there. I wrote to someone named Hanne-Lore Grünberger, who was with 'Lice in Gross-Rosen, and who was sent from there to Bergen-Belsen, but she unfortunately has not yet answered; the situation with the mail is impossible at the moment. My dear Irene, I found out about the women's transport to Belsen yesterday—it robbed me of all hope. As of yesterday I am the poorest of the poor, and I ask myself over and over again: Why? Why did God take this wonderful, gifted girl from me, and why did he allow me to survive this horrible war, why? All of us who went through so many awful things in Germany have only one thing in mind: getting away from this country and from these people. One can no longer live in a country where all of this was possible. For me it will not be easy to leave, especially with four children, but I always believe there will be good people to help me. I would like to begin a new life somewhere else in the world, start from the beginning, and that will not be easy. But I must leave here, because I can never forget.

On January 25, 1945, the Kurzbach camp was evacuated. The women spent eight days in the icy cold on a foot march in rows of five to Gross-Rosen. Two hundred women died along the way. They stayed in the main Gross-Rosen camp for two weeks, sleeping four to a cot and getting soup twice a day. After that they were transported in open cattle cars to Bergen-Belsen. The actual destination was Buchenwald, but that camp was too overcrowded to take in any more prisoners. Near Weimar they were bombarded by the British and there were casualties in the first and last cars. Once they arrived in Bergen-Belsen they had to strip naked and were given lice-infested rags to wear. Many prisoners there died of spotted fever, starvation, or diarrhea. Beate Mohr's sister died of scarlet fever and dystentery.

"Don't be sad," Beate wrote to her mother after liberation. "Other people died too: Lotte Trier, Käte Pegner, Anne Marcus, Felice Schragenheim, Ruth Schönfeld. . . ."

ELEVEN

During the icy cold winter of 1945–46 Lilly had no coal for heating, and moved in with her parents. She spent most of her time there writing in her "book of tears." Weeping as she wrote, she copied all of the letters and poems that Jaguar and Aimée had written to each other. She bartered the fifty pairs of silk stockings Felice had given her for bread. Her older children were sent to Oldenburg as part of the British "Operation Stork," where they were fed and given warm shelter. Only Albrecht remained with her.

"Mutti, Aunt Felice is coming back for sure," he would say in an effort to comfort Lilly. But Aimée was inconsolable.

In the first years after the war Lilly's sons rarely saw their mother when she wasn't crying, or carrying on about how it would be when Felice returned and they would emigrate to America. Lilly went about her household chores perfunctorily, becoming more and more deeply depressed. She often would lie in the living room for hours, reading or writing in her diary, only unwillingly allowing the children to disturb her. They had to knock before entering her room. She took refuge in the synagogue.

Bernd Wust:

Mutti imposed herself, that has to be said. She established contact with some Jewish people or other in Schmargendorf, and joined the Jewish Community. They tolerated her, but blocked any serious efforts on her part to convert.

After the war we were registered at school as Jewish. Mutti explained to us that this was something special, and dragged us to the synagogue on Joachimstaler Strasse. That's how I came to celebrate Sukkoth and other such things. It was interesting. To me it was church, a Jewish church that was called a synagogue. We stayed home from school on Jewish holidays, that was worth it. And no one felt comfortable asking about it. "Why weren't you here yesterday?" the teacher asked me. "Oh, I didn't know," he said, and then apologized deeply. I knew he was a Nazi. I was listed in the class register as being "Mosaic." And I was beaten up for being a Muslim.

I never developed a relationship to Judaism; where would it have come from? I only knew a little more about it than the others did, and I simply know more about the history. I have a colleague at work who, in the language of the Nazi era, is a "half-Jew," and there's a bond between us. That's what it all came to.

The war broke out in Palestine while I was in school. So in class they expected me to stand up for the Jews, that was clear. And they were always at me about the Arabian Legion. The teachers were the same ones as before, of course. I was immediately assigned the role of outsider. In 1945 I went to the Walther Rathenau School. Everyone came from different grade schools, but we all knew each other, we were all from the same neighborhood. So then everybody knew: He's a Jew. There weren't supposed to be any Jews anymore. After all, we had learned as children that they were subhuman and should be exterminated, and all of a sudden there was one left, one they knew personally. In that sense I was pretty interesting, they all stared at me.

And for Eberhard it was a decisive factor. I see it this way: In puberty young people want to show off. If you can find a field in which you're different from the others, then that's the direction you take. And Eberhard always enjoyed being different. The way I explain it to myself is, Mutti laid the groundwork at home, and at fourteen, fifteen, sixteen, when he was trying to adjust, that was what suited him. By the time he graduated, it was all settled.

Eberhard Wust:

I was interested in ancient languages, that was something romantic to me. At the high school for humanities I attended, we started with Latin in the fifth grade, at nine years of age, that is. Three years later Greek was added. After that I said to myself, there are other ancient languages, Hebrew, for example. It must have been 1951–52 when Mutti said to me: We don't have any money as it is, go see the rabbi. So I went to the police station and asked where Rabbi Levinson lived. Were they surprised! And he sent me to an old man who gave religious and Hebrew instruction. I started with him, but he didn't have a teaching method and didn't really know that much Hebrew. But he always took me with him to synagogue, and became a kind of substitute father to me. Well, I studied with him, and joined a Jewish youth group through the synagogue, and then a Jewish student group. In 1958 the World Union of Jewish Students held a conference in Jerusalem, and because I could already speak Hebrew so well I was the representative from Germany. That was my first trip to Israel. And here in Germany I attached myself to anyone who spoke Hebrew. You can't learn a language without talking to people. At school I took notes in Hebrew, which irritated the teacher because he couldn't read them. There were two girls I was friends with; they were a little older than I, and the three of us always sat together and studied Hebrew. We'd read the weekly passage from the Pentateuch and several passages from the Mishnah.

Mutti was happy, of course, that I was interested, and supported me in it. And to that extent. . . . But it has little to do with Germany's past; I couldn't make a direct connection between the two. Up to this day, ninety percent of who I am consists of this interest in ancient languages. I was pretty much of a late bloomer, politically speaking. At fourteen I was still a dreamy kid and basically was still that way at eighteen. At home, at any rate, we were always taught that anything German was bad. In that sense we really enjoyed an anti-German education. My mother was constantly cursing the damned Nazis, and all Germans were Nazis. Which bothered my older brother, because to a certain extent he is proud of his father, not because he was a soldier, but the only pictures of him from that time show him in uniform. Bernd has those. I myself don't have any pictures of my father. It doesn't interest me; I have no connection to him.

On January 26, 1946, Dr. Louis Grünberger wrote to Lilly from Berlin that his daughter, "Puppe," still had not written concerning whether or not she had encountered Felice in Bergen-Belsen. He advised her not to give up hope: "One can always be hopeful where young people are concerned. Two young ladies from Breslau who were in concentration camps arrived here six and two weeks ago, respectively. One had come almost from Asia, the other had been in the Caucasus Mountains."

Finally, on June 5, Hanne-Lore Grünberger wrote from Neustadt-Aisch: " . . . and I regret to have to tell you *once again* that I never met your friend anywhere along the way. Nor did my inquiries to other concentration camp comrades amount to anything. Unfortunately, she probably shared the fate of millions of concentration camp comrades."

During 1946 and 1947 Aimée continued to hope and to search. On February 14, 1948, Jaguar was declared legally dead by the municipal court of Berlin-Charlottenburg. The date of her death was set as December 31, 1944. Their women friends dissociated themselves from Lilly. And the material support Lilly had hoped for failed to appear.

TWELVE

While Aimée was busy waiting for Jaguar, Elisabeth Wust missed the deadline for annulling her divorce. Because she shared responsibility in divorcing Günther Wust, she lost her option to claim a war widow's pension. Her plan to emigrate to Australia failed. And the increasingly testy correspondence with Irene concerning Felice's inheritance came to nothing.

In March 1947 Lilly received a part of Irene's original letters to Felice, forwarded to her by Emmi-Luise Kummer in Aarau, Switzerland. The first package apparently had gotten lost in the mail, for the sender had written the following warning on the envelope: *To the thief of the previous letters: This envelope contains letters from the sister of a very young girl who was killed in a concentration camp. I could only deliver a portion of them during the Hitler period. Is this package not sacred to you as well?*

It was the last sign of life from Emmi-Luise Kummer.

In spring 1949 Lilly swallowed all of the pills she had hoarded up until then. Helene, a friend who for one year had been living on Friedrichshaller Strasse with her baby and who was in love with Lilly, rescued her at the last minute.

But disconsolate Helene was soon to move out to make way for Willi Beimling, the son of Frau Beimling from the back building, the woman who had hidden Felice behind her sofa when the Gestapo came. Willi Beimling had a beer belly, wore a peaked cap and ran an electrical shop around the corner.

Lilly now had to work in his shop all day and cook for her family in the evening. At noon the children would arrive at the shop from school, and Lilly would take them up to the apartment to fix them a hurried lunch.

Lilly's diary, May 6, 1949:

Once I was Aimée, and Lilly, now I am Elisabeth, and unhappy. Now I am "allowed" to do everything for him, with no time or energy left for anything else. He thinks only of himself and of his business, the egotist. But he won't marry me or declare himself. He did everything for his wife, and he will for me, too, I know that. But the children. The way he acts, people would think he's crazy. Oh, I just don't care anymore. The children are such dear sweet things that I think he will get used to them. I have tried to deal with life in as honorable a way as possible. You know that I give my all to the person I have decided to live with, but at what price to myself now? I've

*been pressed into some terrible, obsessive, almost obedi-
ent mold. I could almost laugh at my belief in him. I've
been working in the shop since January. If you could only
see what that means. I am simply no longer a normal
human being. I don't have a penny. I'm a fool. After
our last fight I at least got fifty marks spending money.
I work from eight-thirty in the morning to six in the
evening without a lunch break, then I go home and cook
and wash clothes and mend socks for him late into the
night, in addition to my responsibilities to the children.
It is a crying shame, I know that. If only he had a nice
word for me now and then, but he simply isn't like that.
Oh my beloved girl, I wouldn't be able to take it were
I not so terribly afraid of being alone, of having no one
to be nice to me occasionally, and Willi can be very nice
when he has a mind to. He can't help the tears I shed,
which no one is meant to see. I weep for you, uncontrol-
lably and without shame. Why must I go through life so
tormented? I'll gladly do things I'm not meant for, but
I need to know why. Things simply cannot continue like
this. How often have I told myself that, and then they
do continue. Things continue. Because I cannot be alone
for the rest of my life. And tomorrow I'll go back to the
shop again and worry myself sick and bury my thoughts. I
don't even have enough time for you, you who I love more
than myself. You were and remain the incarnation of
true life. With you, everything worth living for was lost.
Why won't God just destroy me too, or take my insane
love for you away from me. I scream so loudly to you, oh*

*God, you must be able to hear me. I've been screaming
since August 21.*

Lilly and Willi Beimling were married on April 3, 1950.
He virtually kept her behind lock and key in the beginning.
She, who had always had a house full of people, was allowed
neither to receive visitors nor to go out. Willi would not tolerate any strange people in their home, nor did he have any
friends of his own. His entire life revolved around his business,
he was determined to succeed. It was Lilly's desire for a little
love and her wish for financial security that drove her into his
arms. Today, she labels this marriage a last-minute panic.

Willi knew this as well. "You don't need a man at all," he
would tell her.

In the spring of 1953 Lilly once again tried to kill herself.
Following a fight with Willi, who was forcing his wife to work
in his shop despite the fact that she was ill with the flu, she slit
her wrists, slicing across the veins instead of lengthwise. Willi
made a terrible scene, and as Lilly ran out into the corridor
bleeding, he slammed a door on her other hand, smashing it.
Bernd went for the police.

Lilly's diary, August 1953:

*Short, sweet and awful. Briefly: Married Willi April 1950,
divorced—as the innocent party—from Willi February
1951. Willi moved back in in 1952, same old thing, tug-of-
war to marry him again, the old routine, against my better
judgment. Shop, household, Willi and the children. Begin-*

ning of 1953, following the fourth time he had not kept his promise, made it clear to him that I had had enough once and for all. Takes his time leaving, despite my demands. I'm long-suffering, but this is sh———.

Willi finally moved out in December. "I'm finally rid of him, the biggest scoundrel I've ever run across," Lilly wrote in her diary.

After this, Aimée withdrew more and more into herself. The family spent the years of Germany's "economic miracle" in the poorest of circumstances; there was never any money. Whereas in the first years following the war it didn't matter if the children went to school barefoot, Lilly's four sons began to suffer from having to wear worn-out coats passed down from one brother to the next. While Lilly's friends from earlier days slowly began to make something of themselves, Lilly lived on the children's "half-orphan" annuity. She occasionally accepted cleaning jobs, or helped out in a stationery shop at Christmas. Lilly enjoyed the work, but lacked the confidence to make decisions. When asked if she would accept a position in the stationery shop, she thought it over until it was too late. She nevertheless managed to enable Bernd, Eberhard and Reinhard to attend university. When finally she managed to pull herself together enough to apply for state support, she was asked why it was necessary that her children go to college at all.

"Shall I raise my children beneath our standard?"

When the official persisted, Lilly threatened to go and get her sons and sit them down in his office.

"Or can you return their father to me?"

"Well maybe he didn't want to come back to you at all."

In September 1961 Eberhard Wust emigrated to Israel.

In 1963—Lilly was fifty years old—she finally found a job that provided her with insurance benefits. She accepted a position as cleaning woman and attendant to the personnel department of the Zehlendorf Textile Company, a subsidiary of Hoechst. She got up every morning at five o'clock and fell into bed exhausted every night. She had nothing left over for an emotional life or enjoyment. Weekends were spent with her parents.

In mid-1970—all four sons had left home by then—Lilly moved out of her lovely apartment on Friedrichshaller Strasse, afraid of a threatened rent increase and to be closer to her elderly parents. She took a modest one-room apartment in Lichterfelde, with a view of her parents' apartment. But her mother died on October 1, and her father's death followed a few years later.

Günther Wust was officially declared dead in the fall of 1974, thirty years after he had been killed in action in Jassy, Rumania.

On September 21, 1981, as a result of efforts initiated by her son Bernd, Lilly was awarded the German Federal Service Cross.

Lilly:

> When they wanted to give me the medal my first thought was: Turn it down, it won't bring Felice back. But then I thought, perhaps it is for Felice. The day of the ceremony I didn't say anything about it at work, I just didn't show up that Monday.

I didn't want the attention, but then it was in all the newspapers! The media almost drove me crazy. I turned them all
down, I didn't want to create a sensation, God knows. And
then, people reacted to it in a strange way. Management was
great. They gave me this vase here, full of roses. But the people
I was friends with in the factory, I never would have expected
their reaction. Most of them distanced themselves from me
personally. Even here in my neighborhood, you know. It's
not that they didn't speak to me anymore, but I noticed it. I
was marked, and that's something I won't recover from, I'll
die with that mark. That's the reason I withdrew totally. I
didn't trust anyone anymore, anyone. No one wants to take
responsibility, even today! People haven't changed at all, not
them at least. In the many phone calls I have had with Dörthe
we both agreed that we are quite alone. If you followed the
trials, it was horrible—all those people they didn't want to
believe, it was enough to drive you insane. I'm overly sensitive, but even those I helped deserted me later. They promised
me the moon, but they didn't keep their promises. Quite the
contrary. Lucie's sister wrote me a letter—and it showed how
little people abroad knew: "Couldn't you have prevented it?"
I resented that. It was I, after all, who buried Lucie. Even
Countess Malzahn, who hid a huge number of people, said
something once during an interview over Radio Free Berlin
that shook me to the core. She was asked whether the people
she protected, and for whom she constantly had risked her
life, had thanked her, and she answered, "I regret to say that
very few did. They wanted to be done with all of that. To go
away and forget everything." And I too had a plan, to go to

America, to Felice's uncle, her mother's brother. I didn't want to stay in Germany. And I would have gone to Sweden, but I was told it would be enormously difficult with four children. I was always handicapped by the children. I hate the Germans still. There's always something new coming to the surface. For instance, over there is the route taken by our two buses, number 85 and number 96. I used to take them to work. There's a vocational school here now, and one day I'm standing at the bus stop and the children are making a terrible racket. Suddenly one woman says to another, "They're going at it like at the Jew school!" Sometimes I'm glad I won't be around for much longer, truly.

Two weeks after the newspapers ran articles on Lilly having been awarded the German Federal Service Cross, Lilly was leaving her apartment when she almost fell over a large stone that had been placed on her staircase. The door to her apartment had been smeared with urine.

In 1983, when she was seventy, Lilly fainted one day at work, and realized it was finally time to retire. As she had been paying into the social insurance system for only twenty years, the duration of her employment, her pension did not amount to much. Lilly's impoverishment remains a sore point to her. Every other year she is eligible to receive a coat and a pair of shoes, which she refuses to accept. "I have my pride, I'm not going to go begging to them," she says.

Lilly has let herself go. She reads and lives for the moment. She no longer goes to the hairdresser and doesn't buy anything that might afford her pleasure. Make ends meet with your pension for a few years more and then it will be over, she tells herself.

Lilly is a seasoned patient. She has to go to the hospital at least twice a year, for her heart, her circulation, diabetes. Only when she visits Eberhard in Israel does her joy of life return. She feels comfortable in Israel, she's among her own there. She lights candles on the Sabbath in Berlin, too, and thinks of her Jewish son, Eberhard, and of her Jewish love, Felice Schragenheim, always of Felice. Each year as August 21 approaches, she feels the old familiar sadness all over again. Lilly keeps the negatives of the photos of Aimée and Jaguar, taken that day on the Havel River, in the little white plastic bag she carried in Israel to hold the scarf she wore at the Wailing Wall.

To save electricity, she had to turn off one of the two refrigerators that kept separate the dairy and meat products she eats. She now uses it to store her medications.

Every Sabbath she called Dörthe Zivier. The two women hadn't seen each other for over thirty years. "We want to remember each other as we were," Lilly said to Dörthe.

Dörthe Zivier died in July 1992.

Lilly has stored her diaries, Felice's documents and family photographs and all the letters and poems that Aimée and Jaguar wrote to each other in two brimming suitcases that lie ready to hand on her small black-glazed cabinet. On April 2 of every year, their "wedding day," Aimée takes out her "book of tears" and reads herself into the past. Should something happen to her, the documents are to be taken to Eberhard in

Israel. The suitcases were Eberhard's idea: "So the police won't need to do a big search." Lilly carries the keys to the suitcases around her neck. On the little and middle fingers of her right hand she wears the gold wedding ring engraved with the initials F.S. and the date 2.4.43, and the silver ring with the green oval stone, her present to Felice that Felice gave back to her on the day she was deported.

In 1985, four years after she received the Federal Service Cross, she was contacted by an American journalist. The Berlin senate had given him Elisabeth Wust's name because he was planning to write a book on "the good Germans." He convinced Lilly to reveal her secret, and for the first time she told the truth about Aimée and Jaguar—that the "Jewess Schragenheim" was not only her friend, but her life.

"It makes me sad sometimes," Lilly says. "Now it's no longer my story."

ABOUT THE AUTHOR

ERICA FISCHER was born in 1943 in England. Her parents were refugees there and returned to Austria with their two children in 1948. Erica Fischer studied at the Interpreting Institute of the University of Vienna, was a founding member of the second wave women's movement in Vienna, and started working there as a journalist in the mid-1970s. She has been living in Germany since 1988 as a freelance journalist, writer, and translator, residing in Berlin since 1994.